STECK-VAUGHN

WORKING *with* Numbers ALGEBRA

Consultants

Carol K. Duggan
Mathematics Program Leader
Trumbull Public Schools
Trumbull, Connecticut

Chuck Hayden
Mathematics Teacher, Department Chair
San Diego City Schools
San Diego, California

Acknowledgments

Editorial Director: Diane Schnell
Supervising Editor: Donna Montgomery
Editor: Meredith Edgley O'Reilly
Associate Director of Design: Joyce Spicer
Designer: Jim Cauthron

Senior Technical Advisor: Alan Klemp
Editorial Development and Production:
Monotype Composition
Media Researcher: Sarah Fraser
Cover Photo: © Chris Tomaidis/Stone

STECK-VAUGHN
ELEMENTARY · SECONDARY · ADULT · LIBRARY

A Harcourt Company

www.steck-vaughn.com

ISBN 978-0-7398-3543-2
ISBN 0-7398-3543-2

11 12 13 14 0982 11 10 09

Table of Contents

Unit 4 Exponents and Polynomials

Unit 5 Functions and Graphs

Unit 6 Graphs and Systems of Equations

Unit 7 Inequalities, Roots, and Proportions

Name _____ Date _____

Identify all the sets to which each of the following numbers belong: *natural numbers, whole numbers, integers, rational numbers,* **and** *real numbers.*

	a	*b*	*c*	*d*
1.	$^-6$	4	$\frac{5}{8}$	0.3

Find the absolute value of each number.

	a	*b*	*c*	*d*
2.	$|^-26|$	$|126|$	$|^-1.2|$	$\left|^-\frac{1}{2}\right|$

Place the following numbers in order from least to greatest.

	a	*b*	*c*	*d*
3.	$^-1, \ ^-3, \ 0$	$^-9, \ 8, \ 4$	$^-17, \ ^-4, \ 7$	$^-1.3, \ ^-1, \ ^-14$

Simplify.

	a	*b*	*c*	*d*
4.	$63 \div (7-4) \times 2 =$	$4^2 \div 2 - 3 \times 2 =$	$(10+8) \div 9 + 30 =$	$(7-5) \times (2+4) =$

Write an algebraic expression for each verbal expression.

	a	*b*
5.	*y* multiplied by 6 _____	8 decreased by *z* _____

Evaluate each expression if *a* = 8, *b* = 4, **and** *c* = 2.

	a	*b*	*c*	*d*
6.	$ac + b =$	$\frac{a+b}{c} =$	$3b - 2c =$	$a + b - c =$

Solve.

	a	*b*	*c*	*d*
7.	$n = 4(3+2)$	$2s = 10$	$x = 3(2) + 4(1)$	$6 + y = 18$

Name _____ Date _____

Solve.

8. In the formula $A = lw$, find A when l is 5 inches and w is 25 inches.

9. In the formula $A = \pi r^2$, find A when r is 14 centimeters.

10. In the formula $I = prt$, find p when I is $300, r is 4%, and t is 1 year.

11. In the formula $V = lwh$, find w when V is 120 cubic inches, l is 8 inches, and h is 5 inches.

12. In the formula $C = (F - 32)\frac{5}{9}$, find C when F is 59°.

13. In the formula $F = (C \cdot \frac{9}{5}) + 32$, find F when C is 45°.

Simplify.

	a	b	c	d
14.	$6 + (^-16) =$	$^-8 + (^-10) =$	$14 - (^-7) =$	$(^-4)(^-8)$
15.	$^-5(^-7)(^-2)$	$^-35 \div (^-7) =$	$\frac{^-18}{6} =$	$4a + 7a =$
16.	$27xy - 15xy =$	$^-3x + x + (^-7x) =$	$7cd - (^-15cd) =$	$3t(1.5r) =$
17.	$\frac{9z}{3} =$	$3(8 + 6p) =$	$\frac{p}{3}(\frac{q}{6}) =$	$\frac{1}{4}(8a - a) =$

Solve.

	a	b	c	d
18.	$8a - 5 = 3a + 15$	$2b + 6 = b - 4$	$3x - 2 = 2(x + 3)$	$4y - (2y + 6) = 10$
19.	$\frac{x}{3} + 5 = \frac{x}{6} + 2$	$\frac{a}{2} + 3 = \frac{2a}{8}$	$\frac{9}{t} = \frac{3}{5}$	$\frac{s}{4} = \frac{6}{8}$

Write an equation. Solve.

20. Three times a number increased by 15 is equal to 30. What is the number?

21. The length of a rectangle is 3 times the width. The area is 48 square inches. Find the length and width.

Answer _____

Answer _____

Name _____ Date _____

Change each number from scientific notation to standard form.

	a		b		c
22. $2.1 \times 10^3 =$		$0.8 \times 10^4 =$		$1.7 \times 10^{-2} =$	

Simplify.

	a	b	c
23.	$(^-3)^2(2)^3 =$	$2ab^2(3c) =$	$(2x^2y)(^-3xy^3) =$
24.	$(ab^2)^3 =$	$\dfrac{2x^3}{x^2} =$	$\dfrac{^-8a^3b}{4ab^3} =$
25.	$(3a - 3b) + (-a + 5b) =$	$(4a + 2b) - (a + 3b) =$	$4a^2 - 5b^3 + 3a^2 =$
26.	$\dfrac{x}{3y} \cdot \dfrac{3y}{x} =$	$\dfrac{a}{b^2} \div \dfrac{a}{b} =$	$\dfrac{8ab + 10a^2b}{2ab} =$

Multiply.

	a	b	c
27.	$3(2x - y) =$	$(r + s)(2r + s) =$	$2a(a^2 - 3b) =$
28.	$2x^2(x^2 + 3x + 7) =$	$(x + y)^2 =$	$(x + y)(2x - 3y) =$

Make a table of solutions. Graph the equation. Draw a straight line through the points.

a

29. $3x - 5y = 15$

x	y
$^-5$	
0	
5	

b

$2x + 3y = 6$

x	y

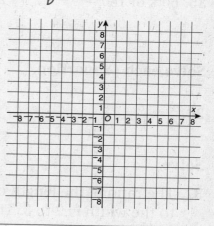

Find the slope of the line that passes through the given points.

	a	b	c	d
30.	$(2, 3)$ and $(4, 5)$	$(1, ^-3)$ and $(^-5, 1)$	$(1, ^-2)$ and $(2, ^-4)$	$(0, 6)$ and $(5, 7)$

Solve each system of equations.

	a	*b*	*c*
31.	$x + y = 6$ $x - y = 4$	$3x + 2y = 26$ $3x - 2y = 10$	$2x + 3y = 9$ $x - 2y = 1$
	Ordered pair _____	Ordered pair _____	Ordered pair _____
32.	$5x - 2y = 3$ $2x + 5y = 7$	$a + 4b = 12$ $2a - b = 6$	$\frac{1}{2}x + y = 6$ $\frac{1}{2}x - y = 2$
	Ordered pair _____	Ordered pair _____	Ordered pair _____

Solve.

	a	*b*	*c*
33.	$4x \leq 28$	$b + 2 > 12$	$\frac{a}{2} \leq {}^-6$

Simplify.

	a	*b*	*c*
34.	$\sqrt{16x^2y^4} =$	$\sqrt[3]{64} =$	$\sqrt[3]{8x^3} =$

Find the percent.

	a	*b*	*c*	*d*
35.	60% of 180 =	25% of 37 =	0.2% of 10 =	65% of 135 =

Solve each proportion.

	a	*b*	*c*
36.	$\frac{x}{4} = \frac{6}{12}$	$\frac{2}{x} = \frac{6}{9}$	$\frac{4}{5} = \frac{x}{20}$

Solve.

37. The ratio of the length of a rectangle to the width is 2 to 3. The area of the rectangle is 96 square inches. Find the dimensions.

38. Elena earns \$30 for working 2 hours. She works 30 hours a week. How much does she earn in a week?

Answer _____

Answer _____

Name _____ Date _____

Find the length of the missing side of each right triangle.
Use the formula $a^2 + b^2 = c^2$.

a	b	c
39. $a = 5$, $b = 12$, $c = ?$	$a = 3$, $b = ?$, $c = 5$	$a = ?$, $b = 6$, $c = 10$

Find the distance between each pair of points.

a	b	c
40. $(1, 3)$ and $(5, 6)$	$(4, {}^{-}1)$ and $(7, 3)$	$(5, 8)$ and $({}^{-}7, 3)$

Find the midpoint between the two points.

a	b	c
41. $({}^{-}2, 5)$ and $(6, 7)$	$(4, 1)$ and $(6, 9)$	$(1, {}^{-}8)$ and $({}^{-}5, 2)$

Factor each polynomial.

a	b	c
42. $x^2 + 2xy + y^2 =$	$9x^2 + 12xy + 4y^2 =$	$2x^2 + 7x - 4 =$

Solve.

a	b	c
43. $x^2 - 7x + 6 = 0$	$2x^2 + 5x + 2 = 0$	$x^2 + 16 = {}^{-}8x$

Solve.

44. The length of a rectangle is 4 inches more than the width. The area of the rectangle is 45 square inches. Find the length and width.

45. The product of two consecutive whole numbers is 600. What are the numbers?

Answer _____

Answer _____

What Is Algebra?

Study the following number sentences to find a pattern.

$$1 \times 3 = 3 \qquad 1 \times 5.7 = 5.7 \qquad 1 \times 12 = 12$$

You can write a general statement about the three number sentences: if a number is multiplied by 1, the product is the number. Here is a way to describe the pattern using a **variable**. Variables are letters or symbols used to represent numbers. The number is represented by the variable n.

$$1 \times n = n \qquad \text{where } n \text{ represents any number}$$

Algebra is the study of variables and the operations of arithmetic with variables. Sometimes more than one variable is needed to describe a pattern.

EXAMPLE 1

Study the three number sentences. Describe the pattern using two variables, a and b.

$22 + 8 = 8 + 22$

$3 + 5 = 5 + 3$

$10 + 2 = 2 + 10$

The pattern is $a + b = b + a$.

EXAMPLE 2

Write three number sentences that fit the pattern $\frac{d}{d} = 1$.

Choose any number for d. Here are three possible number sentences.

$$\frac{4}{4} = 1 \qquad \frac{1.2}{1.2} = 1 \qquad \frac{99}{99} = 1$$

PRACTICE

Describe the pattern using one or two variables.

a	b	c	d
1. $5 \times 6 = 6 \times 5$	$3 - 3 = 0$	$6 + 6 = 2 \times 6$	$0 \times 7 = 0$
$7 \times 10 = 10 \times 7$	$8 - 8 = 0$	$10 + 10 = 2 \times 10$	$0 \times 10 = 0$
$4 \times 8 = 8 \times 4$	$99 - 99 = 0$	$3 + 3 = 2 \times 3$	$0 \times 25 = 0$
$a \times b = b \times a$	_____	_____	_____

Write two number sentences that fit the pattern.

a

2. $n + 0 = n$

b

$3 \times a = a + a + a$

3. $r + 2 = s$

$4 \times m = n$

Sets of Numbers

Every number belongs to a **set** of numbers. Some numbers belong to more than one set. It is helpful to compare the following sets of numbers by using number lines.

Natural Numbers
$\{1, 2, 3, 4, ...\}$

Whole Numbers
$\{0, 1, 2, 3, 4, ...\}$

Integers
$\{... -3, -2, -1, 0, 1, 2, 3, ...\}$

Rational Numbers
{all numbers that can be written in the form $\frac{a}{b}$, where a and b are integers and $b \neq 0$}

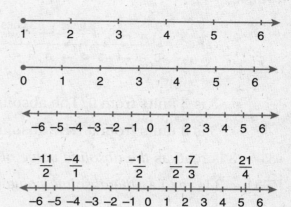

Several rational numbers are shown on the number line. Between any two rational numbers, you can always find another rational number.

EXAMPLE 1

> **Name all the sets to which each of the following numbers belong.**
>
> **5** Natural Numbers, Whole Numbers, Integers, Rational Numbers
>
> $\frac{1}{3}$ Rational Numbers

EXAMPLE 2

> **Write three numbers that belong to each of the following sets.**
>
> **Whole Numbers** 0, 2, 7
>
> **Integers** $^-$8, 0, 5

PRACTICE

Name all the sets to which each of the following numbers belong.
Write *natural numbers, whole numbers, integers,* or *rational numbers.*

	a	b	c	d
1.	13	$^-$5	$\frac{1}{5}$	0
	natural numbers, whole numbers, integers, rational numbers			

Write three numbers that belong to each of the following sets.

2. integers   whole numbers   natural numbers   rational numbers

Understanding Numbers and Absolute Value

The **absolute value** of a number is its distance from 0 on a number line. Look at 3 and $^-3$. They are both 3 units away from 0.

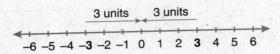

3 is 3 units from 0. The absolute value of 3 is 3.

$^-3$ is 3 units from 0. The absolute value of $^-3$ is 3.

$|3| = 3$ is read as *the absolute value of 3 equals 3.*

$|^-3| = 3$ is read as *the absolute value of $^-3$ equals 3.*

EXAMPLE 1

$$|2| = 2$$

EXAMPLE 2

$$|^-30| = 30$$

EXAMPLE 3

$$|9| = 9$$

EXAMPLE 4

$$|^-4| = 4$$

PRACTICE

Find the absolute value of each number.

	a	b	c	d
1.	$\|^-7\| = \underline{\quad 7 \quad}$	$\|0\| = \underline{\qquad}$	$\|^-17\| = \underline{\qquad}$	$\|22\| = \underline{\qquad}$
2.	$\|6\| = \underline{\qquad}$	$\|^-9\| = \underline{\qquad}$	$\|^-8\| = \underline{\qquad}$	$\|13\| = \underline{\qquad}$
3.	$\|^-12\| = \underline{\qquad}$	$\|^-19\| = \underline{\qquad}$	$\|^-11\| = \underline{\qquad}$	$\|26\| = \underline{\qquad}$
4.	$\|18\| = \underline{\qquad}$	$\|^-3\| = \underline{\qquad}$	$\|10\| = \underline{\qquad}$	$\|^-15\| = \underline{\qquad}$

Name the two numbers that have the given absolute value.

5. 23 $\underline{\quad 23, ^-23 \quad}$	14 $\underline{\qquad}$	32 $\underline{\qquad}$	29 $\underline{\qquad}$
6. 21 $\underline{\qquad}$	40 $\underline{\qquad}$	12 $\underline{\qquad}$	99 $\underline{\qquad}$

Unit 1 Expressions and Formulas

Comparing and Ordering Integers

You can use a number line to compare two or more integers. An integer is **less than** (<) any integer to its right on the number line. An integer is **greater than** (>) any integer to its left. An integer is **greater than or equal to** (≥) itself and any integer to its left. An integer is **less than or equal to** (≤) itself and any integer to its right.

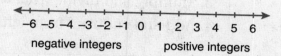

negative integers   positive integers

EXAMPLE 1

6 is to the right of 3.
3 < 6 and 6 > 3

$^-2$ is to the right of $^-4$.
$^-4 < ^-2$ and $^-2 > ^-4$

EXAMPLE 2

3 is to the left of 5.
5 > 3 and 3 < 5

$^-4$ is to the left of $^-3$.
$^-3 > ^-4$ and $^-4 < ^-3$

PRACTICE

Compare. Write <, >, or =.

	a	b	c	d
1.	$^-9$ _< 7	$^-6$ ___ 1	8 ___ 8	0 ___ $^-4$
2.	31 ___ 18	$^-5$ ___ $^-8$	$^-12$ ___ $^-12$	0 ___ 17
3.	$^-13$ ___ $^-9$	$^-11$ ___ $^-11$	$^-3$ ___ 2	$^-6$ ___ $^-2$
4.	45 ___ 54	$^-2$ ___ $^-19$	6 ___ $^-6$	0 ___ 0
5.	$^-1$ ___ $^-1$	9 ___ $^-16$	0 ___ $^-5$	$^-3$ ___ $^-3$

Write in order from least to greatest. Use <.

a	b	c	d
6. 5, 0, $^-6$	17, 18, $^-20$	0, $^-47$, 74	$^-4$, 4, $^-6$
$-6 < 0 < 5$			

Write in order from greatest to least. Use >.

7. 1, $^-6$, 8	$^-13$, $^-31$, 44	$^-2$, $^-9$, 0	7, $^-5$, 0
$8 > 1 > ^-6$			

Order of Operations

When an expression contains more than one operation or makes use of grouping symbols, such as parentheses, follow the correct **order of operations** in order to simplify the expression.

Order of Operations:

1. Complete operations in parentheses or brackets.
2. Complete operations with exponents.
3. Multiply and divide from left to right.
4. Add and subtract from left to right.

EXAMPLE

Simplify.

$6 + (11 - 7)^2 - 1$

$$6 + (11 - 7)^2 - 1 \quad = 6 + (4)^2 - 1 \quad \text{Evaluate inside the parentheses first.}$$

$$= 6 + 16 - 1 \quad \text{Complete the operation with the exponent.}$$
$$4^2 = 4 \times 4 = 16$$

$$= 22 - 1 \quad \text{Add and subtract from left to right.}$$

$$= 21$$

PRACTICE

Simplify.

a	b	c
1. $25 \div (3 + 2) \times 3$ $25 \div 5 \times 3 =$ $5 \times 3 =$ 15	$42 - 2 \times (9 - 3) + 3$	$50 - (35 - 10 \times 2)$
2. $63 \div 7 - 3 \times 2 + 4$	$40 + 3 \times 5 - 8 \div 4$	$(13 - 3) + 5 - 6$
3. $[(19 - 5) \div 2] \times 7$	$8 + [(4 + 5) \times 2]$	$[10 \times (27 - 11) \div 4] \times 3$

Unit 1 Expressions and Formulas

Evaluating Expressions

To **evaluate** an expression means to find a single value for it. If you were asked to evaluate $8 + 2 \cdot 3$, would your answer be 30 or 14? Since an expression has a unique value, be sure to follow the order of operations.

The correct value of $8 + 2 \cdot 3$ is 14 because multiplication should be done before addition. To change the expression so that it has a value of 30, write $(8 + 2) \cdot 3$. The operation within the parentheses must be done first.

EXAMPLE 1

Evaluate:
$12 - 2 \cdot 5$
$12 - 10 = 2$

EXAMPLE 2

Evaluate:
$9(12 + 8)$
$9(20) = 180$

EXAMPLE 3

Evaluate:
$\frac{3 + 6}{1 + 2}$
$\frac{9}{3} = 3$

EXAMPLE 4

Evaluate:
$\frac{1}{2}(3 + 11)$
$\frac{1}{2}(14) = 7$

PRACTICE

Evaluate each expression.

	a	b	c	d
1.	$5 \cdot 2 + 1$	$5(2 + 1)$	$(4 + 6)(8)$	$4 + 6 \cdot 8$
2.	$2(9 + 3)$	$2 \cdot 9 + 3$	$18 - (3 \cdot 6)$	$(18 - 3)(6)$
3.	$8 \cdot 5 - 1$	$8(5 - 1)$	$2 \cdot 10 - 7$	$2(10 - 7)$
4.	$\frac{4 + 8}{3}$	$\frac{7 + 9}{4}$	$\frac{11(2) + 18}{8}$	$\frac{10 - 2(3)}{2}$
5.	$\frac{6 + 10}{2 + 2}$	$\frac{10}{2} - \frac{6}{2}$	$\frac{12}{16} + \frac{21}{4}$	$\frac{12 + 21}{7 - 4}$
6.	$\frac{1}{2}(6 + 26)$	$\frac{1}{2}(6) + \frac{1}{2}(26)$	$\frac{2}{3}(18) - 9$	$\frac{2}{3}(18 - 9)$

Writing Expressions with Variables

An **algebraic expression** consists of one or more numbers and variables, along with arithmetic operations. Here are some examples of algebraic expressions.

$$c - rs \qquad 8 \cdot 3x \qquad 9a(5b) \qquad \frac{a}{f} - 5$$

Remember, $a \times b$, ab, $a \cdot b$, and $a(b)$ all mean to multiply a times b. The fraction $\frac{a}{b}$ means $a \div b$.

Use these examples to help you write algebraic expressions.

Verbal Expression	Operation	Algebraic Expression
the product of 7 and y	multiplication	$7y$
9 more than a	addition	$a + 9$
a number decreased by y	subtraction	$n - y$
a number separated into 5 equal parts	division	$\frac{n}{5}$

PRACTICE

Write an algebraic expression for each verbal expression. Use the variable n when no variable is indicated.

	a		b
1. y multiplied by z	_____	the difference between e and f	_____
2. the sum of p and q	_____	the quotient of b divided by 7	_____
3. 2 more than r	_____	a decreased by 6	_____
4. 12 divided by a number	_____	the product of 3 and a number	_____
5. 8 less than a number	_____	a number increased by 1	_____
6. a number times 100	_____	a number subtracted from 20	_____
7. 32 decreased by t	_____	7 multiplied by a number	_____
8. 28 separated into g equal parts	_____	the difference between 25 and a number	_____

Evaluating Expressions with Variables

If you are given the value of each variable in an expression, you can evaluate the expression by first substituting the value for each variable and then performing the indicated operations.

EXAMPLE 1

Evaluate: $r(r - 2)$ if $r = 6$

$6(6 - 2) = 6(4)$
$\qquad\qquad = 24$

EXAMPLE 2

Evaluate: $7p - \frac{1}{2}q$ if $p = 4$ and $q = 2$

$7(4) - \frac{1}{2}(2) = 28 - 1$
$\qquad\qquad\qquad = 27$

PRACTICE

Evaluate each expression if $a = 9$, $b = 3$, and $c = 7$.

	a	b	c	d
1.	$4a + 7$	$c(c + 3)$	$7b + 2b$	$(7 + 2)b$
2.	$2bc$	$ab + ac$	$a(b + c)$	$ab + c$
3.	$c(a - b)$	$ca - cb$	$ca - b$	$cb - a$
4.	$\frac{a + b}{2}$	$\frac{2a + 2b}{4}$	$\frac{a}{b} + 9$	$\frac{a + 9}{b}$

Evaluate each expression if $x = 10$, $y = 25$, and $z = 20$.

	a	b	c	d
5.	$x + y$	$2y - 3x$	$3xy$	$3yx$
6.	$z + 5x$	$y - 2x$	$(y - z)(z - x)$	$x(x + 2)$
7.	$\frac{2}{3}(y - x)$	$\frac{2(y - x)}{3}$	$\frac{x}{2(y - z)}$	$\frac{x}{2}(y - z)$

Solutions to Equations

If two numbers or expressions are equal, you can write an **equation**. The equation $14 - x = 8$ indicates that the expression $14 - x$ is equal to 8. A **solution** to an equation is a number that, when substituted for the variable, makes the left and right sides of the equation have the same value. For example, 6 is a solution to $14 - x = 8$ since $14 - 6$ is equal to 8. However, 7 is not a solution since $14 - 7$ is 7, which is not equal to 8. To show 7 is not equal to 8, write $7 \neq 8$. See Example 1.

EXAMPLE 1

Is 4 a solution to $7 - y = 0$?

$$7 - 4 = 0?$$

Substitute 4 for y. $\qquad 7 - 4 = 0?$

$$3 \neq 0$$

3 does not equal zero. 4 is not a solution.

EXAMPLE 2

Solve: $\frac{2+8}{1+1} = y$

$$\frac{10}{2} = y$$

$$5 = y$$

The solution is 5.

PRACTICE

Answer each question. Write *yes* or *no*.

	a		b	
1. Is 10 a solution to $2n = 40$?		Is 20 a solution to $2n = 40$?	
2. Is 2 a solution to $6 = 3n$?		Is 3 a solution to $6 = 3n$?	
3. Is 9 a solution to $\frac{36}{n} = 4$?		Is 15 a solution to $3 = \frac{n}{5}$?	
4. Is 8 a solution to $24 = n + 3$?		Is 100 a solution to $n - 9 = 91$?	

Solve.

a	b	c	d
5. $7 + 2 = w$	$32 - 12 = c$	$t = 8(2 + 3)$	$p = 5(8) + 3(9)$
Solution _____	Solution _____	Solution _____	Solution _____
6. $3(8 - 6) = t$	$m = 88 + 3(5)$	$z = 44 + 22$	$k = 75 - 15$
Solution _____	Solution _____	Solution _____	Solution _____
7. $\frac{8+5}{4-3} = n$	$b = \frac{2(5)+6}{2}$	$\frac{3}{4}(6 \cdot 7 + 2) = a$	$\frac{90 - 2(5)}{8} = z$
Solution _____	Solution _____	Solution _____	Solution _____

Missing Addends and Missing Factors

To solve an equation with a missing addend or factor, use the **inverse operation** to isolate the variable on one side of the equal sign. That is, solve for a missing addend by subtracting the known number from both sides of the equation, as in Example 1. Solve for a missing factor by dividing, as in Example 2. Check the solution by substituting the value of the variable in the original equation.

EXAMPLE 1

Solve: $r + 9 = 21$

$$r + 9 = 21$$
$$r + 9 - 9 = 21 - 9$$
$$r = 12$$

The solution is 12.   Check: $12 + 9 = 21$

EXAMPLE 2

Solve: $9n = 99$

$$9n = 99$$
$$\frac{9}{9}n = \frac{99}{9}$$
$$n = 11$$

The solution is 11.   Check: $9(11) = 99$

PRACTICE

Solve. Check.

	a	b	c	d
1.	$b + 9 = 17$	$10 + a = 40$	$8y = 40$	$12n = 48$
	Solution _____	Solution _____	Solution _____	Solution _____
2.	$2a = 8$	$5b = 35$	$z + 14 = 30$	$4x = 100$
	Solution _____	Solution _____	Solution _____	Solution _____
3.	$p + 33 = 333$	$7r = 77$	$b \cdot 6 = 90$	$17 + m = 83$
	Solution _____	Solution _____	Solution _____	Solution _____
4.	$d \cdot 20 = 180$	$9 + n = 9$	$4y = 4$	$f + 12 = 24$
	Solution _____	Solution _____	Solution _____	Solution _____
5.	$7x = 1$	$0 + k = 44$	$5z = 400$	$s + 40 = 555$
	Solution _____	Solution _____	Solution _____	Solution _____
6.	$6r = 3$	$7 + a = 8\frac{1}{2}$	$c + \frac{2}{3} = 5$	$2x = 6$
	Solution _____	Solution _____	Solution _____	Solution _____

Problem-Solving Strategy: Write a Number Sentence

A rope border will be placed along the rectangular boundary of an entire parking lot. The length of the parking lot is 300 feet, and the width is 250 feet. How much rope will be needed?

Understand the problem.

- **What do you want to know?**
  the amount of rope needed for the border

- **What information is given?**
  length 300 feet, width 250 feet

Plan how to solve it.

- **What strategy can you use?**
  You can write a number sentence, using the formula for perimeter.

Solve it.

- **How can you use this strategy to solve the problem?**
  Write a number sentence to show the perimeter of the parking lot to find how much rope is needed. Perimeter = 2(length) + 2(width)

$$2l + 2w = P$$
$$2(300) + 2(250) = P$$
$$600 + 500 = P$$
$$1,100 = P$$

- **What is the answer?**
  The amount of rope needed is 1,100 feet.

Look back and check your answer.

- **Is your answer reasonable?**
  You can check addition using subtraction and check multiplication using division.

  $$1,100 - 500 = 600$$

  $$600 \div 2 = 300 \text{ and } 500 \div 2 = 250$$

  The answer is reasonable.

Write a number sentence to solve each problem.

1. Carla asked 100 people whether they preferred orange juice or grape juice. If 78 people preferred orange juice, how many preferred grape juice?

   Number Sentence _____

   Answer _____

2. Audrey walks each morning around the rectangular block she lives on. The block Audrey lives on is 125 yards long and 60 yards wide. What is the perimeter of the block where Audrey lives?

   Number Sentence _____

   Answer _____

3. A delivery truck follows the same route each day. In 5 days the delivery truck travels a total of 240 kilometers. What is the length of the delivery route?

   Number Sentence _____

   Answer _____

4. Nancy paid $2.72 sales tax on a backpack. If the total with tax was $36.79, what was the price of the backpack without tax?

   Number Sentence _____

   Answer _____

5. One eighth of the students in Mrs. Preston's class had perfect attendance. If 4 students had perfect attendance, how many students are in the class?

   Number Sentence _____

   Answer _____

6. The length of a picture frame is 1.2 times the width. If the length is 27 cm, what is the width?

   Number Sentence _____

   Answer _____

7. Christine is paid the same amount for each hour of work. If the total pay for 7 hours is $87.50, what is the hourly rate?

   Number Sentence _____

   Answer _____

8. The Marietta family drove 624 miles in two days. If they drove 310 miles the second day, how far did they drive the first day?

   Number Sentence _____

   Answer _____

Formula for Area of a Rectangle

Area is the number of **square** units in a figure. A square inch measures 1 inch by 1 inch. The area of a rectangle is found by multiplying the length by the width. This verbal sentence can be written as the formula $A = lw$. To find A, substitute values for l and w into the formula and solve.

The formula for area of a rectangle is

$$A = lw,$$

where A = area, l = length, and w = width.

EXAMPLE

Jaime's bedroom is 12 feet wide and 14 feet long. How many square feet of carpet will be needed to cover the bedroom floor?

Since both measurements are in feet, the area will be in square feet.

$$A = lw$$
$$A = 12(14)$$
$$A = 168$$

Jaime will need 168 square feet of carpet.

PRACTICE

Solve. Use the formula for area of a rectangle.

1. How many square feet of tile are needed to cover a floor measuring 25 feet by 22 feet?

   Answer _____

2. The school's playground measures 30 meters by 50 meters. How many square meters is the playground?

   Answer _____

3. A den measures 20 feet by 12 feet. How many square feet is the den?

   Answer _____

4. A kitchen measures 12 feet by 16 feet. How many square feet is the kitchen?

   Answer _____

5. The dimensions of a professional football field are 120 yards by $53\frac{1}{3}$ yards. How many square yards is a professional football field?

   Answer _____

6. A professional basketball court is 94 feet by 50 feet. How many square feet is a professional basketball court?

   Answer _____

Missing Factors in the Area Formula

You can use the formula for the area of a rectangle to find the length or width if you know the area and the other dimension. Substitute the known values and solve for the unknown value.

EXAMPLE

Find the length when the area is 4,200 square feet and the width is 60 feet.

$$A = lw$$
$$4,200 = 60l$$
$$\frac{4,200}{60} = \frac{60l}{60}$$
$$70 = l$$

The length is 70 feet.

PRACTICE

Solve. Use the formula for area of a rectangle.

a	b	c

1.

a. Find the length when the area is 1,000 square feet and the width is 20 feet.

b. Find the length when the area is 750 square meters and the width is 25 meters.

c. Find the length when the area is 1,800 square centimeters and the width is 30 centimeters.

Answer _____   Answer _____   Answer _____

2.

a. Find the length when the area is 7,500 square yards and the width is 75 yards.

b. Find the width when the area is 1,200 square feet and the length is 40 feet.

c. Find the width when the area is 300 square feet and the length is 15 feet.

Answer _____   Answer _____   Answer _____

3.

a. Find the width when the area is 720 square inches and the length is 60 inches.

b. Find the width when the area is 17.5 square meters and the length is 5 meters.

c. Find the width when the area is 18 square miles and the length is 4.5 miles.

Answer _____   Answer _____   Answer _____

Formula for Volume of a Rectangular Prism

Volume is measured in **cubic** units. A cubic inch measures 1 inch by 1 inch by 1 inch. The volume of a rectangular prism is found by multiplying the length by the width by the height. This verbal sentence can be written as the formula $V = lwh$.

The formula for volume of a rectangular prism is
$$V = lwh,$$
where V = volume, l = length, w = width, and h = height.

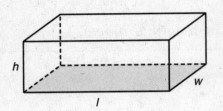

EXAMPLE

What is the volume of a tank that measures 6 meters by 5 meters by 0.5 meters?

$V = lwh$

$V = (6)(5)(0.5)$

$V = 15$

The volume is 15 cubic meters.

PRACTICE

Solve. Use the formula for volume of a rectangular prism.

1. In building a new house, Al dug a basement measuring 30 feet by 32 feet by 9 feet. How many cubic feet of dirt had to be removed?

   Answer _____

2. The floor of a railroad boxcar measures 6 feet by 36 feet. The car has been filled to a depth of 6 feet with grain. How many cubic feet of grain are in the boxcar?

   Answer _____

3. A construction crew dug a ditch 2 meters wide, 3 meters deep, and 150 meters long. What was the volume of the ditch?

   Answer _____

4. The trunk in Tina's car is shaped like a rectangular prism. It measures 4 feet by 2 feet by 3 feet. How many cubic feet is the trunk?

   Answer _____

5. Cut wood is usually sold by the cord. A stack of wood 8 feet long, 4 feet wide, and 4 feet high is a cord. How many cubic feet are there in a cord?

   Answer _____

6. What is the volume in cubic feet of a box whose inside dimensions are 48 inches by 3 feet by 4 feet? (Hint: Change the inches measurement to feet. There are 12 inches in 1 foot.)

   Answer _____

Missing Factors in the Volume Formula

If you know the volume of a rectangular prism and two of the dimensions, you can use the formula $V = lwh$ to solve for the other dimension. Substitute the known values and solve for the unknown value.

EXAMPLE

Find the width when the volume is 1,800 cubic centimeters, the height is 6 centimeters and the length is 30 centimeters.

$$V = lwh$$
$$1,800 = 30 \cdot w \cdot 6$$
$$1,800 = 180w$$
$$\frac{1,800}{180} = \frac{180w}{180}$$
$$w = 10$$

The width is 10 cm.

PRACTICE

Solve. Use the formula for volume of a rectangular prism.

a

b

c

1. Find the height when the volume is 2,100 cubic meters, the length is 20 meters, and the width is 7 meters.

Answer _____

Find the height when the volume is 960 cubic feet, the length is 20 feet, and the width is 8 feet.

Answer _____

Find the height when the volume is 1,500 cubic yards, the length is 25 yards, and the width is 10 yards.

Answer _____

2. Find the length when the volume is 252 cubic meters, the width is 7 meters, and the height is 4 meters.

Answer _____

Find the length when the volume is 480 cubic feet, the width is 4 feet, and the height is 12 feet.

Answer _____

Find the length when the volume is 900 cubic inches, the width is 25 inches, and the height is 6 inches.

Answer _____

3. Find the width when the volume is 480 cubic feet, the length is 20 feet, and the height is 6 feet.

Answer _____

Find the width when the volume is 1,080 cubic meters, the length is 18 meters, and the height is 6 meters.

Answer _____

Find the width when the volume is 800 cubic yards, the length is 40 yards, and the height is 4 yards.

Answer _____

The Circumference Formula

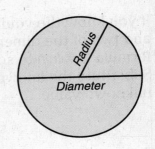

Circumference (*C*) is the perimeter of a circle. You can compute the circumference of a circle if you know the length of the diameter or radius. The **diameter** (*d*) is the distance across the circle and through the center. The **radius** (*r*) is the distance from the center to a point on the circle. The formula $C = \pi d$ means the circumference equals **pi**, or **π**, times the diameter. The value of π is about 3.14. Since $d = 2r$, the formula $C = 2\pi r$ is also true.

Notice that $d = 2r$ and $r = \frac{1}{2}d$.

> The formula for circumference is
> $$C = \pi d,$$
> where C = circumference, d = diameter, and π is about 3.14.

EXAMPLE 1

Find the circumference of a circle if the diameter is 8.2 m.

$C = \pi d$
$C = 3.14(8.2)$
$C = 25.748$

The circumference is about 25.7 meters.

EXAMPLE 2

Find the circumference of a circle if the radius is 6 cm.

First, find the diameter by doubling the radius.

$d = 2r$, so $d = 2 \cdot 6 = 12$
$C = \pi d$
$C = 3.14(12)$
$C = 37.68$ cm

The circumference is about 37.7 cm.

PRACTICE

Solve. Use the formula for circumference of a circle. Let π = 3.14.

1. A botanical garden has a circular flower bed that is 21 feet in diameter. How many feet of border are needed to enclose it?

   Answer _____

2. A zoo has a circular pool that is 28 feet in diameter. How many feet of fence will be needed to enclose the pool?

   Answer _____

3. The radius of Mr. Traskey's pool is 8 feet. What is the circumference of Mr. Traskey's pool?

   Answer _____

4. Ms. Johnson has a pie dish with a radius of 4 inches. What is the circumference of the dish?

   Answer _____

Formula for Area of a Circle

To find the area of a circle, you can use a formula.

The formula for area of a circle is
$$A = \pi r^2,$$
where A = area, r = radius, and π is about 3.14.

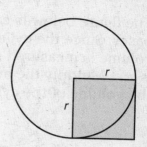

EXAMPLE 1

Find the area of a circle that has a radius of 7 inches. Let $\pi = 3.14$.

$A = \pi r^2$

$A = 3.14(7)^2$

$A = 3.14(49)$

$A = 153.86$ sq in.

EXAMPLE 2

Find A when $d = 7$ in.

First find r by dividing d by 2.

$r = 7 \div 2 = 3.5$

$A = \pi r^2$

$A = 3.14(3.5)^2$

$A = 3.14(12.25)$

$A = 38.465$ sq in.

PRACTICE

Find the area of a circle that has the given radius or diameter. Let $\pi = 3.14$.

a	b
1. $r = 4.5$ cm	$d = 9$ cm
2. $r = 6$ inches	$d = 12$ inches
3. $r = 2\frac{3}{4}$ feet	$d = 7$ feet

Solve.

4. The canvas net used by firefighters is a circular shape and has a diameter of 14 feet. How many square feet of canvas are in the net?

5. A bandstand in the shape of a circle is to be 8 meters across its center. How many square feet of flooring will be required?

Answer _____

Answer _____

Formula for Volume of a Cylinder

The figure below is called a **cylinder**. A cylinder has two circular bases. Since the cylinder is a three-dimensional object, the volume is measured in cubic units. Recall that the area of a circle is πr^2. Multiply the area of the circular base by the height to find the volume of the cylinder ($V = \pi r^2 h$). Use 3.14 for π.

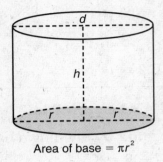

Area of base $= \pi r^2$

> The formula for volume of a cylinder is
> $$V = \pi r^2 h,$$
> where V = volume, r = radius, and h = height.

EXAMPLE

> A cylinder 10 inches high has a base with a radius of 5 inches. How many cubic inches of sand will it hold?
>
> $V = \pi r^2 h$
>
> $V = 3.14(5^2)(10)$
>
> $V = 3.14(25)(10)$
>
> $V = 3.14(250) = 785$
>
> The cylinder will hold 785 cubic inches of sand.

PRACTICE

Solve. Use the formula for volume of a cylinder.

1. A cylindrical water tower is 60 feet high and has a diameter of 14 feet. What is the volume of the water tower (in cubic feet)?

   Answer _____

2. A tank in the shape of a cylinder is 6 meters wide (diameter) and 14 meters high. What is the volume of the tank in cubic meters?

   Answer _____

3. A city water tank has a diameter of 35 feet and a height of 60 feet. How many cubic feet of water will the tank hold?

   Answer _____

4. Two cylinders have the same 20 cm height. One has a radius of 7 cm; the other has a radius of 14 cm. What is the difference in volume between the two cylinders?

   Answer _____

5. A can has a diameter of 3 inches and is 5 inches high. How many cubic inches will it hold?

   Answer _____

6. A coffee can has a diameter of 4 inches and a height of 5.5 inches. How many cubic inches of coffee will it hold?

   Answer _____

Temperature Formulas

There are two commonly used temperature scales, **Fahrenheit** (°F) and **Celsius** (°C). Each can be converted to the other by means of a formula.

To convert Fahrenheit (°F) to Celsius (°C), use the formula $C = (F - 32) \cdot \frac{5}{9}$.	To convert Celsius (°C) to Fahrenheit (°F), use the formula $F = (C \cdot \frac{9}{5}) + 32$.

EXAMPLE 1

Water freezes at 32°F. What is the freezing point on the Celsius scale?

°C = $(32 - 32) \cdot \frac{5}{9}$

°C = 0

The freezing point is 0°C.

EXAMPLE 2

The boiling point of water on the Celsius scale is 100°C. Find the boiling point on the Fahrenheit scale.

°F = $(100 \cdot \frac{9}{5}) + 32$

°F = 180 + 32

°F = 212

The boiling point is 212°F.

PRACTICE

Solve.

1. When a Fahrenheit temperature is 95°, what is the equivalent Celsius temperature?

   Answer _____

2. When a Celsius temperature is 45°, what is the equivalent Fahrenheit temperature?

   Answer _____

3. Find C when F = 68°.

   Answer _____

4. Find F when C = 15°.

   Answer _____

5. Find C when F = 86°.

   Answer _____

6. Find F when C = 30°.

   Answer _____

7. Find C when F = 113°.

   Answer _____

8. Find F when C = 75°.

   Answer _____

9. Find C when F = 77°.

   Answer _____

10. Find F when C = 60°.

    Answer _____

The Simple Interest Formula

When a customer deposits money in a savings account, the bank pays the customer for the use of the money. This payment is called **interest**. Likewise, a customer who borrows money must pay interest to the bank. The formula $I = prt$ is used to find **simple interest**, or interest on a specific amount at a **fixed rate**.

> The formula for simple interest is
> $$I = prt,$$
> where I = interest, p = principal, r = rate, and t = time.

$I = prt$ means multiply the **principal** (money amount) times the rate (a percent or decimal) times the time to find the interest. The rate and time must have corresponding units. That is, if the rate is given per year, the time must be in years. When using the formula, express the rate, r, as a decimal. For example, express 4.5% as 0.045.

EXAMPLE

> **Rachelle borrowed $1,200 at a rate of 7% per year for 6 months. What is the amount of simple interest?**
>
> Change 6 months to $\frac{1}{2}$ or 0.5 year. Also, write 7% as 0.07.
>
> $I = prt$
> $I = (\$1,200)(0.07)(0.5)$ Substitute the data. Multiply.
> $I = \$42$
>
> The interest is $42.

PRACTICE

Find the amount of simple interest.

a

1. Felicia borrowed $200 at a rate of 5% per year for 1 year.

   Interest _____

b

Chris borrowed $2,500 at a rate of $6\frac{1}{2}$% per year for 2 years.

Interest _____

2. Antonio borrowed $300 at a rate of 5% per year for 2 years.

   Interest _____

Chan borrowed $1,000 at a rate of $5\frac{1}{2}$% per year for 1 year.

Interest _____

3. Selena borrowed $500 at a rate of 6% per year for 2 years and 6 months.

   Interest _____

James borrowed $450 at a rate of 10% per year for 3 years and 9 months.

Interest _____

Missing Factors in the Simple Interest Formula

If you know the value for three of the variables in the formula $I = prt$, you can solve for the unknown value. Find the missing factor.

Remember, when using the formula, write r as a decimal.

EXAMPLE

When $p = \$500$, $I = \$25$, and $t = 1$ year, find r.

$$I = prt$$
$$25 = (500)(r)(1)$$
$$25 = 500r$$
$$\frac{25}{500} = \frac{500r}{500}$$
$$\frac{25}{500} = r$$
$$0.05 = 5\% = r$$

The interest rate is 5%.

PRACTICE

Solve. Use the formula for simple interest.

a	b	c
1. Find the principal when the interest is $432, the rate is $6\frac{1}{4}\%$, and the time is 3 years.	Find the principal when the interest for one year amounts to $20 at 5%.	Find the principal when the rate is 5%, the time is 2 years, and the interest is $120.
Answer _____	Answer _____	Answer _____
2. Find the rate when the interest is $300, the time is 3 years, and the principal is $2,000.	Find the rate when the principal is $420, the time is 6 months, and the interest is $12.60. (Hint: $t = \frac{1}{2}$.)	Find the rate when the interest is $24, the time is 2 years, and the principal is $200.
Answer _____	Answer _____	Answer _____
3. Find the time when the principal is $250, the rate is 6%, and the interest is $45.	Find the time when the principal is $50, the rate is 7%, and the interest is $17.50.	Find the time when the principal is $250, the rate is 4%, and the interest is $20.
Answer _____	Answer _____	Answer _____

The Distance Formula

The formula $D = rt$ means distance is equal to the rate times the time. The rate and time must have corresponding units. If r is in miles per hour, then t must be in hours.

> The formula for distance is
> $$D = rt,$$
> where D = distance, r = rate, and t = time.

EXAMPLE

When Ling walks to the post office, she walks at a rate of 4 miles per hour. She walks for 30 minutes. How far does she walk?

Change 30 minutes to 0.5 hours.

$D = rt$

$D = 4 \times 0.5 = 2$

Ling walks two miles.

PRACTICE

Solve. Use the formula for distance.

1. A mail plane left Los Angeles at 2:00 P.M. and arrived in Seattle at 6:00 P.M. During the trip, the average speed was 320 miles per hour. What was the air distance of this trip?

   Answer _____

2. A certain plane flies at a speed of 600 miles per hour. If it requires 4 hours at this rate of speed to make the trip from Kiska to Tokyo, what is the air distance?

   Answer _____

3. A plane flew from Seattle to Toronto in 4 hours, maintaining a speed of 500 miles per hour. What is the air distance between Seattle and Toronto?

   Answer _____

4. A plane flew from San Diego to Honolulu in 6 hours. Due to a head wind, the actual speed traveled was 420 miles per hour. What was the air distance between these two cities?

   Answer _____

5. A plane trip between two cities took 4 hours. A strong head wind slowed the speed of the plane to 390 miles per hour. What was the air distance of the trip?

   Answer _____

6. A plane flew from Newfoundland to Iceland in 4 hours. The average speed of the plane was 530 miles per hour. What was the air distance of this trip?

   Answer _____

Missing Factors in the Distance Formula

If you know the distance and either the rate or the time, you can solve for the unknown value. Use the formula $D = rt$ and substitute the known values. Then find the missing factor.

EXAMPLE

Find r when $D = 50$ mi and $t = 2$ hrs.

$D = rt$

$50 = r(2)$

$\frac{50}{2} = \frac{2r}{2}$

$25 = r$

The rate is 25 miles per hour.

PRACTICE

Solve. Use the distance formula.

1. A plane was sighted over two different observation posts that were 650 miles apart. The plane passed over the first post at 4:00 A.M. and over the second post at 6:30 A.M. At what speed was the plane traveling?

   Answer _____

2. If it took a plane 6 hours to fly from Tampa to Los Angeles, a distance of 2,496 miles, at what rate of speed was the flight made?

   Answer _____

3. Find r when $D = 1,400$ mi and $t = 3\frac{1}{2}$ hr.

   Answer _____

4. Find r when $D = 1,500$ mi and $t = 3$ hr.

   Answer _____

5. Find t when $D = 1,750$ km and $r = 350$ km per hour.

   Answer _____

6. Find t when $D = 180$ km and $r = 45$ km per hr.

   Answer _____

7. Find t when $D = 420$ m and $r = 70$ m per sec.

   Answer _____

8. Find t when $D = 113.5$ ft and $r = 45.4$ ft per sec.

   Answer _____

9. Find r when $D = 2,150$ miles and $t = 5$ hours.

   Answer _____

10. Find r when $D = 247.5$ miles and $t = 4.5$ hours.

    Answer _____

Problem-Solving Strategy: Use a Formula

Margie borrowed $500. The loan was for 6 months, and the interest rate was 10% per year. What was the total amount of interest that Margie paid?

Understand the problem.

- **What do you want to know?**
  the amount of interest Margie paid

- **What information is given?**
  principal = $500
  time = 6 months
  interest rate = 10% per year

Plan how to solve it.

- **What strategy can you use?**
  You can use the formula for simple interest.

Solve it.

- **How can you use this strategy to solve the problem?**
  Use the simple interest formula $I = prt$. Change the rate to a decimal and write the time in years. Then substitute for the variables and multiply to find the amount of interest.

  > The rate is 10%, so $r = 0.10$. The time is 6 months, so $t = \frac{1}{2}$ or 0.5.
  >
  > $I = prt$
  >
  > $I = \$500(0.10)(0.5)$
  >
  > $I = \$25$

- **What is the answer?**
  The amount of interest Margie paid was $25.

Look back and check your answer.

- **Is your answer reasonable?**
  You can check your answer by substituting and solving for a known value such as the principal (p).

  $I = prt$
  $25 = p(0.10)(0.5)$
  $25 = p(0.05)$
  $\frac{25}{0.05} = \frac{0.05p}{0.05}$
  $500 = p$

  The answer is reasonable.

Solve.

1. Darlene has $750 in a savings account paying an interest rate of 4% annually. Find the amount of interest she will earn in 1 year.

   Answer _____

2. The radius of a dinner plate is 5 inches. What is the circumference of the circle? Round the answer to the nearest whole number.

   Answer _____

3. A rectangular flower bed is 2 feet wide and $6\frac{1}{2}$ feet long. What is the area of the flower bed?

   Answer _____

4. The high temperature on Monday was 59°F. What was the equivalent Celsius temperature? (Hint: $C = (F - 32) \cdot \frac{5}{9}$)

   Answer _____

5. A train traveled 240 miles non-stop at an average speed of 80 miles per hour. How long did the trip take?

   Answer _____

6. The dimensions of an apple juice box are as follows: 4.0 cm by 6.3 cm by 10 cm. What is the volume of the box? Round the answer to the nearest whole number.

   Answer _____

7. A poster came in a cardboard tube that was 20 inches long and had a radius of 1.2 inches. What is the volume of the cardboard tube?

   Answer _____

8. Which pool will hold more water: a circular pool 6 feet deep with a diameter of 20 feet or a rectangular pool 8 feet by 12 feet and 6 feet deep?

   Answer _____

Write three number sentences that fit each pattern.

a	b	c	d
1. $n \div n = 1$	$x + y = y + x$	$2x = x + x$	$7 + a = b$
_____	_____	_____	_____
_____	_____	_____	_____
_____	_____	_____	_____

List three numbers that belong to each of the following sets.

a	b	c	d
2. whole numbers	natural numbers	integers	rational numbers
_____	_____	_____	_____

Find the absolute value of each number.

a	b	c	d
3. $|^-7| =$ _____	$|46| =$ _____	$|68| =$ _____	$|^-112| =$ _____

Write the numbers in order from least to greatest.

a	b	c	d
4. $8, 0, {}^-4$	${}^-7, 8, {}^-20$	$0, {}^-4, 7$	${}^-2, {}^-9, {}^-6$

Simplify.

a	b	c
5. $24 \div (9 - 5) \times 4$	$12 \times 3 \div (8 + 4) - 3$	$50 + (36 \div 9 + 22)$

Write an algebraic expression for each verbal expression.

a	b
6. 9 more than b	x decreased by 10
7. the product of 9 and k	r divided by 2

Evaluate each expression.

a	b	c	d
8. $(5 + 2) \times 12$	$2 \cdot 12 + 11$	$\dfrac{20 - 3(4)}{2}$	$\dfrac{16 + 47}{4 + 5}$

Evaluate each expression if $a = 6$, $b = 10$, and $c = 3$.

	a		b		c		d
9. $a + b$		ab		$(c + 2)b$		$\frac{7c - 1}{2b}$	

Solve.

	a		b		c		d
10. $11(9) = w$		$a = \frac{1}{2}(15 + 3)$		$f = 4(4) + 3(10)$		$\frac{15 + 13}{12 - 5} = b$	
Solution _____		Solution _____		Solution _____		Solution _____	
11. $8k = 40$		$x + 23 = 79$		$19 + m = 100$		$4x = 10$	
Solution _____		Solution _____		Solution _____		Solution _____	

Solve.

12. Using the formula $A = lw$, find l when A is 48 square feet and w is 8 feet.

Answer _____

13. Using the formula $C = \pi d$, find C when d is 14 yards.

Answer _____

14. Using the formula $V = lwh$, find V when l is 15 meters, w is 12 meters, and h is 10 meters.

Answer _____

15. Using the formula $V = \pi r^2 h$, find V when r is 3 centimeters and h is 10 centimeters.

Answer _____

16. Using the formula $I = prt$, find I when p is $500, r is $4\frac{1}{2}\%$, and t is 2 years.

Answer _____

17. Use the formula $C = (F - 32) \cdot \frac{5}{9}$ to find C when F is 113°.

Answer _____

UNIT 2 Integers and Monomials

Integers and Opposites

Integers are the set of whole numbers and their **opposites.**
Integers can be shown on a number line. **Positive** integers are
greater than 0. **Negative** integers are less than 0.

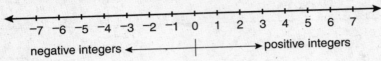

The integer ⁻5 is read *negative five*. The integer 5 can also be
written as ⁺5, or *positive five*. These two integers, 5 and ⁻5,
are opposites.

Positive and negative numbers are used in many everyday
situations.

10° below zero	⁻10
loss of $7	⁻7
gain of 12 yards	⁺12 or 12
profit of $100	⁺100 or 100

PRACTICE

Write the opposite of each integer.

	a	b	c	d
1.	4 ⁻4	⁻7	⁻21	45
2.	⁻19	33	⁻66	0

Write an integer to describe each situation.

	a	b	c
3.	33° above zero ⁺33	8° below zero	deposit of $150
4.	loss of 10 yards	gain of 6 yards	profit of $88
5.	3,500 ft above sea level	50 ft below sea level	up 7 floors
6.	down 4 floors	debt of $30	9 units to the left of 0

Adding Integers with the Same Sign

To add positive integers, think of whole numbers. The sum of $^+2$ and $^+5$ is $^+7$ because $2 + 5 = 7$. To add negative integers, think of moving in the negative direction (left) on the number line. This number line shows the sum of $^-2$ and $^-5$.

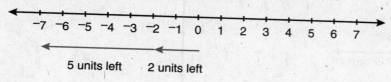

5 units left   2 units left

In order to understand the rules for adding integers with the same sign, you need to know the meaning of **absolute value.** The absolute value of an integer is its distance from 0 on the number line. Distance is always a positive value. Compare $|^-2| + |^-5| = 7$ to the number line above. The sum of $^-2$ and $^-5$ is 7 units to the left, or $^-7$.

> **RULE:** To add integers with the same sign, add the absolute values and give the sum the same sign as the addends.

EXAMPLE 1

Add: $^-8 + (^-4)$

The sum will be negative. Add the absolute values.

$|^-8| + |^-4| =$
$8 + 4 = 12$

Use the sign of the addends for the sum.

$(^-8) + (^-4) = ^-12$

EXAMPLE 2

Add: $9 + 8$

The sum will be positive. Add the absolute values.

$|9| + |8| =$
$9 + 8 = 17$

The addends are positive, so the sum is positive.

EXAMPLE 3

Add: $^-5 + 0$

Adding zero to a number gives the number.

$^-5 + 0 = ^-5$

PRACTICE

Add.

	a	b	c	d
1.	$3 + 1 =$	$^-2 + (^-4) =$	$5 + 4 =$	$^-1 + (^-5) =$
2.	$^-3 + (^-6) =$	$0 + (^-7) =$	$12 + 0 =$	$^-9 + (^-1) =$
3.	$4 + 7 =$	$^-6 + (^-4) =$	$^-9 + (^-5) =$	$^-8 + (^-9) =$
4.	$6 + 8 + 4 =$	$0 + (^-5) + (^-8) =$	$^-7 + 0 + (^-8) =$	$21 + 10 + 65 =$

Adding Integers with Different Signs

To add integers with different signs, think of the number line.
This number line shows the sum of -4 and 7. Remember that
$|^-4| = 4$ and $|7| = 7$.

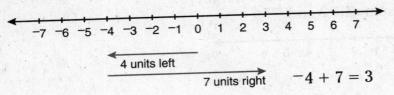

4 units left

7 units right $-4 + 7 = 3$

The sum is 3 units right, or $^+3$. Notice that the absolute value
of 7 is greater than the absolute value of $^-4$. This is why the
sum is positive.

> **RULE:** To add two integers with different signs, subtract the
> lesser absolute value from the greater absolute value.
> The result will have the same sign as the number
> with the greater absolute value.

EXAMPLE 1

Add: $^-9 + 3$

Subtract the absolute values. The sum will be negative.

$^-(9 - 3) = ^-6$

EXAMPLE 2

Add: $7 + (^-2)$

Subtract the absolute values. The sum will be positive.

$^+(7 - 2) = 5$

EXAMPLE 3

Add: $^-2 + 4 + (^-5) + 9$

Combine the integers with the same signs.

$= ^-(2 + 5) + (4 + 9)$

$= ^-7 + 13$

$= 6$

PRACTICE

Add.

	a	b	c	d
1.	$6 + (^-3) =$	$5 + (^-9) =$	$^-4 + 3 =$	$^-2 + 7 =$
2.	$8 + (^-1) =$	$^-4 + 11 =$	$7 + (^-6) =$	$^-8 + 8 =$
3.	$^-9 + 1 =$	$1 + (^-7) =$	$^-12 + 7 =$	$8 + (^-15) =$
4.	$11 + (^-9) =$	$^-4 + 16 =$	$^-18 + 7 =$	$^-19 + 6 =$
5.	$14 + (^-14) =$	$^-7 + 13 =$	$14 + (^-8) =$	$^-17 + 9 =$
6.	$^-3 + (^-4) + 6 =$	$^-2 + 0 + 9 + (^-4) =$	$^-10 + 7 + 3 =$	$7 + (^-6) + (^-5) =$

Subtracting Integers

To subtract an integer, add its opposite. To subtract $10 - (^-4)$, add $10 + 4 = 14$.

> **RULE:** To subtract an integer, add its opposite.

When adding two integers with the same sign, add the absolute values. The sum will have the same sign as the addends.

EXAMPLE 1

Subtract: $6 - (^-2)$

The opposite of -2 is 2.
$6 - (^-2) = 6 + 2$
$\qquad\qquad = 8$

EXAMPLE 2

Subtract: $^-2 - 1$

The opposite of 1 is -1.
$^-2 - 1 = {}^-2 + (^-1)$
$\qquad\quad = {}^-(2 + 1)$
$\qquad\quad = {}^-3$

EXAMPLE 3

Subtract: $^-8 - (^-9)$

The opposite of $^-9$ is 9.
$^-8 - (^-9) = {}^-8 + 9$
$\qquad\qquad = +(9 - 8)$
$\qquad\qquad = 1$

PRACTICE

Subtract.

	a	b	c	d
1.	$5 - (^-2) =$	$^-4 - 3 =$	$1 - 7 =$	$9 - 3 =$
2.	$^-7 - (^-4) =$	$^-5 - 4 =$	$4 - (^-9) =$	$11 - (^-5) =$
3.	$8 - 17 =$	$^-14 - (^-9) =$	$^-9 - 12 =$	$^-17 - 8 =$
4.	$^-13 - (^-3) =$	$^-15 - 7 =$	$4 - (^-14) =$	$16 - 9 =$
5.	$7 - 17 =$	$5 - (^-14) =$	$10 - 18 =$	$15 - (^-9) =$
6.	$13 - 23 =$	$^-18 - 25 =$	$^-29 - 19 =$	$11 - (^-29) =$
7.	$18 - (^-18) =$	$25 - (^-17) =$	$^-14 - 28 =$	$35 - 29 =$
8.	$^-43 - (^-29) =$	$47 - 53 =$	$^-37 - (^-45) =$	$^-54 - 54 =$

Adding and Subtracting Integers

Recall the rules for adding and subtracting integers.

- To add integers with the same sign, add the absolute values and give the sum the same sign as the addends.
- To add two integers with different signs, subtract the lesser absolute value from the greater absolute value. The result will have the same sign as the number with the greater absolute value.
- To subtract an integer, add its opposite.

PRACTICE

Add or subtract.

	a	b	c
1.	$^-9 + (^-21) =$	$^-11 - (^-11) =$	$32 + (^-13) =$
2.	$14 + (^-17) =$	$^-8 - 9 =$	$38 + (^-50) =$
3.	$^-10 - (^-6) =$	$5 - (^-12) =$	$^-5 + (^-9) =$
4.	$12 - (^-3) =$	$24 - (^-21) =$	$(^-14) - (^-27) =$
5.	$^-10 + (^-1) + 2 =$	$14 + (^-5) + (^-12) =$	$^-5 + 4 + (^-9) =$
6.	$16 - (^-4) + 3 =$	$(^-5) - (^-8) + 19 =$	$^-9 - 6 + (^-10) =$
7.	$(^-11) - (^-7) - 6 =$	$3 + (^-5) - (^-12) =$	$(^-7) + 4 - (^-2) =$
8.	$15 + (^-9) + 2 + (^-3) =$	$2 + 3 + (^-8) + (^-1) =$	$^-8 + (^-3) + (^-4) + 7 =$

Multiplying Integers

Recall that one way to multiply is to add repeatedly. For example, you can find 3 times $^-6$ by adding $(^-6) + (^-6) + (^-6)$. So, $3(^-6) = ^-18$. Notice that 3 and $^-6$ have different signs and that the product is negative.

> **RULE:** The product of two integers with different signs is negative.

If you multiply two positive integers the product is positive. But what if you multiply two negative integers? You can think of $^-3(^-6)$ as the opposite of $3(^-6)$. Then $^-3(^-6)$ is the opposite of $^-18$, or 18. Again, the product is positive.

> **RULE:** The product of two integers with the same sign is positive.

EXAMPLE 1

Multiply: $^-1(92)$
$$^-(1 \cdot 92) = ^-92$$

EXAMPLE 2

Multiply: $^-8(^-5)$
$$^+(8 \cdot 5) = 40$$

EXAMPLE 3

Multiply: $7(^-2)(6)$
$$= 7(6)(^-2)$$
$$= 42(^-2) = ^-84$$

PRACTICE

Multiply.

	a	b	c	d
1.	$2(5) =$	$^-3(^-6) =$	$5(^-1) =$	$^-2(^-3) =$
2.	$8(4) =$	$^-9(5) =$	$3(^-8) =$	$^-4(^-9) =$
3.	$^-5(^-7) =$	$^-6(8) =$	$^-9(^-7) =$	$8(^-9) =$
4.	$^-4(^-12) =$	$^-13(^-7) =$	$^-5(23) =$	$^-4(16) =$
5.	$2(^-1)(3) =$	$3(^-2)(^-2) =$	$^-2(^-4)(^-3) =$	$^-4(^-1)(4) =$
6.	$^-5(^-7)(^-3) =$	$4(^-9)(^-6) =$	$^-2(^-13)(5) =$	$^-8(^-3)(^-9) =$
7.	$3(^-15) =$	$^-2(^-17) =$	$^-6(21) =$	$^-7(^-11) =$
8.	$6(^-4)(^-3) =$	$^-2(^-3)(^-3) =$	$2(5)(^-2) =$	$^-6(1)(^-7) =$
9.	$^-8(2)(^-4) =$	$9(^-2)(^-3) =$	$^-8(^-3)(7) =$	$^-4(11)(^-9) =$

Dividing Integers

Recall that division and multiplication are inverse operations.
Consider the multiplication sentence $2(^-3) = ^-6$. You can write
two related division sentences: $^-6 \div (^-3) = 2$ and $^-6 \div 2 = ^-3$.
Compare the signs of the **dividend, divisor,** and **quotient.** Notice
that the rules for dividing integers are similar to the rules for
multiplying integers.

> **RULE:** The quotient of two integers with different signs is
> negative. The quotient of two integers with the same
> sign is positive.

EXAMPLE 1

Divide: $^-30 \div 10$
$^-(30 \div 10) = ^-3$

EXAMPLE 2

Divide: $^-45 \div ^-9$
$^+(45 \div 9) = 5$

EXAMPLE 3

Divide: $\frac{48}{^-6}$
$^-(48 \div 6) = ^-8$

PRACTICE

Divide.

	a	b	c	d
1.	$8 \div (^-4) =$	$^-14 \div 2 =$	$^-16 \div (^-4) =$	$15 \div 3 =$
2.	$^-45 \div (^-9) =$	$28 \div (^-4) =$	$^-48 \div (^-8) =$	$36 \div (^-6) =$
3.	$^-63 \div (^-9) =$	$^-20 \div 2 =$	$^-55 \div (^-5) =$	$54 \div 3 =$
4.	$104 \div (^-4) =$	$^-72 \div (^-3) =$	$^-84 \div (^-7) =$	$120 \div (^-12) =$
5.	$^-126 \div 9 =$	$234 \div (^-13) =$	$^-240 \div (^-15) =$	$483 \div (^-21) =$
6.	$\frac{^-18}{6} =$	$\frac{24}{^-8} =$	$\frac{^-40}{^-5} =$	$\frac{81}{^-9} =$
7.	$\frac{70}{^-5} =$	$\frac{^-66}{3} =$	$\frac{^-108}{^-6} =$	$\frac{153}{^-9} =$
8.	$\frac{198}{^-11} =$	$\frac{^-350}{^-14} =$	$\frac{312}{13} =$	$\frac{^-450}{^-18} =$

Unit 2 Integers and Monomials

Multiplying and Dividing Integers

Recall the rules for multiplying and dividing integers.

- The product of two integers with different signs is negative.
- The product of two integers with the same sign is positive.
- The quotient of two integers with different signs is negative.
- The quotient of two integers with the same sign is positive.

PRACTICE

Multiply or divide.

	a	b	c	d
1.	$^-9(^-12)$	$56 \div (^-7)$	$\frac{^-75}{^-25}$	$^-8(4)$
2.	$^-100 \div (^-20)$	$^-3(^-4)(^-12)$	$\frac{200}{^-40}$	$^-72 \div 8$
3.	$7(^-3)(5)$	$^-8(2)(^-3)$	$^-10(^-3)(2)$	$^-9(^-2)(3)$
4.	$\frac{^-27}{3}$	$150 \div (^-6)$	$\frac{^-20}{^-2}$	$\frac{^-84}{^-12}$
5.	$^-8(^-4)(^-1)$	$^-96 \div (^-3)$	$\frac{^-160}{^-10}$	$^-21(^-5)$
6.	$^-91 \div 7$	$^-3(^-8)(^-3)$	$\frac{^-300}{^-15}$	$^-117 \div 13$
7.	$7(^-8)(6)$	$^-5(^-6)(2)(^-3)$	$^-10(^-35)(0)(20)$	$^-6(1)(^-2)(3)$
8.	$\frac{6(^-8)}{3}$	$^-196 \div (^-14)$	$\frac{^-4(^-5)}{^-2}$	$\frac{3(^-4)}{^-2(3)}$

Problem-Solving Strategy: Choose an Operation

The temperature one morning at dawn was $^-6°F$. By noon the temperature had risen to 20°F. What was the change in temperature?

Understand the problem.

- **What do you want to know?**
  the change in temperature from dawn to noon

- **What information is given?**
  the temperature at dawn ($^-6°F$) and the temperature at noon (20°F)

Plan how to solve it.

- **What strategy can you use?**
  You can choose an operation to find the change in temperature.

Add to combine groups.	**Multiply** to combine equal groups.
Subtract to separate into groups.	**Divide** to separate into equal groups.

Solve it.

- **How can you use this strategy to solve the problem?**
  To find the change in temperature from dawn to noon, you need to subtract the temperature at dawn from the temperature at noon.

  Let c = the change in temperature.

  noon temp. − dawn temp. = c

  $$20° - (^-6°) = c$$
  $$20° + 6° = 26°$$

- **What is the answer?**
  The change in temperature was 26° degrees.

Look back and check your answer.

- **Is your answer reasonable?**
  You can check subtraction with addition.

  dawn temp. + c = noon temp.

  $$^-6° + 26° = 20°$$

  The answer is reasonable.

Solve.

1. A submarine descended to a depth of 53 meters below sea level. Later it rose 15 meters. At what depth was the submarine?

   Let d = depth.
   ⁻53 + 15 = d
   ⁻38 = d

   Answer _____38 meters below sea level_____

2. Kareem scuba dived 23 feet below sea level. He then swam 8 feet more toward the sea floor. How far below sea level was Kareem?

   Let d = depth.
   ⁻23 + ⁻8 = d
   ⁻31 = d

   Answer _____

3. A stock's value decreased the same amount each day for 4 days. If the total change in value was ⁻16, what was the change each day?

   Answer _____

4. Barbara bought 36 apples. If she uses 6 apples to make an apple pie, how many apple pies can Barbara make?

   Answer _____

5. One morning, the temperature rose 15 degrees Fahrenheit between sunrise and 9:00 A.M. If the temperature at 9:00 A.M. was 60°F, what was the temperature at sunrise?

   Answer _____

6. The winning football team scored 14 points in each quarter of the game. How many points did the football team score by the end of the fourth quarter?

   Answer _____

7. In Quebec, the temperature one cold evening at 8:00 P.M. was 0°C. Between then and midnight, the temperature dropped 3°C each hour. What was the temperature at midnight?

   Answer _____

8. Roberta and Helen were exploring a cave. They descended to a depth 74 feet from the entrance, and discovered a large cavern. The ceiling of the cavern was 17 feet above them. At what depth below the cave entrance was the cavern ceiling?

   Answer _____

Terms, Coefficients, and Monomials

An algebraic expression has different parts.

A **term** is a number, a variable, or a product or quotient of numbers and variables.

EXAMPLES OF TERMS

$\frac{a}{b}$	$^-6x^2$	5	a	$8mn$

An **expression** consists of one or more terms and one or more operations.

EXAMPLES OF EXPRESSIONS

$4 + b$	$ab - c$	$x + \frac{b}{t}$	$2a + 7ab - 1$

Constants are terms that do not contain variables.

EXAMPLES OF CONSTANTS

$^-7$	2	$\frac{3}{4}$	0.8	π

The **coefficient** of a term is the numerical factor. When there is no number in front of a variable, the coefficient 1 is understood. Coefficients may be integers, fractions, or decimals.

EXAMPLES OF COEFFICIENTS

Term:	^-7y	m	$-x$	$\frac{3}{4}x$ or $\frac{3x}{4}$
Coefficient:	$^-7$	1	$^-1$	$\frac{3}{4}$ or 0.75

A **monomial** is a number, a variable, or a product of numbers and variables. So, the terms $\frac{s}{t}$ and $\frac{4}{5b}$ are not monomials because division is indicated by the variables in the denominators.

EXAMPLES OF MONOMIALS

$9xy$	0.5	^-7k	$\frac{4}{5}b$

PRACTICE

Circle the constants.

a	b	c	d	e	f	g	h
1. $^-7$	$4m$	9	$\frac{1}{10}$	$-m$	14	$x + y$	$2x$

Circle the monomials.

2. $5x$	a	$a + b$	$2xy$	$x - 2y$	$\frac{1}{3}a$	$a - 2b$	$\frac{12}{z}$

Circle the coefficient of each term.

3. $5a$	$4s$	πd	^-42b	$1{,}250r$	$1.5n$	^-9m	$\frac{2}{3}x$

Write the coefficient of each term.

4. $\frac{x}{2}$	$\frac{^-3y}{4}$	z	$\frac{3a}{2}$	$0.4r$	$\frac{m}{4}$	$-a$	$\frac{3b}{5}$

Unit 2 Integers and Monomials

Adding Like Terms

Like terms are terms that have the same variable or variables. For example, $4m$ and $3m$ are like terms. However, $2x$ and $6y$ are not like terms. To find the sum of $4m$ and $3m$, try writing the multiplication in each term as addition.

$$4m + 3m = (m + m + m + m) + (m + m + m) = 7m$$

Another way to write this is $4m + 3m = (4 + 3)m = 7m$.

> **RULE:** The coefficient of the sum of two like terms is the sum of the coefficients.

EXAMPLE 1

Add: $7x + x$
$$= (7 + 1)x$$
$$= 8x$$

EXAMPLE 2

Add: $^-8mn + 3mn$
$$= (^-8 + 3)mn$$
$$= \,^-5mn$$

EXAMPLE 3

Add: $3x + 4y$

These are not like terms, so they cannot be combined.

PRACTICE

Add.

	a	b	c	d
1.	$2y + 4y =$	$6n + 5n =$	$3m + 15m =$	$13yz + 12yz =$
2.	$5x + x =$	$2a + a =$	$st + 6st =$	$m + 3m =$
3.	$28y + 52y =$	$12b + 16b =$	$29s + 15s =$	$20mn + 10mn =$
4.	$3x + (^-2x) =$	$^-4t + (^-6t) =$	$^-3cd + (^-7cd) =$	$^-5v + (^-7v) =$
5.	$^-2ab + 7ab =$	$^-4t + 2t =$	$^-8rs + 12rs =$	$^-43y + 12y =$
6.	$\frac{1}{2}a + \frac{1}{2}a =$	$\frac{1}{3}n + \frac{1}{3}n =$	$\frac{13}{4}x + \frac{1}{4}x =$	$d + \frac{1}{2}d =$
7.	$0.5b + 1.3b =$	$3.2y + 0.8y =$	$0.8k + 0.2k =$	$0.05t + 0.07t =$
8.	$3a + 2a + 4a =$	$5xy + xy + 8xy =$	$6m + 9m + 3m =$	$7h + h + 2h =$

Subtracting Like Terms

The following rule can be used to subtract like terms, as shown in Example 1. However, sometimes it is easier to subtract by adding the opposite. Write the opposite of a term by changing the sign of the coefficient. Then use the rule for adding like terms.

RULE: The coefficient of the difference of two like terms is the difference of the coefficients.

EXAMPLE 1

Add: $6x - 5x$

$= (6 - 5)x$

$= x$

EXAMPLE 2

Add: $^-9ab - 3ab$

$= {}^-9ab + ({}^-3ab)$

$= ({}^-9 + {}^-3)ab$

$= {}^-12ab$

EXAMPLE 3

Add: $\frac{1}{6}n - (\frac{^-3}{6}n)$

$= \frac{1}{6}n + \frac{3}{6}n$

$= (\frac{1}{6} + \frac{3}{6})n$

$= \frac{4}{6}n = \frac{2}{3}n$

PRACTICE

Subtract.

	a	b	c	d
1.	$7y - 5y =$	$8a - 7a =$	$14rt - 7rt =$	$20w - 14w =$
2.	$3h - 5h =$	$8yz - 11yz =$	$2f - 9f =$	$8mn - 17mn =$
3.	$^-2x - 7x =$	$^-4g - 8g =$	$^-5z - 9z =$	$^-24b - 35b =$
4.	$6n - n =$	$4p - p =$	$^-3k - k =$	$^-5r - 5r =$
5.	$7t - 5t =$	$m - 7m =$	$a - 12a =$	$xy - 28xy =$
6.	$^-5ab - (^-9ab) =$	$^-4k - (^-8k) =$	$^-7t - (^-6t) =$	$^-8x - (^-3x) =$
7.	$\frac{3}{4}t - \frac{1}{4}t =$	$\frac{4}{5}x - \frac{3}{5}x =$	$\frac{2}{3}h - \frac{1}{3}h =$	$\frac{3}{2}b - \frac{1}{2}b =$
8.	$0.3n - 0.12n =$	$3.2a - 2.7a =$	$5.4k - 4.7k =$	$6st - 4.2st =$

Unit 2 Integers and Monomials

Adding and Subtracting Like Terms

Recall the rules for adding and subtracting monomials with like terms.

- The coefficient of the sum of two like terms is the sum of the coefficients.
- The coefficient of the difference of two like terms is the difference of the coefficients.

PRACTICE

Add or subtract.

	a	b	c	d
1.	$^-3xy - 2xy =$	$5a + a =$	$6.5s + 3.5s =$	$^-7mn + (14mn) =$
2.	$^-13k - (^-4k) =$	$10y - 8y =$	$0.7c - 0.3c =$	$15pq + (^-25pq) =$
3.	$h - 3h =$	$10ab - 9ab =$	$^-9v - (^-8v) =$	$15ab + ab + 6ab =$
4.	$2.8n - 3.5n =$	$\frac{3}{5}b + \frac{2}{5}b =$	$18pr - (4pr) =$	$^-9wx - 9wx =$
5.	$25z - 8z + (^-3z) =$	$^-5lm - {}^-9lm =$	$10u + (^-15u) =$	$7s + (2s) - (19s) =$
6.	$7z + {}^-2z =$	$^-5u - 1.9u =$	$^-6rp + (^-3rp) =$	$^-7b - (^-29b) =$
7.	$^-26ty + (^-4ty) =$	$^-21c + 6c =$	$2.9c + (^-3c) =$	$^-5fg + (^-17fg) =$
8.	$9r - (^-3r) + 12r =$	$^-79h + (^-9h) =$	$^-16ds + (^-9ds) =$	$^-5j + j + (^-14j) =$
9.	$\frac{^-4}{7}en - \frac{3}{7}en =$	$3.01i - 1.52i =$	$^-8w - 6w + 3w =$	$^-20x - 9x =$
10.	$7kl - (^-8kl) + kl =$	$^-13dh + (^-10dh) =$	$^-1.3s + 3s - 4s =$	$^-3q + 7q - 4q =$

Simplifying Expressions

The **simplest form** of an expression has no like terms and no parentheses. Also, the terms are usually arranged in alphabetical order, with the constants last.

To **simplify** an expression means to write it in simplest form. Combine the constants and the like terms until the expression is in simplest form.

EXAMPLE 1

Simplify: $^-2 + 8y + y - 3$
$= (8y + 1y) + [^-2 + (^-3)]$
$= 9y + (^-5)$
$= 9y - 5$

EXAMPLE 2

Simplify: $6 + 7x - 8$
$= 7x + (6 + (^-8))$
$= 7x + (^-2)$
$= 7x - 2$

EXAMPLE 3

Simplify: $^-4ab + 7c + ab$
$= (^-4ab + 1ab) + 7c$
$= ^-3ab + 7c$

PRACTICE

Simplify.

	a	b	c
1.	$5a + 4a - 2a =$	$8g + 3g - 7g =$	$4x - 12x + 7x =$
2.	$6y - 4y + y =$	$3m - 5m + 4m =$	$12b - 8b - 4b =$
3.	$9a - 6a + 3b =$	$7t + 4s + 5t =$	$6ab - 3ac - 8ac =$
4.	$5r - 7r + 8m =$	$11 - 4k - 9k =$	$5x - 7 + 9 =$
5.	$16xy - 18 + 7xy =$	$4f - 9f - 3f + 10 =$	$^-8rs + 9rs + st =$
6.	$^-4g - 5 - 3g + 8 =$	$e + ef + 5ef =$	$3x - 7x - 9x =$
7.	$19 + 15bc - 3bc + 2 =$	$31p - 54p - 82p =$	$^-36 + 74r - 53 + r =$

Multiplying Monomials

Recall that a monomial is a number, a variable, or a product of numbers and variables. To multiply two or more monomials, multiply the coefficients and variables separately.

Remember:

- The product of two numbers with the same sign is positive.
- The product of two numbers with different signs is negative.
- When there is no number in front of a variable, the coefficient 1 is understood.
- $ab = ba$
- In simplest form the variables are in alphabetical order.

EXAMPLE 1

Multiply: $(4b)(8a)$

$= (4 \cdot 8)ab$

$= 32ab$

EXAMPLE 2

Multiply: $^-7(^-4pq)$

$= {^-7}(^-4)pq$

$= 28pq$

EXAMPLE 3

Multiply: $3t(^-7m)(-a)$

$= 3(^-7)(^-1)amt$

$= 21amt$

PRACTICE

Multiply.

	a	b	c	d
1.	$4(5a) =$	$5(6b) =$	$9m(6) =$	$3(7a) =$
2.	$3(7xy) =$	$(9mn)(4) =$	$2(6rs) =$	$(8ab)(8) =$
3.	$(^-4)(^-5x) =$	$(7a)(^-4) =$	$(3b)(^-9) =$	$^-2(^-25c) =$
4.	$(4a)(3b) =$	$5t(10s) =$	$(^-4x)(^-9z) =$	$2mn(^-7p) =$
5.	$\frac{1}{2}y(6) =$	$4(\frac{1}{2}x) =$	$20t(\frac{1}{4}a) =$	$25(\frac{1}{2}m) =$
6.	$3s(0.4r) =$	$5c(0.6b) =$	$5v(0.8t) =$	$6(0.7z) =$
7.	$6(3b)(2c) =$	$7(5t)(3r) =$	$(4x)(3y)(9z) =$	$(^-3)(4m)(10n) =$
8.	$(^-19rs)(^-5t)(^-3) =$	$(^-4f)(16e)(12) =$	$^-35y(^-4x)(5z) =$	$t(32s)(4r) =$

Dividing Monomials by Integers

To divide a monomial by an integer, divide the coefficient by the integer and write the variable or variables just as they are in the monomial.

Remember:

- The quotient of two numbers with the same sign is positive.
- The quotient of two numbers with different signs is negative.

EXAMPLE 1

Divide: $\dfrac{^-8k}{2}$

$= \dfrac{^-8}{2}(k)$

$= {}^-4k$

EXAMPLE 2

Divide: $\dfrac{^-100ab}{^-20}$

$= \dfrac{^-100}{^-20}(ab)$

$= 5ab$

EXAMPLE 3

Divide: $\dfrac{7.8w}{3}$

$= \dfrac{7.8}{3}(w)$

$= 2.6w$

PRACTICE

Divide.

	a	b	c	d
1.	$\dfrac{20a}{5} =$	$\dfrac{15a}{3} =$	$\dfrac{12x}{4} =$	$\dfrac{16y}{4} =$
2.	$\dfrac{16ab}{4} =$	$\dfrac{30xy}{5} =$	$\dfrac{12mn}{6} =$	$\dfrac{28rs}{4} =$
3.	$\dfrac{^-20a}{^-2} =$	$\dfrac{^-45b}{5} =$	$\dfrac{^-54c}{^-9} =$	$\dfrac{^-125x}{25} =$
4.	$\dfrac{32a}{^-2} =$	$\dfrac{75b}{^-15} =$	$\dfrac{^-64c}{^-4} =$	$\dfrac{^-180d}{^-20} =$
5.	$\dfrac{^-15x}{5} =$	$\dfrac{48a}{^-4} =$	$\dfrac{^-32b}{8} =$	$\dfrac{96c}{^-24} =$
6.	$\dfrac{15x}{^-5} =$	$\dfrac{^-64x}{8} =$	$\dfrac{^-72a}{9} =$	$\dfrac{56b}{^-14} =$
7.	$\dfrac{2.4z}{4} =$	$\dfrac{^-2.1x}{^-3} =$	$\dfrac{1.5a}{5} =$	$\dfrac{2.4n}{8} =$

Multiplying and Dividing Monomials

Remember, to multiply monomials, multiply their coefficients and variables separately.

To divide a monomial by an integer, divide the coefficient by the integer and write the variable or variables.

PRACTICE

Multiply or divide.

	a	b	c	d
1.	$8(8n) =$	$\frac{36y}{-9} =$	$3a(^-5b) =$	$\frac{^-56n}{^-8} =$
2.	$\frac{24ab}{8} =$	$36m(\frac{^-1}{4}n) =$	$\frac{72r}{3} =$	$\frac{^-64p}{16} =$
3.	$4(^-2t)(^-5s) =$	$\frac{150x}{^-15} =$	$(^-9j)(0.2k) =$	$(^-12x)(^-6) =$
4.	$\frac{^-4.5w}{^-5} =$	$(^-7ab)(^-6c)(^-2) =$	$^-16(\frac{1}{2}x) =$	$9pq(^-r) =$
5.	$5(0.13k) =$	$\frac{^-84fg}{^-12} =$	$\frac{2}{3}b(18) =$	$\frac{63cd}{^-7} =$
6.	$\frac{33rs}{^-6} =$	$^-4m(7h) =$	$\frac{^-49g}{^-7} =$	$4(^-12hy) =$
7.	$\frac{^-3}{6}i(42j) =$	$\frac{1.6f}{4}g =$	$\frac{^-78z}{^-13} =$	$\frac{^-2.8r}{^-7} =$
8.	$\frac{^-160t}{^-8} =$	$(^-15w)(\frac{^-ev}{3}) =$	$(^-4v)(^-14d) =$	$(^-18k)(^-mj) =$
9.	$(^-3b)(^-2r)(^-3p) =$	$21(\frac{^-1}{3}t) =$	$^-16dj(^-5q) =$	$^-15ng(\frac{^-1}{5}d) =$
10.	$\frac{70s}{^-14} =$	$\frac{1}{4}m(^-16) =$	$\frac{69n}{^-3} =$	$\frac{3}{11}gt(22) =$

The Distributive Property

To **distribute** means to give something to each member of a group. The **Distributive Property** multiplies a factor by each term within parentheses. A negative sign in front of parentheses indicates multiplication by $^-1$.

Remember:
- The product of two numbers with the same sign is positive.
- The product of two numbers with different signs is negative.

EXAMPLE 1

Simplify: $7(x + 2)$

$= 7(x) + 7(2)$

$= 7x + 14$

EXAMPLE 2

Simplify: $^-(2y + 3)$

$= {}^-1(2y) + (^-1)(3)$

$= {}^-2y - 3$

EXAMPLE 3

Simplify: $y(5x - 4)$

$= 5x(y) - 4(y)$

$= 5xy - 4y$

PRACTICE

Simplify.

	a	b	c	d
1.	$6(y - 1) =$	$r(3 - t) =$	$5(7 + n) =$	$x(2 - a) =$
2.	$^-9(r - 4) =$	$4(c + 2) =$	$^-7(1 + t) =$	$g(4s + 6) =$
3.	$p(7 - 2g) =$	$7(5y - 8) =$	$^-2(6 - 5a) =$	$^-8(1 + 2d) =$
4.	$k(^-10 - 7r) =$	$^-14(a + b) =$	$s(^-4 - 8t) =$	$^-8(3p - 2q) =$
5.	$-m(x + 3) =$	$9(2x + y) =$	$c(^-3e + 9g) =$	$^-(9 - m) =$
6.	$3(2b - 5c + d) =$	$^-3x(9 - 2y) =$	$n(3j - 8k) =$	$t(3x + 2) =$
7.	$5a(2b - 1) =$	$^-9b(1 + 3a) =$	$4(m - 5n) =$	$2r(^-6s + t) =$
8.	$^-5(9s - 2t + v) =$	$^-(p + 2q - r) =$	$2x(3y - 4z) =$	$2k(m + 3n - 7) =$

Simplifying Expressions with Parentheses

A more complex expression involving the Distributive Property might include additional operations or additional expressions within parentheses. Follow the order of operations, the Distributive Property rule, and the rules of combining like terms to simplify the expression. Remember, a negative sign in front of parentheses indicates multiplication by $^-1$.

EXAMPLE 1

Simplify:
$^-3(8a + 5b) + 3b$

$= {}^-3(8a) + (^-3)(5b) + 3b$
$= {}^-24a + (^-15b) + 3b$
$= {}^-24a + (^-15 + 3)b$
$= {}^-24a - 12b$

EXAMPLE 2

Simplify: $4 - (r + 7)$

$= 4 + (^-1)(r + 7)$
$= 4 + (-1)(r) + (^-1)(7)$
$= 4 - r - 7$
$= -r - 3$

EXAMPLE 3

Simplify:
$4(r + s) + 3(r + 2s)$

$= 4r + 4s + 3r + 6s$
$= (4 + 3)r + (4 + 6)s$
$= 7r + 10s$

PRACTICE

Simplify.

	a	b	c
1.	$4(^-7x + 3y - 2z) =$	$^-2(4m + 9n) + 3mn =$	$8(7 - 5ab) - 2ab =$
2.	$^-(4p + 3q) + 7p =$	$^-(6x + y - z) =$	$^-(^-2r + 7s) + 2(r + s) =$
3.	$8y - (3 - 6y) =$	$^-7 + (9x - 8) =$	$2x + 3y - (x + 5y) =$
4.	$2a + 3b + 2(a - 2b) =$	$3x - 5y + 4(x - 3y) =$	$5m + 4n + 3(2m - 5n) =$
5.	$5t - 4s - 3(2t - 3s) =$	$4m + 3n - 2(m + 3n) =$	$7x - 4y - 5(2y - x) =$
6.	$2(3b + 4) - (b - 5) =$	$3(5x - 2y) - (4x + 3y) =$	$3(m + 2n) - 4(2m + n) =$

Simplifying Fractional Expressions

Expressions with negative or positive fractions are simplified using the same rules as for integers. First, separate each fractional coefficient by multiplying the term by the **reciprocal** of the divisor. For example, $\frac{x}{2} = \frac{1}{2}x$ because the reciprocal of 2 is $\frac{1}{2}$. This step allows you to collect like terms or to use the Distributive Property in order to simplify an equation. Dividing by an integer is the same as multiplying by its reciprocal.

EXAMPLE 1

Simplify: $a + \frac{a}{4}$

$= a + \frac{1}{4}a$ Separate the fractional coefficient.

$= (1 + \frac{1}{4})a = 1\frac{1}{4}a$ Add like terms.

EXAMPLE 2

Simplify: $\frac{^{-}8m + 6n}{2}$

$= \frac{1}{2}(^{-}8m + 6n)$ Separate the fractional coefficients.

$= \frac{1}{2}(^{-}8m) + \frac{1}{2}(6n)$ Use the Distributive Property.

$= {^{-}4m} + 3n$

PRACTICE

Simplify.

	a	b	c
1.	$\frac{k}{3} - \frac{4k}{3} =$	$\frac{^{-}x}{7} + \frac{4x}{7} =$	$\frac{^{-}5n}{6} + \frac{5n}{6} =$
2.	$\frac{^{-}r}{4} + s - \frac{3r}{4} =$	$\frac{y}{3} + r - \frac{5y}{3} =$	$c + x + \frac{3x}{4} =$
3.	$\frac{r}{2} - \frac{3r}{2} =$	$\frac{^{-}3a}{5} + x + \frac{3a}{5} =$	$\frac{2y}{3} - c - y =$
4.	$\frac{1}{2}(^{-}16p + 8) =$	$\frac{^{-}1}{3}(6y + 1) =$	$\frac{2}{5}(10a - 5) =$
5.	$\frac{7x + 21y}{7} =$	$\frac{24a + 2b}{4} =$	$\frac{a + 4a}{^{-}5} =$

    Unit 2 Integers and Monomials

Multiplying Fractional Expressions

Expressions with negative or positive fractions are multiplied using the same rules as for integers.

Remember:

- Separate the coefficients from the variables by multiplying the variables by the reciprocal of the divisor.
- Multiply the coefficients and then multiply the variables.
- If the signs of two factors are the same, the product is positive, and if the signs are different, the product is negative.

EXAMPLE

Simplify: $\frac{-y}{4} \cdot \frac{x}{5}$

$= \frac{-1}{4}y \cdot \frac{1}{5}x$ Separate the coefficients from the variables.

$= (\frac{-1}{4} \cdot \frac{1}{5})xy$ Multiply the coefficients and then the variables.

$= \frac{-1}{20}xy$ or $\frac{-xy}{20}$ The signs of the factors are different, so the product is negative.

PRACTICE

Simplify.

	a	b	c
1.	$\frac{-b}{3} \cdot \frac{a}{5} =$	$\frac{-t}{4} \times \frac{-r}{8} =$	$\frac{q}{7} \cdot \frac{-p}{8} =$
2.	$\frac{x}{2} \times \frac{n}{-2} =$	$\frac{h}{5} \cdot \frac{3k}{7} =$	$\frac{x}{8} \times \frac{-4}{7} =$
3.	$\frac{-3y}{4} \cdot \frac{-z}{2} =$	$\frac{9}{10} \times \frac{p}{3} =$	$\frac{-5n}{8} \cdot \frac{2}{-3} =$
4.	$\frac{-8a}{9} \times \frac{3b}{10} =$	$\frac{2z}{3} \cdot \frac{9x}{3} =$	$\frac{3e}{-2} \times \frac{-4f}{9} =$
5.	$\frac{3v}{4} \cdot \frac{-5}{9w} =$	$\frac{3y}{-10} \times \frac{5x}{9} =$	$\frac{-a}{5} \cdot \frac{3b}{-4} =$

Problem-Solving Strategy: Use Estimation

Juan owns 62 shares of a certain company's stock. The value per share is $+12\frac{1}{8}$ dollars. About how much is the total value of Juan's shares?

Understand the problem.

- **What do you want to know?**
  about how much Juan's shares are worth

- **What information is given?**
  the number of shares Juan has (62) and the value per share ($+12\frac{1}{8}$ dollars)

Plan how to solve it.

- **What strategy can you use?**
  You can estimate the number of shares and price per share to find about how much the total value is.

Solve it.

- **How can you use this strategy to solve the problem?**
  Round the number of shares and the value per share to the nearest ten or nearest whole number. Then find the product.

  > Round 62 to 60. Round $12\frac{1}{8}$ to 12.
  > $60(12) = 720$

- **What is the answer?**
  The total value of the shares is about $720.

Look back and check your answer.

- **Is your answer reasonable?**
  You can check your estimate by finding the exact answer.

  $62 \times 12\frac{1}{8} =$

  $62 \times 12.125 = 751.75$

  The answer is reasonable.

Use estimation to solve.

1. A box is 41 cm long, 32 cm wide, and 26 cm high. Is the volume closer to 3,600 or 36,000 cubic cm?

Answer _____

2. The floor of a room has an area of about 196 square feet. The width of the room is $10\frac{1}{4}$ feet. Estimate the length of the room.

Answer _____

3. Brad typed in 48 minutes a report that had 2,876 words. About how many words per minute did Brad type?

Answer _____

4. Teresa borrowed $1,950 to buy a used car. The interest rate is 14.8% per year. If she pays back the full amount in one year, about how much interest will she owe?

Answer _____

5. Lakeesha drives 65 mph on the highway. If she drives at this rate, about how many hours will it take her to drive 367 miles?

Answer _____

6. Estimate the perimeter of a rectangular field that is 734 meters long and 492 meters wide.

Answer _____

7. Pat owns 89 shares of stock in a certain company. The dollar value of each share changed $^-4\frac{3}{8}$ on Friday. About how much money did Pat lose?

Answer _____

8. A submarine left the dock and went to a depth of 103 ft below sea level. Then the submarine moved 37 ft closer to sea level. At about what depth was the submarine?

Answer _____

UNIT 2 Review

Write the opposite of each integer.

	a	b	c	d
1.	8	$^-13$	$^-1$	75

Add, subtract, multiply, or divide.

	a	b	c	d
2.	$^-10 + (^-20) =$	$13 + 8 =$	$^-25 + 42 =$	$^-87 + (^-4) =$
3.	$20 - 17 =$	$11 - 23 =$	$^-5 - (^-3) =$	$^-9 - 2 =$
4.	$8(^-6) =$	$(^-4)(^-22) =$	$\frac{^-75}{^-5} =$	$\frac{^-63}{9} =$

Simplify.

5.	$8k + k =$	$12m - 3m =$	$7ab - 10ab =$	$10n + (^-3n) =$
6.	$5y + 2z - y =$	$^-2b + 4c + 3b =$	$^-t + 2t - 8t =$	$5jk - (^-8jk) + jk =$
7.	$^-3(17q) =$	$^-7(^-26st) =$	$(^-8x)(9y) =$	$(^-5k)(2.4y) =$
8.	$\frac{15x}{5} =$	$\frac{^-25rs}{^-5} =$	$\frac{54y}{^-6} =$	$\frac{105mn}{^-3} =$
9.	$9(r - 3) =$	$w(4 + 6m) =$	$^-4(16p + 8) =$	$a(^-32c - 6d) =$
10.	$\frac{21x}{4} \cdot \frac{2y}{3} =$	$\frac{^-30rs}{^-6} \cdot \frac{p}{5} =$	$\frac{4y}{^-6} \cdot \frac{s}{4} =$	$\frac{10m}{^-3} \cdot \frac{n}{2} =$

Simplify the following expressions.

	a	b	c
11.	$k + 7 - (2k + 5) =$	$r + 2 - 3(5 - 2r) =$	$2(3a + 5b) + 3(5a - 3b) =$
12.	$\frac{a}{2} + b + \frac{a}{2} =$	$\frac{3}{4}(^-12x + 20) =$	$\frac{42b + 70}{7} =$

Unit 2 Integers and Monomials

Find the absolute value of each number.

a	b	c	d
1. $\lvert {}^-16\rvert =$	$\lvert 4.6\rvert =$	$\left\lvert \frac{-3}{7}\right\rvert =$	$\lvert 15\rvert =$

Write an algebraic expression for each verbal expression.

a	b
2. n increased by 10 _____	7 divided by w _____

Evaluate each expression if $x = 9$, $y = 1$, and $z = 5$.

a	b	c	d
3. $xyz =$	$\frac{x + y}{z} =$	$3z + xy =$	$9y - x =$

Solve.

a	b	c	d
4. $8 + 2r = 26$	$5y = \frac{33}{3} - 1$	$9x = 90$	$22 - 3b = {}^-50$

Simplify.

a	b	c	d
5. $({}^-2)({}^-13) =$	$({}^-7)(11) =$	$\frac{54}{{}^-6} =$	$\frac{{}^-100}{{}^-5} =$
6. $2a + 7a + 5a =$	$15x - 7x + 4y =$	$4b - ({}^-9b) =$	${}^-16rs + 12rs + 4rs =$
7. $3(15a) =$	$\frac{{}^-32ab}{4} =$	$\frac{1.6t}{4} \cdot \frac{s}{2} =$	$\frac{18y}{5} \cdot \frac{15x}{3} =$
8. $4(7a + 10) =$	$\frac{2}{5}(10m - 4n) =$	$\frac{{}^-12s - 27}{{}^-3} =$	$\frac{{}^-4m + 20}{{}^-4} =$

Solve.

9. In the formula $V = lwh$, find V when l is 10 feet, w is 6 feet, and h is 2 feet.

10. In the formula $D = rt$, find t when D is 240 miles and r is 80 miles per hour.

Answer _____

Answer _____

Solving Addition Equations

To solve the equation $4 + x = 10$, find the value of x that makes the equation true. Since x is a missing addend, the solution is $10 - 4$, or 6. It is important to check the solution by substituting 6 for x in the original equation. Since $4 + 6$ is 10, the solution is correct.

When an addition equation involves integers, a slightly different process is used to find the solution. You can add the same number to both sides of an equation without changing its solution. The goal is to isolate the variable on one side of the equation, with the constants on the other side, so the solution will be obvious. In Example 1, the number 4 is added to both sides because 4 is the opposite of $^-4$. The left side of the equation becomes $x + 0$, or simply x.

EXAMPLE 1

Solve: $x + (^-4) = 9$

$x + (^-4) + 4 = 9 + 4$

$x = 13$

The solution is 13.

Check: $13 + (^-4) = 9$

EXAMPLE 2

Solve: $5 + n = {}^-2$

$^-5 + 5 + n = {}^-5 + (^-2)$

$n = {}^-7$

The solution is $^-7$.

Check: $5 + (^-7) = {}^-2$

EXAMPLE 3

Solve: $a + 9 = 7$

$a + 9 + (^-9) = 7 + (^-9)$

$a = {}^-2$

The solution is $^-2$.

Check: $^-2 + 9 = 7$

PRACTICE

Solve. Check.

	a	b	c	d
1.	$x + 2 = 5$	$x + (^-15) = 3$	$x + 4 = 8$	$x + (^-2) = {}^-9$
2.	$x + 23 = 23$	$a + 4 = {}^-1$	$n + (^-5) = 1$	$t + (^-33) = 30$
3.	$r + 15 = 2$	$h + (^-9) = -9$	$y + 12 = 0$	$d + 7 = 9$
4.	$k + (^-10) = 1$	$c + 17 = 27$	$x + 54 = 36$	$m + (^-9) = 72$
5.	$f + 19 = 0$	$m + (^-5) = 19$	$z + 9 = {}^-10$	$x + (^-3) = 3$

Solving Subtraction Equations

To isolate the variable in a subtraction equation, you can add the same number to both sides. Or, you can rewrite the equation as addition and then solve.

EXAMPLE 1

Solve: $x - 6 = 4$

$x - 6 + 6 = 4 + 6$

$x = 10$

The solution is 10.

Check: $10 - 6 = 4$

EXAMPLE 2

Solve: $n - (^-4) = 8$

$n + 4 = 8$

$n + 4 + (^-4) = 8 + (^-4)$

$n = 4$

The solution is 4.

Check: $4 - (^-4) = 8$

EXAMPLE 3

Solve: $z - 9 = 0$

$z - 9 + 9 = 0 + 9$

$z = 9$

The solution is 9.

Check: $9 - 9 = 0$

PRACTICE

Solve. Check.

	a	b	c	d
1.	$x - 13 = 15$ $x - 13 + 13 = 15 + 13$ $x = 28$ Check: $28 - 13 = 15$	$z - 7 = 4$	$y - (^-12) = ^-10$	$r - 66 = 100$
2.	$y - 3 = 3$	$m - 9 = ^-7$	$z - 48 = 84$	$x - (^-25) = 10$
3.	$x - (^-3) = ^-3$	$p - 6 = ^-4$	$y - 82 = 70$	$h - 16 = 15$
4.	$r - (^-12) = 5$	$t - 61 = ^-21$	$a - (^-1) = 0$	$b - (^-2) = ^-1$

Solving Multiplication Equations

One way to solve a multiplication equation such as $7n = 28$ is to think of the missing factor. The solution to $7n = 28$ is $28 \div 7$, or 4.

Remember that another way to solve an equation is to isolate the variable so the solution is obvious. You can multiply or divide both sides of an equation by any number (except zero) without changing its solution. For $7n = 28$, multiply both sides by $\frac{1}{7}$, the reciprocal of n's coefficient. The equation becomes $(\frac{1}{7})7n = (\frac{1}{7})(28)$, or $1n = \frac{28}{7}$. So, $n = 4$.

EXAMPLE 1

Solve: $4x = {}^-32$
$(\frac{1}{4})4x = (\frac{1}{4})({}^-32)$
$x = -8$
The solution is $^-8$.
Check: $4({}^-8) = {}^-32$

EXAMPLE 2

Solve: $-m = 5$
$({}^-1)(-m) = ({}^-1)(5)$
$m = {}^-5$
The solution is $^-5$.
Check: $-({}^-5) = 5$

EXAMPLE 3

Solve: $^-3y = {}^-3$
$(\frac{-1}{3})({}^-3y) = (\frac{-1}{3})({}^-3)$
$y = 1$
The solution is 1.
Check: $^-3(1) = {}^-3$

PRACTICE

Solve. Check.

	a	b	c	d
1.	$6x = 36$	$^-8y = 48$	$-n = 9$	$3m = {}^-10$
2.	$^-2x = 16$	$23y = 92$	$3x = 18$	$2a = {}^-24$
3.	$25k = 50$	$^-3x = {}^-9$	$6r = 24$	$^-14y = 56$
4.	$^-7x = {}^-14$	$-m = {}^-2$	$3n = {}^-18$	$5x = 25$

Solving Division Equations

To solve division equations, use the same methods as for multiplication equations. To isolate the variable in a division equation, you can multiply both sides by the same number (except zero).

EXAMPLE 1

Solve: $\frac{x}{2} = 6$

$(2)\frac{x}{2} = (2)6$

$x = 12$

Check: $\frac{12}{2} = 6$

EXAMPLE 2

Solve: $\frac{-b}{3} = 9$

$(^-3)\left(\frac{-b}{3}\right) = (^-3)9$

$b = ^-27$

Check: $-\left(\frac{-27}{3}\right) = 9$

EXAMPLE 3

Solve: $\frac{y}{5} = 0$

$(5)\frac{y}{5} = (5)0$

$y = 0$

Check: $\frac{0}{5} = 0$

PRACTICE

Solve. Check.

	a	b	c	d
1.	$\frac{x}{4} = 8$	$\frac{x}{3} = ^-2$	$\frac{w}{5} = 2$	$\frac{z}{9} = 10$
2.	$\frac{-f}{8} = ^-8$	$\frac{p}{9} = ^-9$	$\frac{t}{6} = 3$	$\frac{h}{7} = 0$
3.	$\frac{a}{10} = 7$	$\frac{b}{2} = ^-20$	$\frac{-m}{1} = 6$	$\frac{z}{1} = 1$
4.	$\frac{-y}{15} = 1$	$\frac{-w}{4} = 20$	$\frac{d}{25} = 4$	$\frac{-r}{36} = ^-2$

Mixed Practice Solving Equations

Remember that when isolating the variable in an equation, you can add, subtract, multiply, or divide both sides by the same number. Always check your solution in the original equation.

PRACTICE

Solve. Check.

	a	b	c	d
1.	$a + (^-5) = 8$	$r - 9 = 13$	$\frac{y}{2} = 5$	$3m = 9$
2.	$t + 2 = 1$	$b - (^-4) = 0$	$\frac{n}{3} = {}^-2$	$7k = 7$
3.	$s + 6 = 0$	$z - 6 = {}^-3$	$\frac{^-d}{3} = {}^-9$	$-x = 4$
4.	$\frac{k}{3} = 5$	$r + 7 = {}^-1$	$^-2c = 4$	$y - 5 = 7$
5.	$w - 18 = 27$	$9m = 12$	$\frac{s}{4} = 5$	$b + 12 = 11$
6.	$\frac{^-h}{3} = 8$	$t - 9 = {}^-4$	$f + 7 = {}^-11$	$7y = {}^-35$
7.	$g + 5 = 4$	$-z = 12$	$\frac{a}{3} = 0$	$m - 5 = 7$
8.	$5b = {}^-8$	$l + 24 = {}^-2$	$z - 3 = {}^-15$	$\frac{n}{12} = 9$
9.	$x + 73 = 27$	$7r = {}^-49$	$\frac{^-a}{13} = {}^-1$	$h - 81 = 9$
10.	$c + 15 = {}^-93$	$t - 1 = {}^-60$	$16x = {}^-4$	$\frac{^-a}{1} = 8$

The Fractional Equation

One method for solving an equation such as $\frac{3x}{4} = 15$ is to multiply both sides by 4 and then divide both sides by 3. This is shown in Example 1.

A simpler method to solve the same equation is to think of $\frac{3x}{4}$ as $\frac{3}{4}x$. This is a multiplication equation with a fractional coefficient. It can be solved by multiplying both sides by the reciprocal of $\frac{3}{4}$, which is $\frac{4}{3}$. This method is shown in Example 2 and Example 3.

EXAMPLE 1

Solve: $\frac{3x}{4} = 15$

$(4)\frac{3x}{4} = (4)15$

$3x = 60$

$\left(\frac{1}{3}\right)3x = \left(\frac{1}{3}\right)60$

$x = 20$

EXAMPLE 2

Solve: $\frac{3x}{4} = 15$

$\left(\frac{4}{3}\right)\frac{3x}{4} = \left(\frac{4}{3}\right)15$

$x = 20$

Check: $\frac{3(20)}{4} = 15$

EXAMPLE 3

Solve: $\frac{2n}{3} = {}^-4$

$\left(\frac{3}{2}\right)\frac{2n}{3} = \left(\frac{3}{2}\right)({}^-4)$

$n = {}^-6$

Check: $\frac{2({}^-6)}{3} = {}^-4$

PRACTICE

Solve. Check.

	a	b	c	d
1.	$\frac{2n}{3} = 14$	$\frac{7r}{3} = 7$	$\frac{n}{4} = {}^-6$	$\frac{2a}{5} = 8$
2.	$\frac{3x}{5} = {}^-12$	$\frac{2y}{5} = 24$	$\frac{2r}{7} = 12$	$\frac{3y}{7} = 6$
3.	$\frac{3a}{4} = 15$	$\frac{3z}{10} = 9$	$\frac{5x}{8} = {}^-10$	$\frac{4z}{5} = 24$
4.	$\frac{5a}{8} = 25$	$\frac{{}^-7m}{10} = 21$	$\frac{3x}{10} = 3$	$\frac{{}^-2r}{5} = 48$

Solving Equations with Like Terms

Some equations contain the same variable in more than one term. Combine the like terms on each side of the equation. Then solve and check.

EXAMPLE 1

Solve: $5a + 4a = 45$

$$9a = 45$$
$$\left(\tfrac{1}{9}\right)9a = \left(\tfrac{1}{9}\right)45$$
$$a = 5$$

Check: $5(5) + 4(5) = 45$

$$25 + 20 = 45$$

EXAMPLE 2

Solve: $3b - 5b = 4$

$$^-2b = 4$$
$$\left(-\tfrac{1}{2}\right)(^-2b) = \left(-\tfrac{1}{2}\right)4$$
$$b = ^-2$$

Check: $3(^-2) - 5(^-2) = 4$

$$^-6 + 10 = 4$$

EXAMPLE 3

Solve: $4r + r = {}^-5$

$$5r = {}^-5$$
$$\left(\tfrac{1}{5}\right)5r = \left(\tfrac{1}{5}\right)(^-5)$$
$$r = {}^-1$$

Check: $4(^-1) + (^-1) = {}^-5$

$$^-4 + {}^-1 = {}^-5$$

PRACTICE

Solve. Check.

	a	b	c	d
1.	$^-15c + 10c = 100$	$4m + 7m = 66$	$^-2x + 3x = 24$	$5z + 2z = 41 - 6$
2.	$8a - 5a = 60$	$15a - 3a = 60$	$^-8x + 6x = 38$	$^-8z - 3z = 24 - 2$
3.	$14b - 6b = 48$	$^-6b + 5b = 55$	$3x - x = 46$	$3r + 2r = 31 - 6$
4.	$5x - 2x = 120$	$14b - 9b = 65$	$7x - 3x = 12$	$x - 3x = 18 + 6$

Writing Equations to Solve Problems

A problem may include information about the relationship between a number and an unknown quantity. To solve such a problem, first define a variable to represent the unknown quantity. Then write and solve an equation to find the value for the unknown.

EXAMPLE

Three fifths of a certain number is 18. What is the number?

Define a variable.	Write an equation.	Solve the equation.	Check:
Let n = the number.	Three fifths of n is 18. $\frac{3}{5}n = 18$	$\left(\frac{5}{3}\right)\frac{3}{5}n = \left(\frac{5}{3}\right)18$ $n = 30$	$\frac{3}{5}(30) = 18$ The number is 30.

PRACTICE

Write an equation. Solve. Check.

1. Three fourths of a number is 36. What is the number?

   Answer _____

2. One fifth of what number is 14?

   Answer _____

3. One third of a certain number is equal to 15. What is the number?

   Answer _____

4. Five times a certain number is equal to 35. What is the number?

   Answer _____

5. A certain number when divided by 3 is equal to 20. What is the number?

   Answer _____

6. Two times a certain number plus three times the number is 30. What is the number?

   Answer _____

Equations with More Than One Unknown

A problem may contain more than one unknown quantity. Sometimes the unknown quantities might be related in such a way to allow the use of one variable. Use the following steps to solve such a problem.

1. Define a variable to represent one unknown quantity. Then use the same variable to write an expression for the other unknown.
2. Write and solve an equation.
3. State the answer to the question that is asked. Sometimes the answer must include both unknowns.

EXAMPLE

Jeffrey's father is three times as old as Jeffrey. The sum of their ages is 60 years. How old is each?

Define a variable.

Let a = Jeffrey's age.

$3a$ = his father's age

Write an equation.

The sum of a and $3a$ is 60.

$a + 3a = 60$

Solve the equation.

$a + 3a = 60$

$4a = 60$

$a = 15$, so $3a = 45$

Answer: Jeffrey is 15 years old. His father is 45 years old.

PRACTICE

Write an equation. Solve. Check.

1. Quanisha's father is four times as old as Quanisha, and the sum of their ages is 50 years. How old is each?

   Answer _____

2. Leroy and Aaron have $7.20. Aaron has five times as much as Leroy. How much does each boy have?

   Answer _____

3. Together, Thomas and Tyrone have $24.00. Thomas has three times as much as Tyrone. How much does each have?

   Answer _____

4. Ling is twice as old as her sister. The sum of their ages is 42 years. How old is each?

   Answer _____

5. Deidra and Shelby inherited an estate of $3,000. Deidra is to receive two times as much as Shelby. How much does each receive?

   Answer _____

6. From Kansas City to Denver is twice as far as from Kansas City to St. Louis. The two distances together total 900 miles. What are the two distances?

   Answer _____

Solving Two-Step Equations

Some equations require two steps in order to find the solution. First, add or subtract from both sides to isolate the constants on one side. Then multiply both sides by the reciprocal of the coefficient (or divide by the coefficient) in order to isolate the variable. Check the solution against the original equation.

EXAMPLE 1

Solve: $2x - 5 = 71$

Step 1 $2x = 71 + 5$

           $2x = 76$

Step 2 $x = 76\left(\frac{1}{2}\right)$

           $x = 38$

Check: $2(38) - 5 = 71$

           $71 = 71$

EXAMPLE 2

Solve: $4a + 7 = {}^-49$

Step 1 $4a = {}^-49 - 7$

           $4a = {}^-56$

Step 2 $a = {}^-56\left(\frac{1}{4}\right)$

           $a = {}^-14$

Check: $4({}^-14) + 7 = {}^-49$

           ${}^-49 = {}^-49$

EXAMPLE 3

Solve: ${}^-3y - 4 = 11$

Step 1 ${}^-3y = 11 + 4$

           ${}^-3y = 15$

Step 2 $y = 15\left(\frac{{}^-1}{3}\right)$

           $y = {}^-5$

Check: ${}^-3({}^-5) - 4 = 11$

           $11 = 11$

PRACTICE

Solve. Check.

	a	b	c	d
1.	$3x - 5 = 16$	${}^-14r - 7 = 49$	$25a - 4 = 96$	$60y - 7 = 173$
2.	$7x + 3 = -4$	$23y + 6 = 75$	$17a + 9 = 77$	${}^-2m + 9 = 7$
3.	$8a - 7 = 65$	$19b - 4 = 72$	$52x + 4 = {}^-100$	${}^-6z + 15 = 3$
4.	$2r + 45 = 15$	$33b - 3 = 96$	${}^-75x + 5 = 230$	$35z + 12 = 82$

Problem-Solving Strategy: Work Backwards

Some people get on an elevator on the ground floor of an office building. On the second floor, 3 people get off the elevator. On the third floor, 4 people get off the elevator, and 2 get on. On the fifth floor, 5 people get off the elevator, and 1 gets on. On the top floor, 6 people get off the elevator, leaving the elevator empty. How many people were on the elevator on the ground floor?

Understand the problem.

- **What do you want to know?**
  the number of people on the elevator on the ground floor

- **What information is given?**
  the number of people that got on and off the elevator on different floors and the number of people remaining on the elevator at the top floor

Plan how to solve it.

- **What strategy can you use?**
  You can work backwards to find out how many people were on the elevator on the ground floor.

Solve it.

- **How can you use this strategy to solve the problem?**
  Work backwards, beginning with the empty elevator at the top floor. If people got off the elevator, put them back on by adding. If people got on the elevator, take them off by subtracting.

Top floor	Put 6 people on.	$0 + 6 = 6$
Fifth floor	Put 5 people on and take 1 off.	$6 + 5 - 1 = 10$
Third floor	Put 4 people on and take 2 off.	$10 + 4 - 2 = 12$
Second floor	Put 3 people on.	$12 + 3 = 15$

- **What is the answer?**
  There were 15 people on the elevator when it started.

Look back and check your answer.

- **Is your answer reasonable?**
  You can check your answer by starting with the elevator on the ground floor, adding when people get on the elevator and subtracting when people get off the elevator. The elevator should be empty at the top floor.

Second floor	Take 3 people off.	$15 - 3 = 12$
Third floor	Take 4 people off and put 2 on.	$12 - 4 + 2 = 10$
Fifth floor	Take 5 people off and put 1 on.	$10 - 5 + 1 = 6$
Top floor	Take 6 people off.	$6 - 6 = 0$

The answer is reasonable.

Solve.

1. Miguel went shopping at a factory outlet. He bought a sweater for $39.99, a pair of pants for $35.95, and a shirt for $29.99. After paying for it all, he had $9.15 left. How much did Miguel have before he bought the clothes?

Answer _____

2. Latasha was born in New York. She moved to California and lived there twice as long as she lived in New York. Then she moved to Toronto, where she has been living for 8 years. She is now 62 years old. How long did she live in New York?

Answer _____

3. If you divide Uncle Wilbert's age by 4 and then subtract 11, the answer will be the number of eggs in a dozen. How old is Uncle Wilbert?

Answer _____

4. Shanelle bought a new car for a total price of $28,152.25. The extra features she picked cost $3,150. The sales tax was $2,007.25. What was the price of Shanelle's car before the extra features and tax were added?

Answer _____

5. Darren wants to save $1,125.00 for his vacation. When he has saved 3 times as much as he has already saved, he will need only $27 more. How much has he saved so far?

Answer _____

6. Kiersten bought 2 loaves of bread at $1.45 each, 3 cans of soup at $0.80 each, and a pound of butter for $2.75. She gave the cashier a bill and got $1.95 in change. What bill did she give the clerk?

Answer _____

Variables on Both Sides of Equations

Sometimes you need to rewrite an equation so that a variable is on only one side of the equation. To accomplish this, add the opposite of the term to both sides of the equation. Then add, subtract, multiply, or divide in order to isolate the variable.

EXAMPLE 1

Solve: $4x - 5 = 3x + 1$

$4x - 5 + (^-3x) = 3x + 1 + (^-3x)$

$\qquad x - 5 = 1$

$\qquad x - 5 + 5 = 1 + 5$

$\qquad\qquad x = 6$

Check: $4(6) - 5 = 3(6) + 1$

$\qquad\qquad 19 = 19$

EXAMPLE 2

Solve: $3x + 5 = x + 13$

$3x + 5 - 5 = x + 13 - 5$

$\qquad 3x = x + 8$

$\qquad 3x - x = x + 8 - x$

$\qquad 2x = 8$

$\qquad x = 4$

Check: $3(4) + 5 = 4 + 13$

$\qquad\qquad 17 = 17$

EXAMPLE 3

Solve: $7x - 1 = 15 + 3x$

$7x - 1 + 1 = 15 + 3x + 1$

$\qquad 7x = 16 + 3x$

$\qquad 7x - 3x = 16 + 3x - 3x$

$\qquad 4x = 16$

$\qquad x = 4$

Check: $7(4) - 1 = 15 + 3(4)$

$\qquad\qquad 27 = 27$

PRACTICE

Solve. Check.

	a	b	c	d
1.	$8x + 4 = 5x - 11$	$2x - 1 = 4x + 3$	$3x - 5 = x - 7$	$4x + 3 = 8 - x$
2.	$7x - 16 = x + 8$	$6x + 3 = 5x + 3$	$15x + 5 = 10x - 15$	$2x + 3 = x + 10$
3.	$8x - 9 = 19 + x$	$3x + 6 = 8 + x$	$9x + 20 = 4x - 25$	$5x - 6 = 12 + 2x$
4.	$x - 2 = 2x - 4$	$4x - 12 = 2x + 2$	$5x + 1 = 10 + 2x$	$2x - 4 = x + 8$

Clearing Fractions

When an equation contains fractions on both sides, it is helpful to multiply both sides by a **common denominator** of the fractions. This process of eliminating fractions is called **clearing fractions**.

EXAMPLE 1

Solve: $\frac{x}{2} + 5 = \frac{x}{3} + 8$

$(6)\left(\frac{x}{2} + 5\right) = (6)\left(\frac{x}{3} + 8\right)$

$3x + 30 = 2x + 48$

$3x - 2x = 48 - 30$

$x = 18$

Check: $\frac{18}{2} + 5 = \frac{18}{3} + 8$

$9 + 5 = 6 + 8$

$14 = 14$

EXAMPLE 2

Solve: $\frac{3x}{2} + 2 = \frac{x}{2} + 4$

$(2)\left(\frac{3x}{2} + 2\right) = (2)(\frac{x}{2} + 4)$

$3x + 4 = x + 8$

$3x - x = 8 - 4$

$2x = 4$

$x = 2$

Check: $\frac{3(2)}{2} + 2 = \frac{2}{2} + 4$

$5 = 5$

EXAMPLE 3

Solve: $\frac{2x}{3} - 6 = \frac{x}{9} + 4$

$(9)\left(\frac{2x}{3} - 6\right) = (9)\left(\frac{x}{9} + 4\right)$

$6x - 54 = x + 36$

$6x - x = 36 + 54$

$5x = 90$

$x = 18$

Check: $\frac{2(18)}{3} - 6 = \frac{18}{9} + 4$

$6 = 6$

PRACTICE

Solve. Check.

	a	b	c
1.	$\frac{5x}{4} + 2 = \frac{x}{4} + 7$	$\frac{x}{2} - 3 = \frac{x}{7} + 2$	$\frac{x}{5} + 7 = \frac{x}{10} + 8$
2.	$\frac{x}{3} + 5 = \frac{x}{6} - 6$	$\frac{x}{2} + 4 = \frac{x}{4} - 1$	$\frac{x}{4} + 5 = \frac{x}{8} + 6$
3.	$\frac{x}{3} - 6 = \frac{x}{9}$	$\frac{x}{7} + 8 = 4 + \frac{3x}{7}$	$\frac{2x}{3} + 12 = \frac{5x}{2} - 10$

Fractions and Cross-Multiplication

If an equation contains only one fraction, the fraction can be cleared by multiplying both sides by the denominator. When there are two fractions, the fractions can be cleared by multiplying both sides by the common denominator. For equations that contain only one fractional term on each side, a faster method is to **cross-multiply**. With this shortcut, each numerator is multiplied by the opposite denominator.

EXAMPLE 1

Solve: $\frac{2x}{3} = \frac{12}{9}$

$9(2x) = 3(12)$

$18x = 36$

$x = 2$

Check: $\frac{2(2)}{3} = \frac{12}{9}$

$\frac{4}{3} = \frac{4}{3}$

EXAMPLE 2

Solve: $\frac{x}{2} = \frac{3}{4}$

$4x = 2(3)$

$4x = 6$

$x = \frac{3}{2}$

Check: $\frac{3}{2}\left(\frac{1}{2}\right) = \frac{3}{4}$

$\frac{3}{4} = \frac{3}{4}$

EXAMPLE 3

Solve: $\frac{3}{x} = \frac{6}{4}$

$4(3) = x(6)$

$12 = 6x$

$2 = x$

Check: $\frac{3}{2} = \frac{6}{4}$

$\frac{3}{2} = \frac{3}{2}$

PRACTICE

Solve. Check.

	a	b	c	d
1.	$\frac{x}{3} = \frac{2}{5}$	$\frac{x}{4} = \frac{1}{3}$	$\frac{x}{5} = \frac{3}{4}$	$\frac{2x}{9} = \frac{2}{3}$
2.	$\frac{3x}{10} = \frac{3}{5}$	$\frac{5c}{12} = \frac{5}{6}$	$\frac{4x}{7} = \frac{3}{5}$	$\frac{2a}{5} = \frac{3}{8}$
3.	$\frac{x}{6} = \frac{7}{12}$	$\frac{x}{7} = \frac{5}{8}$	$\frac{3}{4} = \frac{x}{8}$	$\frac{4}{5} = \frac{16}{m}$
4.	$\frac{3x}{7} = \frac{4}{9}$	$\frac{10}{x} = \frac{5}{2}$	$\frac{3}{x} = \frac{3}{5}$	$\frac{5}{x} = \frac{2}{8}$

Equations with Parentheses

When an equation contains parentheses, simplify each side before solving the equation. When you remove parentheses, remember to multiply each term within the parentheses by the factor in front of the parentheses. If the factor is negative, the sign of each term within the parentheses must be changed when the parentheses are removed.

EXAMPLE 1

Solve: $5(x + 4) = 4(x + 6)$

$$5x + 20 = 4x + 24$$
$$5x - 4x = 24 - 20$$
$$x = 4$$

Check: $5(4 + 4) = 4(4 + 6)$

$$40 = 40$$

EXAMPLE 2

Solve: $5b - 3(4 - b) = 2(b + 21)$

$$5b - 12 + 3b = 2b + 42$$
$$5b + 3b - 2b = 42 + 12$$
$$6b = 54$$
$$b = 9$$

Check: $5(9) - 3(4 - 9) = 2(9 + 21)$

$$60 = 60$$

PRACTICE

Solve. Check.

	a	b	c
1.	$3(x + 2) = 2(x + 5)$	$3x - (2x - 7) = 15$	$2b - 7(3 + b) = b + 3$
2.	$4(x - 3) = 2(x - 1)$	$7x - (x - 1) = 25$	$9a - 3(2a - 4) = 15$
3.	$4(x - 1) = 2(x + 4)$	$7 - 12(3 + b) = 31$	$5x - 2(4 - x) = 20$
4.	$5x + 3 = 4(x + 2)$	$5x - (x + 6) = 10$	$4(2x - 5) - 3(x + 10) = {}^-15$
5.	$3(x - 1) = 2x + 3$	$3x - (x + 2) = 4$	$2(x + 5) - (x - 3) = 8$

Writing Equations to Solve Problems

When there is a problem to be solved, use a variable to represent an unknown quantity. Then write and solve an equation using the variable, and be sure to answer the question in the problem.

EXAMPLE

If 5 is added to 4 times a number, the result is 21. What is the number?

Let x = the number.   Choose a variable.

$$5 + 4x = 21$$ Write an equation.

$$^-5 + 5 + 4x = ^-5 + 21$$ Solve the equation.

$$4x = 16$$

$$\left(\tfrac{1}{4}\right)4x = 16\left(\tfrac{1}{4}\right)$$

$$x = 4$$

The number is 4.

GUIDED PRACTICE

Solve.

1. Together, Theodore and Derrick have $33.10. Theodore has $3.05 more than 4 times as much as Derrick. How much does each have?

   Let x = Derrick's money.
   4x + 3.05 = Theodore's money
   x + (4x + 3.05) = $33.10
   5x + 3.05 − 3.05 = $33.10 − 3.05
   5x = $30.05
   x = $6.01
   4x + $3.05 = $27.09

   Answer _Derrick $6.01, Theodore $27.09_

2. If 10 less than a number is multiplied by 3, the result is equal to 2 times the number. What is the number?

   Let x = the number.
   3(x − 10) = 2x

   Answer _____

3. If 15 is added to twice a number, the result will be equal to the number increased by 23. Find the number.

   Answer _____

4. Frank is 4 times as old as Lin. The difference in their ages is equal to Lin's age plus 8. How old is each?

   Answer _____

Solve.

1. The length of a building is three times the width. The perimeter is 560 feet. Find the length and width. (Hint: $2l + 2w = P$)

   Let x = width.
   3x = length
   2(3x) + 2x = 560
   6x + 2x = 560
   8x = 560
   x = 70, so 3x = 210

   Answer <u>Length = 210 ft, Width = 70 ft</u>

2. The sum of two consecutive numbers is 85. Find the numbers.

   Let x = the first number.
   x + 1 = the second number
   x + x + 1 = 85
   2x + 1 = 85
   2x = 84
   x = 42, so x + 1 = 43

   Answer <u>First number = 42, Second number = 43</u>

3. The perimeter of a rectangular-shaped parking lot is 420 meters. The length is twice the width. Find both dimensions.

   Answer _____

4. Three numbers added together total 180. The second number is twice the first, and the third is three times the first. Find each number.

   Answer _____

5. The length of a rectangular-shaped garden is four times the width. The perimeter is 100 feet. Find both dimensions.

   Answer _____

6. Three numbers added together total 500. The second number is four times the first, and the third is five times the second. Find each number.

   Answer _____

7. The width of a rectangle is one-fifth as much as the length. The perimeter is 120 cm. Find the length and width.

   Answer _____

8. The sum of three consecutive numbers is 42. What are the numbers?

   Answer _____

Problem-Solving Strategy: Identify Substeps

Kira needs to drive 595 miles to reach her destination. She has been driving for $4\frac{1}{2}$ hours at a rate of 60 miles per hour. She will drive at an average rate of 65 miles per hour for the rest of the trip. How much longer must she drive to reach her destination?

Understand the problem.

- **What do you want to know?**
  how much longer Kira must drive

- **What information is given?**
  595 total miles, 60 miles per hour for $4\frac{1}{2}$ hours, and 65 miles per hour for the rest of the trip

Plan how to solve it.

- **What strategy can you use?**
  You can identify the substeps needed to solve the problem.

Solve it.

- **How can you use this strategy to solve the problem?**
  There are 3 substeps needed:

  1. Find how far Kira drove in the first $4\frac{1}{2}$ hours.

  2. Find how far Kira has yet to drive.

  3. Find how long it will take Kira to drive the rest of the trip.

  > **1.** Distance = rate $\times$ time ($D = rt$), so
  > $60 \times 4\frac{1}{2} = \frac{60}{1} \times \frac{9}{2} = 270$ miles so far
  >
  > **2.** $595 - 270 = 325$ miles to go
  >
  > **3.** $D = rt$, so
  >
  > $$325 = 65t$$
  > $$5 = t$$

- **What is the answer?**
  Kira must drive 5 hours longer to reach her destination.

Look back and check your answer.

- **Is your answer reasonable?**
  You can check your answer by setting up and working an equation for the original problem.

  $(4\frac{1}{2} \text{ hr.} \times 60 \text{ mph}) + (5 \text{ hr} \times 65 \text{ mph}) = 595 \text{ mi.}$

  $\quad\quad 270 \text{ mi.} \quad\quad + \quad\quad 325 \text{ mi.} \quad = 595 \text{ mi.}$

  The answer is reasonable.

Understand, Plan, Solve, Look back

Solve.

1. A rectangle with a perimeter of 72 inches is half as wide as it is long. What is the area of the rectangle?

Answer ______________________

2. When Randy started his job, he earned $8.00 per hour. Now he makes $450 for working a 40-hour week. How much more does he earn per hour than he did when he started?

Answer ______________________

3. Pencils sell for $1.98 per dozen. A teacher bought 288 pencils for his math classes. How much did the pencils cost?

Answer ______________________

4. There are 88 keys on a piano. Thirty-six of the keys are black and the rest are white. How many more white keys are there than black keys?

Answer ______________________

5. Mrs. Kwan is three times as old as her daughter Ling. Her son Chan, who is 5 years old, is half as old as Ling. How old is Mrs. Kwan?

Answer ______________________

6. One week Ginny worked 36 hours at $11.00 per hour. The next week she worked 40 hours at $12.00 per hour. How much more did she earn the second week than the first week?

Answer ______________________

Solve. Check.

a	*b*	*c*
1. $a + (^-25) = 75$	$x - 37 = 94$	$r + (^-12) = 3$
2. $5x = 45$	$^-15y = 105$	$25x = 10$
3. $\frac{2a}{3} = 4$	$\frac{x}{2} = 6$	$5x - 2x = 9$
4. $5x + 6x = 1$	$4r - 3 = 3$	$5x + 7 = 2x + 8$
5. $3m + 1 = 6m - 5$	$\frac{3x}{4} = 7 + \frac{x}{6}$	$\frac{5x}{2} - 10 = \frac{x}{4} - 1$
6. $\frac{3x}{10} = \frac{9}{5}$	$5y - 2(y + 2) = 5$	$6y - 4 = 2(2y + 1)$

Solve.

7. Together, Leslie and Lakita have $15.25. Lakita has $0.25 more than Leslie. How much does each have?

8. Marcos is 7 years older than his sister, Rosa. The sum of their ages is 1 less than 3 times Rosa's age. How old is each?

Answer _____

Answer _____

Simplify.

a	*b*	*c*
1. $(^-2)(^-7) =$	$5(^-8 + 9) =$	$\frac{4 + 6(2)}{4} =$
2. $^-3a + 4(a + 2) =$	$7(^-3a) + 6(^-a) =$	$3(a + 3b) - (a + 2b) =$

Solve. Check.

a	*b*	*c*
3. $r + 17 = 20$	$\frac{a}{5} + 7 = ^-2$	$x - 10 = 35$
4. $5x = 90$	$\frac{y}{9} = ^-8$	$\frac{2a}{5} = 4$
5. $8x + 5 = 5x - 10$	$8a - 6a + 3 = 7$	$\frac{3x}{2} + 2 = \frac{x}{4} + 7$
6. $\frac{2a}{7} = \frac{2}{3}$	$\frac{x}{8} = \frac{15}{24}$	$3(x + 2) = 2(x + 5)$

Solve.

7. In the formula $V = lwh$, find l when $h = 4$ in., $w = 7$ in., and $V = 252$ cu in.

Answer _____

8. In the formula $I = prt$, find p when $I = \$20$, $r = 5\%$, and $t = 1$ year.

Answer _____

9. Twice a number decreased by 8 is equal to the number increased by 10. Find the number.

Answer _____

10. The sum of two consecutive numbers is 95. What are the numbers?

Answer _____

Squares and Exponents

Recall that the area of a rectangle is $A = lw$. A square is a rectangle that has equal dimensions. Let s represent the side of a square. The formula for area of a square is $A = s \times s$, or $A = s^2$ (read as s squared). In the expression s^2, s is the **base** and 2 is the **exponent**. The exponent indicates the number of times the base is used as a factor.

When no exponent is used, the exponent of each variable is understood to be 1. If an expression contains repeated factors, you can rewrite the expression using exponents.

Remember, $y \times y$, $y \cdot y$, and $(y)(y)$ all show multiplication of y by itself.

EXAMPLE 1

Write $(p)(p)$ using exponents.

$(p)(p) = p^2$

EXAMPLE 2

Write y using exponents.

$y = y^1$

EXAMPLE 3

A square has sides 4 inches long. What is the area?

$4^2 = 4 \times 4 = 16$

The area is 16 square inches.

PRACTICE

Write using exponents.

	a	b	c
1.	$(3)(3) = 3^2$	$n \times n =$	$10 \cdot 10 =$
2.	$m =$	$1 \times 1 =$	$(5)(5) =$
3.	$x \cdot x =$	$g =$	$2 \times 2 =$
4.	$w =$	$9 =$	$15 \times 15 =$

Solve.

5. Find the area of a square with sides 5 inches long.

$A = s^2$
$A = 5^2$
$A = 25$ square inches

6. Find the area of a square with sides z inches long.

Cubes and Exponents

Recall that the formula for finding the volume of a rectangular prism is $V = lwh$. A **cube** is a rectangular prism that has equal dimensions. Let s represent the length of each edge of the cube. The formula for volume of a cube is $V = s \times s \times s$, or $V = s^3$ (read s cubed).

EXAMPLE 1

Write $r \cdot r \cdot r$ using exponents.

$r \cdot r \cdot r = r^3$

EXAMPLE 2

Write $(2)(2)(2)$ using exponents.

$2 \cdot 2 \cdot 2 = 2^3$

EXAMPLE 3

A cube has edges 5 inches long. What is its volume?

$5^3 = 5 \times 5 \times 5 = 125$

The volume is 125 cubic inches.

PRACTICE

Write using exponents.

	a	b	c
1.	$8 \times 8 \times 8 =$	$4 \times 4 \times 4 =$	$(y)(y)(y) =$
2.	$b \times b \times b =$	$a \cdot a \cdot a =$	$g \cdot g \cdot g =$
3.	$9 \times 9 \times 9 =$	$(n)(n)(n) =$	$p =$
4.	$s \cdot s =$	$1 \times 1 \times 1 =$	$15 \times 15 =$
5.	$(3)(3)(3) =$	$w \cdot w =$	$(7)(7)(7) =$

Solve.

6. Find the volume of a cube with edges 3 inches long.

$V = s^3$
$V = 3^3$
$V = 27$ cubic inches

7. Find the volume of a cube with edges 2 inches long.

8. Find the volume of a cube with edges 6 inches long.

9. Find the volume of a cube with edges g inches long.

Powers of Integers

The exponent in an expression indicates the number of times the base is used as a factor. Sometimes the exponent is called the **power**. For example, the expression a^2 can be read as *a to the second power*.

If a non-zero number is written to the zero power, the value is 1. For example, $27^0 = 1$.

> **RULE:** Any number, except zero, to the zero power is 1.

EXAMPLE 1

Simplify: $(^-2)^4$

$(^-2)^4 = (^-2)(^-2)(^-2)(^-2)$

$\qquad = 4 \cdot 4$

$\qquad = 16$

EXAMPLE 2

Simplify: $(8)^0$

$(8)^0 = 1$

EXAMPLE 3

Simplify: $^-2^4 \cdot 3^2$

$^-2^4 \cdot 3^2 = {}^-(2 \cdot 2 \cdot 2 \cdot 2)(3 \cdot 3)$

$\qquad = {}^-16 \cdot 9$

$\qquad = {}^-144$

PRACTICE

Simplify.

	a	b	c	d
1.	$(^-4)^3 =$ $(^-4)(^-4)(^-4) =$ $(16)(^-4) = {}^-64$	$7^2 =$	$(^-1)^2 =$	$5^2 =$
2.	$3^3 =$	$^-6^3 =$	$(^-5)^3 =$	$1^5 =$
3.	$^-8^2 =$	$0^3 =$	$(^-10)^2 =$	$9^2 =$
4.	$2^5 =$	$(^-3^4) =$	$4^0 =$	$^-3^5 =$
5.	$2^2 \cdot 3^2 =$	$7^0 \times 5^2 =$	$(^-3)^3 \cdot 4^2 =$	$8^2 \times 2^3 =$
6.	$10^2 \times 5^3 =$	$(^-9)^2 \cdot 3^2 =$	$^-6^2 \times 7^3 =$	$(^-1)^2 \cdot 5 =$
7.	$(^-3^4)(2^2) =$	$(4^3)(7^2) =$	$(6^2)(4^2) =$	$(8^2)(^-8^3) =$

Scientific Notation

When writing large or small numbers, you can use **scientific notation** as an alternate form. A number in scientific notation is expressed as the product of two factors. The first factor is at least 1 but less than 10, and the second factor is a power of 10.

When a number is converted from **standard form** to scientific notation, the power of 10 is positive if the decimal moves left. If the decimal moves right, the power is negative.

When a number is converted from scientific notation to standard form, the decimal moves left if the power of 10 is negative. If the power of 10 is positive, the decimal moves right.

Express the following in scientific notation.

5,870

Move the decimal point 3 places to the left to get a number between 1 and 10. The power of 10 is 3.

$5,870 =$ 5.87 $\times 10^3$

0.00015

Move the decimal point 4 places to the right to get a number between 1 and 10. The power of 10 is −4.

$0.00015 =$ 1.5×10^{-4}

Express the following in standard form.

4.2×10^6

Because the power of 10 is 6, move the decimal point 6 places to the right.

$4.2 \times 10^6 =$ 4,200,000

3.6×10^{-4}

Because the power of 10 is −4, move the decimal point 4 places to the left.

$3.6 \times 10^{-4} =$ 0.00036

PRACTICE

Express each number in scientific notation.

	a	b	c
1.	4,100 4.1×10^3	0.0000054	9,920,000
2.	0.008	70,500	0.000301

Express each number in standard form.

	a	b	c
3.	5×10^2 500	1.45×10^5	6.072×10^6
4.	4.8×10^{-3}	7.41×10^{-5}	1.9×10^{-4}

Problem-Solving Strategy: Find a Pattern

Anna drew a diagram of her family tree. She wrote her own name in the bottom row and her parents' names in the row above. Then she wrote her grandparents' and great-grandparents' names in the rows above her parents'. Suppose she continued until there were 7 rows in all. How many names would there be in the seventh row?

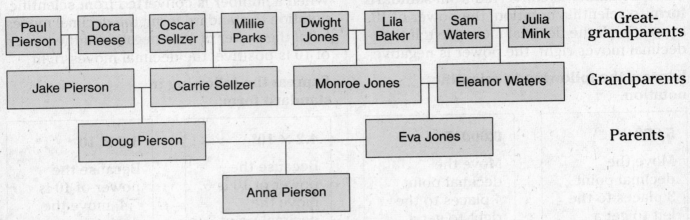

| Paul Pierson | Dora Reese | Oscar Sellzer | Millie Parks | Dwight Jones | Lila Baker | Sam Waters | Julia Mink | Great-grandparents |

Jake Pierson — Carrie Sellzer · Monroe Jones — Eleanor Waters — Grandparents

Doug Pierson · Eva Jones — Parents

Anna Pierson

Understand the problem.

• **What do you want to know?**
the number of names in the seventh row of Anna's family tree

• **What information is given?**
the first three rows in the diagram of Anna's family tree

Plan how to solve it.

• **What strategy can you use?**
You can find and complete the pattern.

Solve it.

• **How can you use this strategy to solve the problem?**
Count the number of names in each row, starting at the bottom. Anna has 2 parents, 4 grandparents, and 8 great-grandparents. The pattern is doubling the number of names. The fifth row from the bottom would have 2×8, or 16, names. The sixth row from the bottom would have 2×16, or 32, names. The seventh row from the bottom would have 2×32, or 64, names.

• **What is the answer?**
The seventh row from the bottom would have 64 names.

Look back and check your answer.

• **Is your answer reasonable?**
The number of names in each row can be expressed using exponents.

Rows	1	2	3	4	5	6	7
Number of Names	1	2	4	8	16	32	64
Powers of 2		2^0	2^1	2^2	2^3	2^4	2^5	2^6

Since $2^6 = 2 \times 2 \times 2 \times 2 \times 2 \times 2 = 64$, the answer is reasonable.

Find a pattern. Solve.

1. The number of students at Jefferson High School has been decreasing steadily from 911 two years ago to 862 last year to 813 today. If the trend continues, how many students will be at Jefferson High School next year?

Answer _____

2. Leonard's hourly wage has increased steadily every 6 months. It has gone from $16.50 per hour to $17.25 per hour to $18.00 per hour. If the pattern continues, how much will he make in another 6 months?

Answer _____

3. Suppose one day a person gave a card to six friends. Suppose the next day each of the six friends gave a card to six of their friends and so on. How many people will receive a card on the fourth day?

Answer _____

4. Suppose that ten 9s are multiplied together.

$$9 \times 9 \times 9 \times 9 \times 9 \times 9 \times 9 \times 9 \times 9 \times 9$$

What is the ones digit of the answer? (Hint: Multiply two nines together; three nines; four nines. Look for a pattern in the ones digit.)

Answer _____

5. Devante wrote the following number pattern: 0.00054, 0.0054, 0.054. Using scientific notation, write the next number in the pattern.

Answer _____

6. Luciana had 3 employees in 1997. Her business grew to 9 employees in 1998. Then there were 27 employees in 1999. At this growth rate, how many employees were there in 2001?

Answer _____

Multiplying Monomials with the Same Base

To multiply monomials that have the same base, add their exponents. For example, $(2^3)(2^2) = 2^{3+2} = 2^5$, because $(2^3)(2^2) = (2 \cdot 2 \cdot 2)(2 \cdot 2) = 2^5$. Therefore, $(a^6)(a^3) = a^{6+3} = a^9$.

When the monomials have coefficients other than 1, multiply the coefficients first.

EXAMPLE 1

Simplify: $s \cdot s$

$s^1 \cdot s^1 = s^{1+1}$

$\quad = s^2$

EXAMPLE 2

Simplify: $(3m^4)(3m^3)$

$(3m^4)(3m^3) = (3 \cdot 3)m^{4+3}$

$\quad = 9m^7$

EXAMPLE 3

Simplify: $(d^3ef)(de^4)$

$(d^3ef)(de^4) = (d^{3+1})(e^{1+4})(f^1)$

$\quad = d^4e^5f$

PRACTICE

Simplify.

	a	b	c	d
1.	$(a^3)(a^5) =$	$(b^3)(b^4) =$	$(c^6)(c^6) =$	$(d^3)(d^7) =$
2.	$5^2 \cdot (5^3 \cdot 5^1) =$	$(a^3b)(ab^2) =$	$(m^5n)(m^2n) =$	$(x^6y)(xy^3) =$
3.	$(abc)(a) =$	$(xyz)(x^2) =$	$(rst)(s^2) =$	$(def)(e^5) =$
4.	$(a^3xy)(ay^2) =$	$(a^4bc)(ab^2) =$	$2(4^3 \cdot 4^2) =$	$(b^3df^3)(b^5d) =$
5.	$(7m^2n^2)(m^6n^2) =$	$(6a^5b^6)(3ab) =$	$(8b^3cd)(2b) =$	$(5x^2y^3)(5x^2y^3) =$
6.	$(9ay)(^-8y) =$	$(^-6ab^2)(^-9bc) =$	$(2xy^3)(6x^4) =$	$2mr(^-6mr^6) =$
7.	$(4z^5)(12yz) =$	$3^2(4^1 \cdot 4^2) =$	$(^-16z^3)(9yz) =$	$(^-15r^6)(^-5r^3s) =$
8.	$(15x^3y^2)(2axy) =$	$(^-10bc^3d)(^-5bcd) =$	$(6x^3y)(^-6axy) =$	$(8c^2d)(6abd^2) =$

Powers of Powers

When a base with an exponent is raised to another exponent, such as $(2^2)^3$, simplify by multiplying the two exponents. You can check the multiplication by showing the factors and adding the exponents.

Remember to multiply the exponents of *all* the factors in each expression, including coefficients. If no exponent is used, the exponent 1 is understood.

EXAMPLE 1

Simplify: $(2^2)^3$

$(2^2)^3 = 2^{2 \cdot 3} = 2^6 = 64$

Check:

$(2^2)^3 = (2^2 \cdot 2^2 \cdot 2^2)$

$= 2^{2+2+2} = 2^6 = 64$

EXAMPLE 2

Simplify: $(3x^3)^3$

$(3x^3)^3 = (3^{1 \cdot 3})(x^{3 \cdot 3})$

$= 3^3 x^9 = 27x^9$

Check:

$(3x^3)^3 = (3 \cdot 3 \cdot 3)(x^3 \cdot x^3 \cdot x^3)$

$= 27x^{3+3+3} = 27x^9$

EXAMPLE 3

Simplify: $(2ab^2)^2(a^2)^3$

$(2ab^2)^2(a^2)^3 = (2^2 a^2 b^4)(a^6)$

$= 2^2 a^{2+6} b^4$

$= 4a^8 b^4$

PRACTICE

Simplify.

	a	b	c	d
1.	$(3^2)^3 =$	$(4^2)^2 =$	$(5^2)^3 =$	$(6^3)^2 =$
2.	$(2a^4)^2 =$	$(3h^3)^4 =$	$(2n^5)^4 =$	$(5k^7)^3 =$
3.	$(a^4 b)^4 =$	$(st)^6 =$	$(xy^3 z)^5 =$	$(m^2 np)^8 =$
4.	$(a^4 b)^2 =$	$(y^2 z)^2 =$	$(mn^4)^3 =$	$(p^6 q)^3 =$
5.	$(m^2 n^4)^2 =$	$(p^5 q^2)^2 =$	$(r^2 s^4)^3 =$	$(x^4 y^2)^4 =$
6.	$(2c^2 de^3)^2 =$	$(4x^3 y^2 z)^2 =$	$(2mn^5 p^3)^4 =$	$(5r^4 s^2 t^3)^3 =$

Simplify.

	a	b	c
7.	$(ab^4)(a^2 b)^2 =$	$(m^2 n)(m^6 n)^2 =$	$(j^2 k^3)(j^2 k^2)^3 =$
8.	$(xy)^2(x^3 y^2)^3 =$	$(mn^2)^3(m^2 n^3)^4 =$	$(g^4 h)^3(g^4 h^2)^3 =$
9.	$(^-3y^2)^2(x^2 y^2)^3 =$	$(7pq^3)^2(p^4 q^6)^3 =$	$(3x)^3(xy^4)^2 =$

Dividing Monomials with the Same Base

Division is the inverse of multiplication. When monomials are multiplied, exponents of like bases are added. When monomials are divided, exponents of like bases are subtracted. Study the examples. When monomials have coefficients other than 1, remember to divide the coefficients.

Recall that expressions such as $\frac{5}{5}$ and $\frac{a}{a}$ equal 1. If you use the rule for dividing monomials, you will see why $a^0 = 1$.

$\frac{a}{a} = a^{1-1} = a^0 = 1.$

EXAMPLE 1

Simplify: $\dfrac{a^7}{a^4}$

$\dfrac{a^7}{a^4} = a^{7-4} = a^3$

Check:

$$\dfrac{a^7}{a^4} = \dfrac{\overset{1}{\cancel{a}} \cdot \overset{1}{\cancel{a}} \cdot \overset{1}{\cancel{a}} \cdot \overset{1}{\cancel{a}} \cdot a \cdot a \cdot a}{\underset{1}{\cancel{a}} \cdot \underset{1}{\cancel{a}} \cdot \underset{1}{\cancel{a}} \cdot \underset{1}{\cancel{a}}}$$

$= a^3$

EXAMPLE 2

Simplify: $\dfrac{b^3}{b}$

$\dfrac{b^3}{b} = \dfrac{b^3}{b^1} = b^{3-1} = b^2$

Check: $\dfrac{b^3}{b} = \dfrac{\overset{1}{\cancel{b}} \cdot b \cdot b}{\underset{1}{\cancel{b}}} = b^2$

EXAMPLE 3

Simplify: $\dfrac{3c^2}{c^2}$

$\dfrac{3c^2}{c^2} = 3c^{2-2} = 3c^0 = 3(1) = 3$

Check:

$\dfrac{3c^2}{c^2} = \dfrac{3}{1} \cdot \dfrac{\overset{1}{\cancel{c}} \cdot \overset{1}{\cancel{c}}}{\underset{1}{\cancel{c}} \cdot \underset{1}{\cancel{c}}} = 3$

PRACTICE

Simplify.

	a	b	c	d	e
1.	$\dfrac{a^4}{a^4} =$	$\dfrac{d^6}{d^3} =$	$\dfrac{b^8}{b^4} =$	$\dfrac{m^8}{m^3} =$	$\dfrac{c^9}{c^5} =$
2.	$\dfrac{x^5}{x^3} =$	$\dfrac{y^5}{y^3} =$	$\dfrac{a^6}{a^4} =$	$\dfrac{m^7}{m^2} =$	$\dfrac{s^5}{s^2} =$
3.	$\dfrac{x^2}{x} =$	$\dfrac{a^5}{a^4} =$	$\dfrac{c^7}{c^4} =$	$\dfrac{c^9}{c^3} =$	$\dfrac{m^2}{m^2} =$
4.	$\dfrac{4z}{2z} =$	$\dfrac{3a^5}{a^3} =$	$\dfrac{5e^5}{e} =$	$\dfrac{9t}{t} =$	$\dfrac{6d^4}{3d} =$
5.	$\dfrac{2x^3}{x^2} =$	$\dfrac{10a^2}{a^2} =$	$\dfrac{20b^3}{4b^2} =$	$\dfrac{2d^6}{d^4} =$	$\dfrac{3b^5}{b^4} =$
6.	$\dfrac{4a}{2} =$	$\dfrac{2y^3}{y} =$	$\dfrac{5e^6}{5e} =$	$\dfrac{6d^6}{6} =$	$\dfrac{8f^8}{2f^2} =$

Fractions and Negative Exponents

When subtracting exponents, you may get a negative exponent.
A negative exponent means that the variable will remain in the denominator.

EXAMPLE 1

Simplify: $\dfrac{x^2}{x^3}$

$\dfrac{x^2}{x^3} = x^{2-3} = x^{-1} = \dfrac{1}{x}$

Check:

$\dfrac{x^2}{x^3} = \dfrac{\overset{1}{\cancel{x}} \cdot \overset{1}{\cancel{x}}}{\underset{1}{\cancel{x}} \cdot \underset{1}{\cancel{x}} \cdot x} = \dfrac{1}{x}$

EXAMPLE 2

Simplify: $\dfrac{18y^2}{9y^4}$

$\dfrac{18y^2}{9y^4} = \dfrac{18}{9}(y^{2-4})$

$= 2 \cdot y^{-2} = 2 \cdot \dfrac{1}{y^2} = \dfrac{2}{y^2}$

Check:

$\dfrac{18y^2}{9y^4} = \dfrac{18}{9} \cdot \dfrac{\overset{1}{\cancel{y}} \cdot \overset{1}{\cancel{y}}}{\underset{1}{\cancel{y}} \cdot \underset{1}{\cancel{y}} \cdot y \cdot y}$

$= 2 \cdot \dfrac{1}{y \cdot y} = \dfrac{2}{y^2}$

EXAMPLE 3

Simplify: $\dfrac{^-30x}{15x^3}$

$\dfrac{^-30x}{15x^3} = \dfrac{^-30}{15} \cdot x^{1-3}$

$= ^-2 \cdot x^{-2} = \dfrac{^-2}{x^2}$

Check:

$\dfrac{^-30x}{15x^3} = \dfrac{^-30}{15} \cdot \dfrac{\overset{1}{\cancel{x}}}{\underset{1}{\cancel{x}} \cdot x \cdot x}$

$= ^-2 \cdot \dfrac{1}{x \cdot x} = \dfrac{^-2}{x^2}$

PRACTICE

Simplify.

	a	b	c	d	e
1.	$\dfrac{x^3}{x^8} =$	$\dfrac{y^2}{y^3} =$	$\dfrac{a^2}{a^5} =$	$\dfrac{b}{b^2} =$	$\dfrac{s^2}{s^4} =$
2.	$\dfrac{x^4}{x^6} =$	$\dfrac{a^3}{a^4} =$	$\dfrac{y^2}{y^7} =$	$\dfrac{b^9}{b^{10}} =$	$\dfrac{d^{12}}{d^{14}} =$
3.	$\dfrac{^-y}{y^2} =$	$\dfrac{^-x^2}{x^6} =$	$\dfrac{^-z}{z^3} =$	$-\dfrac{r^3}{r^5} =$	$-\dfrac{d}{d^4} =$
4.	$\dfrac{15c}{5c^2} =$	$\dfrac{21x}{7x^3} =$	$\dfrac{27b}{3b^4} =$	$-\dfrac{18r^2}{6r^3} =$	$\dfrac{12e^2}{2e^4} =$
5.	$\dfrac{12x^4}{6x^5} =$	$\dfrac{15y}{5y^2} =$	$\dfrac{6a^4}{a^8} =$	$\dfrac{10b^2}{2b^6} =$	$\dfrac{27z^2}{9z^5} =$

Simplify using a negative exponent.

	a	b	c	d	e
6.	$\dfrac{-12a^2}{4a^3} =$ $^-3(a^{2-3})$ $= ^-3a^{-1}$	$\dfrac{16b^4}{-4b^6} =$	$\dfrac{^-18x^3}{2x^9} =$	$\dfrac{^-90r^2}{10r^4} =$	$\dfrac{^-14z^3}{^-7z^4} =$

Reducing Algebraic Fractions to Lowest Terms

Algebraic fractions can be reduced to lowest terms. First, reduce the fraction formed by the coefficients to lowest terms and then divide the like bases.

Remember, when dividing, subtract the exponents.

EXAMPLE 1

Reduce: $\dfrac{20x^3y}{5x^2y^2}$

$\dfrac{20x^3y}{5x^2y^2} = \dfrac{20}{5} \cdot x^{3-2} \cdot y^{1-2}$

$= 4x^1 \cdot y^{-1} = 4x \cdot \dfrac{1}{y} = \dfrac{4x}{y}$

EXAMPLE 2

Reduce: $\dfrac{a^2b^3c}{a^3b^5}$

$\dfrac{a^2b^3c}{a^3b^5} = a^{2-3} \cdot b^{3-5} \cdot c^1$

$= a^{-1} \cdot b^{-2} \cdot c^1 = \dfrac{1}{a} \cdot \dfrac{1}{b^2} \cdot c$

$= \dfrac{c}{ab^2}$

EXAMPLE 3

Reduce: $\dfrac{8rst^3}{16st^2}$

$\dfrac{8rst^3}{16st^2} = \dfrac{8}{16} \cdot r^1 \cdot s^{1-1} \cdot t^{3-2}$

$= \dfrac{1}{2} \cdot r^1 \cdot s^0 \cdot t^1 = \dfrac{rt}{2}$

Remember, $s^0 = 1$.

PRACTICE

Reduce to lowest terms.

	a	b	c	d	e
1.	$\dfrac{x^3y^2}{x^2y^2} =$	$\dfrac{a^2b^2}{a^3b} =$	$\dfrac{a^4b^2}{a^2b^4} =$	$\dfrac{x^6y^3z}{x^4yz^2} =$	$\dfrac{xy^3z^6}{x^2y^2z^4} =$
2.	$\dfrac{6x^2y^4}{2x^3y^2} =$	$\dfrac{12x^3y^5}{3x^4y^2} =$	$\dfrac{8ab^2c^3}{16a^2b^2c^3} =$	$\dfrac{25a^3b^2c^3}{5ab^2c^3} =$	$\dfrac{6a^4b^2c}{24a^2b^3c^4} =$
3.	$\dfrac{15x^3y}{^-5x^3y^2} =$	$\dfrac{^-5x^2y}{10xy^2} =$	$\dfrac{16x^4y}{^-4x^3y^2} =$	$\dfrac{10x^3y^2}{^-5x^4y} =$	$\dfrac{^-8xy^5}{24x^2y^3} =$
4.	$\dfrac{4ab^2}{^-20a^3b} =$	$\dfrac{^-15x^2y^3}{5x^3y^2} =$	$\dfrac{^-24x^2y^4}{6x^4y^2} =$	$\dfrac{7a^3b^2}{^-35a^2b^3} =$	$\dfrac{^-48xy^2z^3}{8x^3y^2z} =$
5.	$\dfrac{^-15xy}{^-5x^2y^2} =$	$\dfrac{^-6xy^3z^5}{^-36x^2y^2z^4} =$	$\dfrac{^-7x^4y^3}{^-14x^2y^4} =$	$\dfrac{^-16a^3b^4}{^-8a^4b^3} =$	$\dfrac{^-35ab^3}{^-7a^2b} =$
6.	$\dfrac{8a^2y}{12ay^2} =$	$\dfrac{16xy^2}{10x^3y} =$	$\dfrac{12ab^2c}{18a^2bc} =$	$\dfrac{10ab^2c^3}{15a^3b^2c} =$	$\dfrac{14a^4b^2c}{12a^3b^3c^3} =$

Adding Binomials

A **binomial** is the sum or difference of two monomials. An example of a binomial is $5a + bc$ or $4x^2 - 2y$. To add two binomials together, group the like terms and add their coefficients.

EXAMPLE 1

Add: $(a + b) + (a - b)$

$= (a + a) + (b - b)$

$= 2a + 0$

$= 2a$

EXAMPLE 2

Add: $(5a + 3b) + (3a - b)$

$= (5a + 3a) + (3b - b)$

$= 8a + 2b$

EXAMPLE 3

Add: $(8xy - 2y) + (^-5y)$

$= 8xy + (^-2y + ^-5y)$

$= 8xy + (^-7y)$

$= 8xy - 7y$

PRACTICE

Add.

	a	b	c
1.	$(4a - 2b) + (4a + 2b) =$	$(3x - y) + (3x + y) =$	$(6m - 7n) + (4m - 7n) =$
2.	$(5y + 4z) + (3y - 3z) =$	$(6x - 3y) + (x + 4y) =$	$(2ab - a) + (^-2ab + a) =$
3.	$(^-7a + b) + (^-3a - b) =$	$(9r - s) + (4r - s) =$	$(6m - n) + (^-3m + 3n) =$
4.	$(r + 5st) + (r + st) =$	$(4b - 3cd) + (^-b - cd) =$	$(^-6xy - 8z) + (^-8z - 6xy) =$
5.	$(7x + 2y) + (^-3y + x) =$	$(cd + d) + (cd + d) =$	$(7ab - 6yz) + (^-9yz + 3ab) =$
6.	$(5m - 6n) + (^-2m - n) =$	$(xy - x) + (x - xy) =$	$(18p - 19q) + (10p - 14q) =$
7.	$(xyz + z) + (xyz - z) =$	$(-rst + t) + (6rst + 6t) =$	$(6ab - abc) + (ab + 6abc) =$
8.	$(7y - yz) + (7y - yz) =$	$(10xy - z) + (xy - 10z) =$	$(5ab - abc) + (5ab - abc) =$

Subtracting Binomials

Recall that subtracting is the same as adding the opposite. To subtract a binomial, add its opposite. Do this by first changing the sign of each term of the binomial being subtracted. Then group the like terms and add.

EXAMPLE 1

Subtract:

$(x + y) - (2x + y)$

$= (x + y) + (-2x - y)$

$= (x - 2x) + (y - y)$

$= -x + 0$

$= -x$

EXAMPLE 2

Subtract:

$(x + y) - (^-3x + y)$

$= (x + y) + (3x - y)$

$= (x + 3x) + (y - y)$

$= 4x + 0$

$= 4x$

EXAMPLE 3

Subtract:

$(^-7rs - 5t) - (5rs + t)$

$= (^-7rs - 5t) + (^-5rs - t)$

$= (^-7rs - 5rs) + (^-5t - t)$

$= ^-12rs + (^-6t)$

$= ^-12rs - 6t$

PRACTICE

Subtract.

	a	b	c
1.	$(x + y) - (x - y) =$	$(2a + 4b) - (3a - b) =$	$(8m + 6n) - (7m - 5n) =$
2.	$(x - y) - (x + y) =$	$(3a - b) - (6a + 2b) =$	$(10m - n) - (6m + 2n) =$
3.	$(x - y) - (-x + y) =$	$(b - 4c) - (^-3b - c) =$	$(^-6r - 2s) - (-r - 3s) =$
4.	$(3a - 2cd) - (2b + 3cd) =$	$(6m + 2np) - (3m - 5np) =$	$(8rs - t) - (6t + 5rs) =$
5.	$(^-2x + yz) - (x - 5yz) =$	$(6pq - 4rs) - (6pq - 4rs) =$	$(^-7rs - 5t) - (5t + rs) =$
6.	$(8x - 5yz) - (-x - 4yz) =$	$(7x + 5wy) - (^-2x + 3wy) =$	$(^-8mn + 6p) - (^-5mn + 6p) =$
7.	$(^-4 + xyz) - (5 + xyz) =$	$(4p - 5qt) - (^-5qt + 4p) =$	$(-t + rs) - (t - rs) =$
8.	$(10z + xyz) - (10xyz + z) =$	$(3abc - c) - (2abc + c) =$	$(rst - 2rs) - (3rst - 4rs) =$

Unit 4 Exponents and Polynomials

Simplifying Polynomials with Exponents

A **polynomial** is an expression that can be written as a sum of monomials. A binomial is one kind of polynomial. Simplifying polynomials with exponents is done by adding and subtracting like terms. Like terms must have the same variables raised to the same exponents.

Remember, to subtract terms in parentheses, add the opposite. Be sure to change the sign of each term within the parentheses. Then group like terms and add.

EXAMPLE 1

Simplify:

$3x^2 + 5y + 2x^2 + y$

$= (3x^2 + 2x^2) + (5y + y)$

$= 5x^2 + 6y$

EXAMPLE 2

Simplify:

$8x^3 - 5y^2 - (3x^3 + 2y^2 + y)$

$= 8x^3 + -5y^2 + (-3x^3 - 2y^2 - y)$

$= (8x^3 - 3x^3) + (-5y^2 - 2y^2) - y$

$= 5x^3 - 7y^2 - y$

EXAMPLE 3

Simplify:

$2x^4 + 3x^3 - (^-6x^4) + 2$

$= (2x^4 + 6x^4) + 3x^3 + 2$

$= 8x^4 + 3x^3 + 2$

PRACTICE

Simplify.

	a	b	c
1.	$4x^3 + 3y^2 + 3x^3 + 4y^2 =$	$5a^2 + 4b^2 + 3a^2 + 5b^2 =$	$b^2 + 9c^2 + 4b^2 + 3c^2 =$
2.	$9m^2 + n - (m^2 + 6n^2) =$	$5x^2 + 3y - (3x^2 + 5y) =$	$9a^2 + 4b - (6a^2 + 7b) =$
3.	$5b^2 - 7b - (3b^2 - 9b) =$	$7m^2 - 3n^4 - (4m^2 - 7n^4) =$	$4x^2 - 5y - (3x^2 - 2y) =$
4.	$9x^3 - 4y^2 - (-x^3 - 3y^2) =$	$5a^3 - 4b^2 - (^-3a^3 - 5b^2) =$	$8b^3 - 7b^2 - (^-b^3 - b^2) =$
5.	$^-4m^2 - 3m - (^-4m^2 - 2m) =$	$^-5x^2 + 4y^3 - (3x^2 + 2y^3) =$	$^-6x + 9y^2 - (^-6x - 2y^2) =$
6.	$^-(8a^3 + 7a^2 + a) + 3a^2 + 5a =$	$^-(4b^3 - 5b^2) + b^3 - b^2 + b =$	$^-(9m + 9m^2) + 3m^2 + 3m =$
7.	$^-(3 + 2x^2 + 4x^4) - (4x^4) =$	$^-(c^2 - b^2) + c^2 + b^2 + 1 =$	$^-(^-4 - x^2) - (^-2 + 4x^2 + x) =$
8.	$^-3x^4 - x^3 + 3x^2 - (3x^4 + x^3) =$	$^-(15m - 6m^2) + (^-5m + 4m) =$	$^-(7a^4 - 7a^4) + (3a^4 + 9a^4) =$

Multiplying Algebraic Fractions

Algebraic fractions are multiplied in exactly the same way as fractions with integers. Simplify whenever possible. Then multiply the numerators and multiply the denominators. When negative numbers are multiplied, remember the following rule.

> **RULE:** The product of two factors with the same sign is positive. The product of two factors with different signs is negative.

EXAMPLE 1

Simplify: $\dfrac{x}{a} \cdot \dfrac{a}{b}$

$$\dfrac{x}{\overset{1}{\underset{1}{\cancel{a}}}} \cdot \dfrac{\overset{1}{\cancel{a}}}{b} = \dfrac{x}{b}$$

EXAMPLE 2

Simplify: $\dfrac{-x^2}{a^2} \cdot \dfrac{a}{b}$

$$\dfrac{-x^2}{a^2} \cdot \dfrac{a}{b} = \dfrac{-x^2}{a \cdot \underset{1}{\cancel{a}}} \times \dfrac{\overset{1}{\cancel{a}}}{b}$$

$$= \dfrac{-x^2}{ab}$$

EXAMPLE 3

Simplify: $\dfrac{-2xy}{a^2} \cdot \dfrac{-a^4}{x^2}$

$$= \dfrac{-2xy}{\underset{1\ \ 1}{a \cdot a}} \cdot \dfrac{-\overset{1\ \ 1}{(a \cdot a \cdot a \cdot a)}}{\underset{1}{x \cdot x}}$$

$$= \dfrac{(-2y)}{1} \cdot \dfrac{(-a^2)}{x} = \dfrac{2a^2y}{x}$$

PRACTICE

Simplify.

	a	b	c
1.	$\dfrac{p}{q} \cdot \dfrac{q}{p} =$	$\dfrac{x}{2a} \times \dfrac{2a}{9y} =$	$\dfrac{3x^2}{4b} \cdot \dfrac{40y}{x^2} =$
2.	$\dfrac{x^2}{4} \times \dfrac{4a}{2x} =$	$\dfrac{a^2}{x^3} \cdot \dfrac{1}{a} =$	$\dfrac{6a^2}{x^3} \times \dfrac{12x^3}{b} =$
3.	$\dfrac{-4b^2}{x} \cdot \dfrac{2x^5}{b} =$	$\dfrac{-9a^2}{y} \times \dfrac{6y}{15a} =$	$\dfrac{-15c}{6b^2} \cdot \dfrac{12b^3}{5c} =$
4.	$\dfrac{-5x^2}{12a} \times \dfrac{-6x}{10a} =$	$\dfrac{-9a^3}{4x^2} \cdot \dfrac{-8x^4}{3a} =$	$\dfrac{5a}{-6x^2} \times \dfrac{3x^3}{-10a^2} =$
5.	$\dfrac{4ab}{c} \cdot \dfrac{c}{2a} =$	$\dfrac{3y^2z}{4x} \times \dfrac{2xz}{9y^2} =$	$\dfrac{p}{pq^2} \cdot \dfrac{pq^2}{p^2} =$
6.	$\dfrac{a+b}{c} \times \dfrac{c}{a+b} =$	$\dfrac{3(x+y)}{x-y^2} \cdot \dfrac{2(x-y^2)}{3} =$	$\dfrac{5}{a^2+b^2} \times \dfrac{-(a^2+b^2)}{10x} =$

Dividing Algebraic Fractions

To divide fractions with integers, multiply by the reciprocal of the second fraction. Use this same method for algebraic fractions. Remember to simplify when possible.

EXAMPLE 1

Simplify: $\dfrac{3a^2}{x} \div \dfrac{3a}{x^2}$

$= \dfrac{\overset{a}{\cancel{3a^2}}}{\underset{1}{\cancel{x}}} \cdot \dfrac{\overset{x}{\cancel{x^2}}}{\underset{1}{\cancel{3a}}} = ax$

EXAMPLE 2

Simplify: $\dfrac{2x^2y}{3} \div 4a$

$= \dfrac{\overset{1}{2x^2y}}{3} \cdot \dfrac{1}{\underset{2}{\cancel{4a}}} = \dfrac{x^2y}{6a}$

EXAMPLE 3

Simplify: $\dfrac{a+b}{2} \div \dfrac{a+b}{4}$

$= \dfrac{\overset{1}{(a+b)}}{\underset{1}{2}} \cdot \dfrac{\overset{2}{\cancel{4}}}{(a+b)} = 2$

PRACTICE

Simplify.

	a	b	c
1.	$\dfrac{x^2}{a} \div \dfrac{x^4}{a^2} =$	$\dfrac{m}{n^3} \div \dfrac{m^3}{n} =$	$\dfrac{z^4}{b^2} \div \dfrac{z}{b^3} =$
2.	$\dfrac{2x^2y}{3} \div \dfrac{4xy^2}{15} =$	$\dfrac{6ab}{7xy} \div \dfrac{18a^2b^2}{28x^2y^2} =$	$\dfrac{15x^2y}{9ab} \div \dfrac{5xy^2}{3ab} =$
3.	$\dfrac{2xy}{9} \div 4 =$	$\dfrac{5ab}{6x} \div 10 =$	$\dfrac{9x^2y^2}{ab} \div 3 =$
4.	$\dfrac{10x^2y}{3} \div 5xy =$	$\dfrac{9a^2b^2}{6} \div 3ab =$	$\dfrac{3ab^3}{2} \div 6b^2 =$
5.	$\dfrac{^-12a^3}{5} \div 4 =$	$\dfrac{^-15x^2y}{2} \div 5xy =$	$\dfrac{^-16xy^2}{3} \div 4xy =$
6.	$\dfrac{18a^2}{5} \div \dfrac{1}{10} =$	$\dfrac{15x^2y}{4} \div \dfrac{1}{2} =$	$\dfrac{21a^3b^2}{5} \div \dfrac{3}{20} =$
7.	$\dfrac{a+b}{2} \div \dfrac{2(a+b)}{4a} =$	$\dfrac{a-b}{4a} \div \dfrac{a-b}{8} =$	$\dfrac{a^2+b^2}{6} \div \dfrac{a^2+b^2}{12x} =$

Multiplying Polynomials by Monomials

To multiply a polynomial by a monomial, multiply each term of the polynomial by the monomial.

Remember:

- When like bases are multiplied, add the exponents.
- Use the rules for products of negative and positive numbers.

EXAMPLE 1

Simplify: $a(a + b)$

$a(a + b) = (a \cdot a) + (a \cdot b)$
$= a^2 + ab$

EXAMPLE 2

Simplify: $2a^2(a + b + 2c)$

$= (2a^2 \cdot a) + (2a^2 \cdot b) + (2a^2 \cdot 2c)$
$= 2a^3 + 2a^2b + 4a^2c$

EXAMPLE 3

Simplify: $^-2xy(5x^2 + 2y)$

$= (^-2xy \cdot 5x^2) + (^-2xy \cdot 2y)$
$= ^-10x^3y - 4xy^2$

PRACTICE

Simplify.

a	b	c
1. $x(x + y) =$	$y(2x + y) =$	$x^3(x + 2y) =$
2. $2x(x + y) =$	$3x(2x + 3y) =$	$6a^3(2a - b) =$
3. $^-2b(2a + b) =$	$^-2b(3a + b) =$	$^-3b^3(^-4a + 3b) =$
4. $4x(x^2 + y) =$	$2b(2b^2 - a^2) =$	$^-5c^2(^-3c^3 - 4) =$
5. $2x(3x - 5y - 2z) =$	$^-2y(^-2x + 3y - 4z) =$	$3b^2(5a + 4b - 2c) =$
6. $4b(4a^2 - 5b^2 - 3c^2) =$	$^-2b(7a - 3b^4 - 1) =$	$^-3c^2(^-4c^2 - 3c + 2) =$
7. $2xy(5x - 2y + 3z) =$	$xz(x + y - z) =$	$^-2ab^2(^-4a - 4b - 4) =$
8. $-xyz(5x - 3y + 4z) =$	$2abc(a^2 + b^2 + c^2) =$	$^-4xy^2z(xy + yz) =$

Dividing Polynomials by Monomials

When dividing a polynomial by a monomial, divide each term of the polynomial by the monomial. Divide each term separately.

Remember, when dividing, subtract exponents of like bases.

EXAMPLE 1

Simplify: $\dfrac{x^2 + xy}{x}$

$= \dfrac{x^2}{x} + \dfrac{xy}{x}$

$= x^{2-1} + (x^{1-1}y)$

$= x + y$

EXAMPLE 2

Simplify:

$\dfrac{^-6a^3 + 12a^2 - 9a}{3a}$

$= \dfrac{^-6a^3}{3a} + \dfrac{12a^2}{3a} - \dfrac{9a}{3a}$

$= {}^-2a^2 + 4a - 3$

EXAMPLE 3

Simplify:

$\dfrac{^-9a^3y + 12a^2y^2 - 6ay^3}{^-3ay}$

$= \dfrac{-9a^3y}{-3ay} + \dfrac{12a^2y^2}{-3ay} + \dfrac{-6ay^3}{-3ay}$

$= 3a^2 - 4ay + 2y^2$

PRACTICE

Divide.

	a	b	c
1.	$\dfrac{a^2 + a}{a} =$	$\dfrac{6xy - 4z}{2} =$	$\dfrac{8xy + 6xy}{2x} =$
2.	$\dfrac{10ab + 15ac + 20ad}{5a} =$	$\dfrac{18x^2 + 24xy + 16xz}{2x} =$	$\dfrac{6a^2y + 12ay^2 + 18ay^3}{6a} =$
3.	$\dfrac{^-4a^2 + 10a + 2}{2} =$	$\dfrac{12x^4 - 16x^3 - 24x^2}{4x^2} =$	$\dfrac{^-25x^3 - 20x^2 + 15x}{5x} =$
4.	$\dfrac{9x^4 + 15x^3 + 21x^2}{^-3x^2} =$	$\dfrac{18a^3y + 24a^2y^2 + 30ay^3}{^-6ay} =$	$\dfrac{10x^2y + 15xy^2 + 20y^2}{^-5y} =$
5.	$\dfrac{^-12x^3 - 9x^2 - 15x}{^-3x} =$	$\dfrac{^-16a^4 - 24a^3 - 16a^2}{^-8a} =$	$\dfrac{^-24x^3y - 12x^2y^2 - 18xy^3}{^-6xy} =$
6.	$\dfrac{4x^2y + 12xy - 8xy^2}{2xy} =$	$\dfrac{^-15x^3y + 12x^2y^2 - 18xy^3}{^-3xy} =$	$\dfrac{^-18c^2d - 24c^2d^2 + 12cd^3}{^-6cd} =$

Problem-Solving Strategy: Use Logic

Adam, Brenda, and Charles live in New York, Toronto, and Los Angeles, although not necessarily in that order. Adam is the uncle of the person who lives in Los Angeles. Either Brenda or Charles lives in New York. Charles has no uncles. In which city does each person live?

Understand the problem.

- **What do you want to know?**
  in which city each person lives

- **What information is given?**
  Clue 1: Adam is the uncle of the person who lives in Los Angeles.
  Clue 2: Either Brenda or Charles lives in New York.
  Clue 3: Charles has no uncles.

Plan how to solve it.

- **What strategy can you use?**
  You can organize all the possibilities in a chart. Then you can use logic to match the clues to the possibilities.

Solve it.

- **How can you use this strategy to solve the problem?**
  Use what you learned from the clues to logically fill in the parts of the chart. For example, if Adam is the uncle of the person who lives in Los Angeles and Charles has no uncles, the logical conclusion is that Adam and Charles do not live in Los Angeles. Therefore, Brenda lives in Los Angeles. Reread the clues as necessary to help you complete the chart.

	New York	Toronto	Los Angeles
Adam	no	Yes	no
Brenda	no	no	Yes
Charles	Yes	no	no

- **What is the answer?**
  Adam lives in Toronto, Brenda lives in Los Angeles, and Charles lives in New York.

Look back and check your answer.

- **Is your answer reasonable?**
  Make sure your answers agree with the given clues. If Charles has no uncle then Brenda does. So Brenda lives in Los Angeles. Either Brenda or Charles lives in New York. So Charles lives in New York, and Adam lives in Toronto.

  The answer is reasonable.

Unit 4 **Exponents and Polynomials**

Set up a logic chart. Solve.

1. The hobbies of Janet, Katrina, and Latavia are bowling, swimming, and basketball, although not necessarily in that order. Janet often has lunch with the bowler. Latavia is either the basketball player or the swimmer. Janet does not enjoy basketball. Which person has which hobby?

	Bowling	Swimming	Basketball
Janet			
Katrina			
Latavia			

Bowling _____

Swimming _____

Basketball _____

2. Montez, Norman, Omar, and Patrick live in houses of four different colors. The colors are white, yellow, green, and blue. Patrick lives in the green or blue house. Norman's friend lives in the yellow house. The color of Omar's house is blue. Use the clues to figure out which person lives in which house.

	White	Yellow	Green	Blue
Montez				
Norman				
Omar				
Patrick				

White _____ Yellow _____

Green _____ Blue _____

3. Four cars are parked along a street. The colors of the cars are silver, black, tan and red. Here are the license numbers: AB 7641, 340 MDY, GX 2378, and 816 ZPN. The license numbers of the red car and the silver car have a 6 in them. The tan car's license number does not have four digits. The silver car's license number has the letters after the numbers. What is the license number for each car?

Silver _____

Black _____

Tan _____

Red _____

4. Alvin, Shane, Carlos, and Dwight are the names of Derrick's son, father, brother, and grandfather, but not necessarily in that order. Carlos is younger than Alvin. Dwight is older than Shane. Dwight's grandfather is Alvin. Write the name of each of Derrick's relatives.

Son _____

Father _____

Brother _____

Grandfather _____

Identifying Common Monomial Factors

If one factor of a number is known, division can be used to find another factor. For example, since 3 is a factor of 24, divide 24 by 3 to find another factor, 8. Similarly, if one factor of a polynomial is known, divide to find another factor.

The **common monomial factor** of a polynomial is a monomial that is a factor of all the terms in the polynomial. In the example below, the common factors are 3 and a, since 3 and a are factors of each term. The common monomial factor of the entire polynomial is $3a$. To find the other factor, divide the polynomial by $3a$.

EXAMPLE

Find the common monomial factor of $12ab - 6ac + 3ad$. Divide to find another factor. Write the polynomial as the product of the monomial and a polynomial.

Since 3 and a are factors of each term, the common monomial factor is $3a$. Divide by $3a$.

$$\frac{12ab - 6ac + 3ad}{3a} = 4b - 2c + d \qquad \text{The two factors are } 3a \text{ and } 4b - 2c + d.$$

$$12ab - 6ac + 3ad = 3a(4b - 2c + d)$$

PRACTICE

Find the common monomial factor. Divide to find another factor. Then write the polynomial as the product of the monomial and a polynomial.

a   *b*

1. $7mn - 14mp - 21mq =$ $5x^3 - 10x^2 + 15x =$

2. $4ax + 8ay - 12az =$ $6a^3b - 12a^2b^2 + 18ab^3 =$

3. $10x^3 + 8x^2 - 2x =$ $9a^2b^2 + 6ab + 15 =$

4. $8x^2y + 4xy - 12xy^2 =$ $10x^3 - 12x^2 - 6x =$

5. $20a^3b - 15a^2b^2 + 10ab^3 =$ $16xy^3 - 12x^2y^2 + 20x^2y^3 =$

6. $3a^2 - 15a^3y + 18a^4y^2 =$ $20ab^3 - 15a^2b^2 - 25a^3b =$

Multiplying Polynomials by Binomials

Multiplying binomials by binomials may be thought of as multiplying a binomial by two monomials. Parentheses are often used to show multiplication of binomials. Multiply each term of the first binomial by each term of the second binomial. Combine like terms. Two polynomials are multiplied in the same way as two binomials.

Remember, when multiplying different variables, put them in the product in alphabetical order. This will make it easier to find like terms.

EXAMPLE 1

Multiply:
$(4a + 3b)(2a + b)$

$= 4a(2a + b) + 3b(2a + b)$

$= 8a^2 + 4ab + 6ab + 3b^2$

$= 8a^2 + 10ab + 3b^2$

EXAMPLE 2

Multiply:
$(x - y^2)(x - y^2)$

$= x(x - y^2) - y^2(x - y^2)$

$= x^2 - xy^2 - xy^2 + y^4$

$= x^2 - 2xy^2 + y^4$

EXAMPLE 3

Multiply:
$(a + c)(a + b + c)$

$= a(a + b + c) + c(a + b + c)$

$= a^2 + ab + ac + ac + bc + c^2$

$= a^2 + ab + 2ac + bc + c^2$

PRACTICE

Multiply.

a	b	c
1. $(a + b)(a + b) =$	$(^-ab + c)(^-ab - c) =$	$(2x + y)(2x + y) =$
2. $(3a - 2b)(3a - 2b) =$	$(x^2y - z)(xy + z) =$	$(^-2c + d)(c + 2d) =$
3. $(x - 4y)(^-3x - 2y) =$	$(^-a + 2b)(a - 2b) =$	$(^-2abc + d)(3a - 4) =$
4. $(-y - 2z)(y - 2z) =$	$(3a - 4b)(a + 3b) =$	$(^-6x + 2y)(6x - y) =$
5. $(xy + z)(xy + z) =$	$(2ab - c)(4ab - 3c) =$	$(3xy^4 + y^3)(4x^3y - x) =$
6. $(ac + b - d)(a^2 - c) =$	$(2x - y)(x - y + z) =$	$(gk - 2k - m)(g - 2k) =$
7. $(x + y)(2x^2 - x + 1) =$	$(2d^2 + h - 2w)(3h + d) =$	$(4x^2 - 2xy - y^2)(x - y) =$

Dividing Polynomials by Binomials

Polynomials are divided by binomials in much the same way that numbers are divided. Look at Example 1. Divide the first term of the dividend (a^2) by the first term of the divisor (a). The result is a. Place the a in the quotient, multiply both terms of the divisor by a, and subtract. Continue in this manner until the remainder is zero.

EXAMPLE 1

Divide.

$$
\begin{array}{r}
a + b \\
a + b \overline{)a^2 + 2ab + b^2} \\
\underline{a^2 + ab} \quad\downarrow \\
ab + b^2 \\
\underline{ab + b^2} \\
0
\end{array}
$$

EXAMPLE 2

Divide.

$$
\begin{array}{r}
a - b \\
a - b \overline{)a^2 - 2ab + b^2} \\
\underline{a^2 - ab} \quad\downarrow \\
-ab + b^2 \\
\underline{-ab + b^2} \\
0
\end{array}
$$

EXAMPLE 3

Divide.

$$
\begin{array}{r}
x + 3 \\
2x + 7 \overline{)2x^2 + 13x + 21} \\
\underline{2x^2 + 7x} \quad\downarrow \\
6x + 21 \\
\underline{6x + 21} \\
0
\end{array}
$$

PRACTICE

Divide.

	a	b	c
1.	$a - 2b \overline{)a^2 - 4ab + 4b^2}$	$x - y \overline{)x^2 - 2xy + y^2}$	$a + 2b \overline{)a^2 + 4ab + 4b^2}$
2.	$x - 5 \overline{)x^2 - 4x - 5}$	$3x - 2y \overline{)9x^2 - 12xy + 4y^2}$	$5a + 2b \overline{)25a^2 + 20ab + 4b^2}$
3.	$5 + x \overline{)25 + 10x + x^2}$	$4 + 2x \overline{)16 + 16x + 4x^2}$	$2x + 3y \overline{)4x^2 + 12xy + 9y^2}$

Multiplying and Dividing Polynomials

Multiply.

	a	*b*	*c*
1.	$2b(3b^2 - 4b + 6) =$	$3xy(4x^2 - 2xy - 3y^2) =$	$4x^2(10 + 3y^2) =$
2.	$(x + 2)(x^2 - 3x + 5) =$	$(2a + 3b)(2a^2 - 3ab + b^2) =$	$(2x - 1)(3x^3 - 2x^2 - x) =$
3.	$3x - 2(2x^2 - 5x) =$	$3x(2x^2 - 5x + 4) - 2 =$	$2(6 + 2a - 3a^2) - 12 =$
4.	$3(x - y + z)(x + y + z) =$	$(6x^2 - x)(2y + 3)3y =$	$7b(^-4b^2) + 3b(b^2 + 2b) =$

Divide.

	a	*b*	*c*
5.	$\dfrac{x^2 + 4x}{x} =$	$\dfrac{6x^2 + 3x}{3x} =$	$\dfrac{2y^2 - 4y}{2y} =$
6.	$\dfrac{2x(x + 2x)}{2x^2} =$ $= \dfrac{2x(3x)}{2x^2} = \dfrac{6x^2}{2x^2} = 3$	$\dfrac{6y(3y^2 - xy + x^2y)}{y^2} =$	$\dfrac{xy(12 + 9x - 6x^2)}{3x} =$
7.	$x + 1\overline{)x^2 + 3x + 2}$	$6x - 6\overline{)6x^2 - 24x + 18}$	$3 - 2x\overline{)6 + 5x - 6x^2}$

Simplify.

	a	b	c
1.	$5^2 =$	$(^-9)^3 =$	$(^-10)^2 \cdot 3^2 =$

Change each number from scientific notation to standard form.

	a	b	c
2.	$1.8 \times 10^{-4} =$	$2.7 \times 10^6 =$	$3.45 \times 10^{-3} =$

Simplify.

	a	b	c
3.	$(cd^3)(c^2) =$	$(^-5xy^3)(5x^5y) =$	$(xy^3z^4)^3 =$
4.	$\dfrac{m^9}{m^3} =$	$\dfrac{^-8a^3b^2c}{12ab^2c^3} =$	$(xy - x) + (5xy + 3x) =$
5.	$(^-b - 4) - (b + 2) =$	$^-(15m^2 + 6m^3) - (^-5m) =$	$\dfrac{4ab}{6a} \cdot \dfrac{3b}{2ab} =$
6.	$\dfrac{3x^2y}{z} \cdot \dfrac{z^2}{3} =$	$\dfrac{^-12x^3}{5} \div 4x =$	$\dfrac{x^2 - x}{x} =$
7.	$\dfrac{10xy + 4z}{2} =$	$\dfrac{16a^4 - 12a^2 - 4a}{4a} =$	$x(x - y) =$
8.	$^-2y(^-2x^2 + y + 3) =$	$(3a + 4b)(a - 6b) =$	$(a^2 + b^2 + 3)(ab - b) =$

Divide.

	a	b	c
9.	$x + 1\overline{)x^2 - x - 2}$	$x + 2y\overline{)x^2 + 4xy + 4y^2}$	$2x - 3y\overline{)4x^2 - 12xy + 9y^2}$

Find the common monomial factor. Divide to find another factor. Then write the polynomial as the product of the monomial and a polynomial.

	a	b
10.	$12az - 8bz + 16cz =$	$9fy + 15gy - 27y =$

Solve.

	a	b	c
1.	$y - 35 = {}^-100$	$7 + 37 = 2k$	$^-11 - 3r = {}^-2$
2.	$5(a + 3) = 25$	$7b - 10b = {}^-18$	$3(n - 2) = -n - 10$
3.	$5x = 135$	$\dfrac{x}{4} = \dfrac{3}{8}$	$\dfrac{2s}{3} = 16$

Simplify.

	a	b	c
4.	$2(4 + 3) - 6(0) =$	$^-16 - ({}^-34) =$	$^-6({}^-4)({}^-8) =$
5.	$\dfrac{^-135}{^-3} =$	$\left|\,^-15\,\right| =$	$({}^-1)^{99}({}^-2)^4 =$
6.	$(4a^2x)^2 =$	$3a(2b^3 + c^2) =$	$\dfrac{^-125rs^5}{^-25s^3} =$
7.	$\dfrac{a}{4} + \dfrac{3a}{4} - \dfrac{1}{2} =$	$\dfrac{^-15a^4b^{10}c^6}{^-3ab^2c^3} =$	$\dfrac{3a}{4} \div \dfrac{9a^4}{16} =$
8.	$\dfrac{4ab^2}{3} \div \dfrac{12a^2b^2}{a} =$	$\dfrac{10x^3}{(a + b)} \cdot \dfrac{6(a + b)}{20x^2} =$	$(4a + 2b)(3a - b + b^2) =$
9.	$\dfrac{^-9a^3}{x^4} \cdot \dfrac{3x^4}{a} =$	$\dfrac{^-24x^2y - 20y^4z^6 + 10y}{^-2y} =$	$5x - 6\overline{)5x^2 + 9x - 18} =$

Solve.

10. The sum of three consecutive numbers is 279. Find the numbers.

11. Find the circumference of a circle if the diameter is 24 feet. ($C = \pi d$)

Answer _____

Answer _____

UNIT 5 Functions and Graphs

Functions and Relations

A pair of numbers such as (x, y) is called an **ordered pair.** In an ordered pair, the x-value is always given first. A **relation** is a set of ordered pairs. The x-values in a relation make up the **domain,** and the y-values make up the **range.** A **function** is a relation in which each x-value has only one y-value.

EXAMPLE 1

Identify the domain and range of the relation $\{(3, 4), (^-1, 2), (^-2, 4)\}$.

The domain is $\{^-1, ^-2, 3\}$.

The range is $\{2, 4\}$.

EXAMPLE 2

Is this relation a function?
$\{(7, 8), (^-1, 5), (2, 6), (^-1, 3)\}$

No, because the x-value $^-1$ has more than one y-value.

PRACTICE

Identify the domain and range for each relation.

a

1. $\{(0, ^-3), (2, 5), (^-4, 2)\}$

Domain: $\{0, 2, ^-4\}$

Range: $\{^-3, 5, 2\}$

b

$\{(^-9, 1), (3, 1), (0, 3)\}$

Domain: _____

Range: _____

2. $\{(9, ^-5), (^-1, ^-2), (^-3, ^-5), (1, ^-2)\}$

Domain: _____

Range: _____

$\{(4, ^-1), (^-8, ^-1), (^-4, ^-1), (8, ^-1)\}$

Domain: _____

Range: _____

3. $\{(6, 2), (0, ^-4), (1, ^-3), (4, 0)\}$

Domain: _____

Range: _____

$\{(1, 3), (^-1, 1), (^-4, ^-2), (3, 5)\}$

Domain: _____

Range: _____

Determine whether each of the following relations is a function.

a

4. $\{(0, ^-3), (2, 5), (^-4, 2)\}$ ___yes___

5. $\{(1, ^-6), (3, 4), (^-1, ^-6), (6, 7)\}$ _____

b

$\{(0, ^-8), (0, ^-2), (^-5, 1)\}$ _____

$\{(4, ^-1), (5, ^-1), (4, 6), (7, 8)\}$ _____

Graphing Ordered Pairs

Ordered pairs can be graphed on a **coordinate plane.**
In the coordinate plane at the right, the line labeled *x* is
the **horizontal axis,** or *x*-axis. The line labeled *y* is the
vertical axis, or *y*-axis. The point where the axes cross,
or intersect, is the **origin.** The two axes divide the
coordinate plane into four **quadrants.** The quadrants
are numbered counterclockwise 1–4, starting with the
top right quadrant. The position of a point on the graph
is determined by its ordered pair, or **coordinates.**
The *x*-coordinate tells the distance right or left of the
origin. The *y*-coordinate tells the distance up or down.

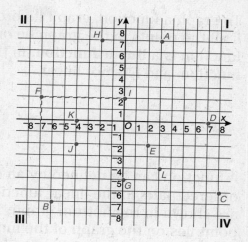

EXAMPLE 1

What are the coordinates of Point F?

To get from the origin to Point F, count
7 units left and 2 units up.

Point F has coordinates ($^-$7, 2).

EXAMPLE 2

What are the coordinates of Point L?

To get from the origin to Point L, count
3 units right and 4 units down.

Point L has coordinates (3, $^-$4).

PRACTICE

Give the coordinates of each point. Refer to the graph above.

	a	b	c	d	e
1.	E (___, ___)	B (___, ___)	H (___, ___)	K (___, ___)	C (___, ___)
2.	D (___, ___)	G (___, ___)	J (___, ___)	A (___, ___)	I (___, ___)

Plot each point on the graph provided.

3. A (2, 6)
B (3, $^-$5)
C ($^-$5, 3)
D ($^-$4, $^-$6)
E (0, 1)

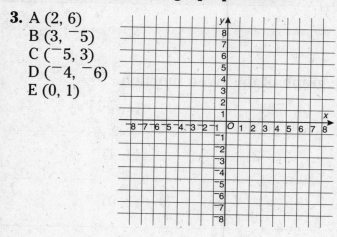

4. F ($^-$5, $^-$8)
G (0, 8)
H ($^-$8, 0)
I (0, $^-$7)
J (0, 0)

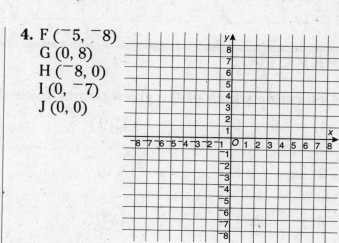

Linear Functions

To graph a function, graph its ordered pairs, or coordinates. If all the points in the graph lie on a straight line, then that function is a **linear function.** In the top graph, f_1 is a linear function, and f_2 is not linear.

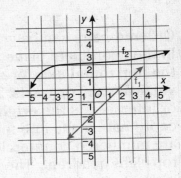

A function can be defined by an equation. Some of the ordered pairs in the linear function defined by $x - y = 4$ are shown in the bottom graph. To determine whether a point lies on the graph of the function, substitute the first coordinate for x and the second coordinate for y. If these substitutions make the equation true, then that point lies on the line. For example, (5, 1) lies on the line, since $5 - 1 = 4$. (1, 5) does not lie on the line, since $1 - 5 \neq 4$.

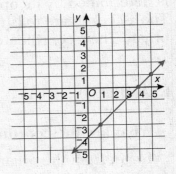

EXAMPLE

Determine which of the given points lies on the graph of the function $2x + 2y = 20$.

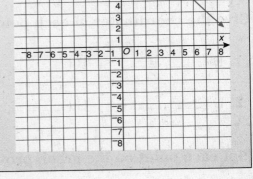

(2, 8)

$2x + 2y = 20$

$2(2) + 2(8) = 20$?

$4 + 16 = 20$?

$20 = 20$

(2, 8) lies on the graph.

(1, 6)

$2x + 2y = 20$

$2(1) + 2(6) = 20$?

$2 + 12 = 20$?

$14 \neq 20$

(1, 6) does not lie on the graph.

PRACTICE

Determine which of the given points lie on the graph of the given function.

1. $x - 5y = 6$	(11, 1)	(4, $^-2$)	(1, $^-1$)
2. $3x - y = 8$	(3, 0)	($^-2$, $^-2$)	(4, 4)
3. $y = {}^-2x + 4$	(1, 2)	(0, $^-4$)	(2, 0)
4. $3x + 2y = 12$	(3, 2)	(2, 3)	(4, 0)

Equations with Two Variables

The equation $x + 2y = 15$ has two variables and many solutions. To find a solution, choose a value to substitute for one of the variables, then solve the equation for the other variable. Each solution may be written as an ordered pair in the form (x, y).

EXAMPLE 1

Solve: $x + 2y = 15$ when $x = 7$

$$7 + 2y = 15$$
$$2y = 15 - 7$$
$$2y = 8$$
$$\frac{2y}{2} = \frac{8}{2}$$
$$y = 4$$

The equation $x + 2y = 15$ is true when x is 7 and y is 4. (7, 4) is a solution.

EXAMPLE 2

Solve: $x + 2y = 15$ when $y = 9$

$$x + 2(9) = 15$$
$$x + 18 = 15$$
$$x = 15 - 18$$
$$x = {}^-3$$

The equation $x + 2y = 15$ is true when x is $^-3$ and y is 9. ($^-3$, 9) is a solution.

PRACTICE

Solve each equation using the given value of x or y.
Write the ordered pair which makes the equation true.

	a	b	c
1.	$x + 2y = 10$ when $x = 0$ $0 + 2y = 10$ $y = 5$ Ordered pair ___(0, 5)___	$x + 2y = 10$ when $y = 3$ Ordered pair _____	$x + 2y = 10$ when $x = 2$ Ordered pair _____
2.	$2x + 2y = 4$ when $y = 0$ Ordered pair _____	$2x + 2y = 4$ when $y = 2$ Ordered pair _____	$2x + 2y = 4$ when $x = 4$ Ordered pair _____
3.	$x + y = {}^-1$ when $x = 3$ Ordered pair _____	$x + y = {}^-1$ when $x = {}^-1$ Ordered pair _____	$x + y = {}^-1$ when $y = 4$ Ordered pair _____

Graphing Solutions

You can graph solutions to equations with two variables.

EXAMPLE

Graph the solutions to $2x - y = 6$, when $x = 0, 1, 3,$ and 4.

Substitute each value for x into the equation and then solve for y. Write each solution in a table. Plot each coordinate pair solution on the coordinate graph.

Find y when $x = 0$.

$$2(0) - y = 6$$
$$0 - y = 6$$
$$y = {}^-6$$

Find y when $x = 1$.

$$2(1) - y = 6$$
$$2 - y = 6$$
$$y = {}^-4$$

x	y
0	$^-6$
1	$^-4$
3	0
4	2

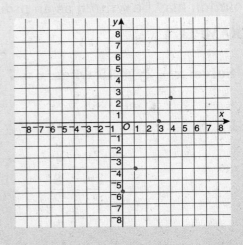

Find y when $x = 3$.

$$2(3) - y = 6$$
$$6 - y = 6$$
$$y = 0$$

Find y when $x = 4$.

$$2(4) - y = 6$$
$$8 - y = 6$$
$$y = 2$$

PRACTICE

Complete each table of solutions to the given equation. Graph each solution.

1. $3x + 4y = 12$

x	y
$^-4$	___
0	___
4	___
8	___

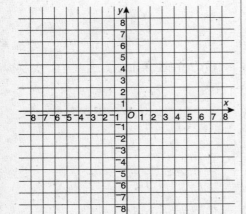

2. $3x - 3y = 15$

x	y
$^-2$	___
0	___
5	___
2	___

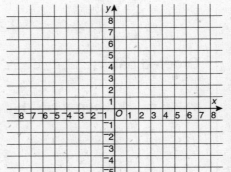

3. $y = 4 - 2x$

x	y
0	___
___	0
1	___
___	$^-2$

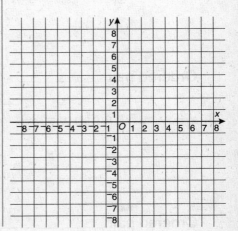

Graphing Linear Equations

For the 2-variable equations that we have studied, the graphs of all the solutions lie on a line. For this reason, equations of this type are called **linear equations**. To graph a linear equation, begin by choosing a value to substitute for either x or y. Then solve for the other variable. Repeat this process to find three or more ordered-pair solutions. Finally, graph the solutions and draw the line through those points.

EXAMPLE

Draw a graph of the solutions to the equation $x - 2y = 6$.

Select values of x and find the corresponding values of y. Try starting with $x = 0$. Make a table like the one below.

x	y
0	$^-3$
2	$^-2$
6	0

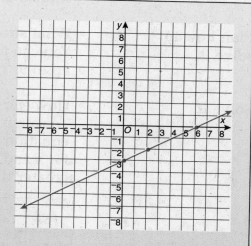

Plot the points and draw a straight line through them to show the graph of the solutions.

PRACTICE

Make a table of 3 solutions. Graph each solution. Draw a straight line through the points.

1. $4x - y = 4$

x	y

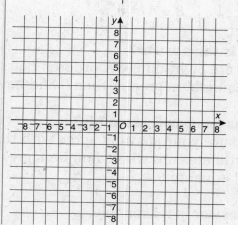

2. $2x + 3y = 6$

x	y

3. $x + y = {}^-8$

x	y

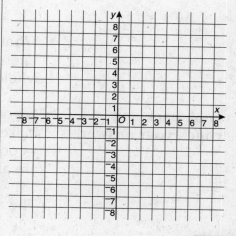

Problem-Solving Strategy: Make a List

How many different ordered pairs have whole number coordinates greater than 0 and have a sum of 9?

Understand the problem.

- **What do you want to know?**
  the number of ordered pairs whose coordinates are whole numbers greater than 0 and have a sum of 9

- **What information is given?**
  whole numbers greater than 0; sum is 9

Plan how to solve it.

- **What strategy can you use?**
  You can make a list of whole number x- and y-coordinates that add up to 9. Then count the ordered pairs.

Solve it.

- **How can you use this strategy to solve the problem?**
  To satisfy the given information, the coordinates must fit the equation $x + y = 9$. Starting with $x = 1$, choose increasing values for x and then solve for y. Remember, both x and y must be greater than 0. Count the number of ordered pairs.

x	y	$x + y = 9$
1	8	$1 + 8 = 9$
2	7	$2 + 7 = 9$
3	6	$3 + 6 = 9$
4	5	$4 + 5 = 9$
5	4	$5 + 4 = 9$
6	3	$6 + 3 = 9$
7	2	$7 + 2 = 9$
8	1	$8 + 1 = 9$

- **What is the answer?**
  There are eight different ordered pairs whose coordinates are whole numbers greater than 0 and have a sum of 9.

Look back and check your answer.

- **Is your answer reasonable?**
  Make sure your answers agree with the conditions. All the x- and y-coordinates are whole numbers greater than zero, and their sums are all equal to 9.

  The answer is reasonable.

Make a list. Solve.

1. Juanita is thinking of two positive whole numbers. The sum of the whole numbers is 15. How many possible whole number combinations are there?

Answer _____

2. Dwight offers one-hour piano lessons and one-hour guitar lessons. He works 10 hours a week in all. How many different ways can he divide his time giving lessons in both instruments?

Answer _____

3. In one linear function, when you subtract each y-coordinate from the x-coordinate, the difference is 3. If the x-coordinate is not greater than 10 and the y-coordinate is a positive whole number, how many ordered pairs are there?

Answer _____

4. In one linear function, the y-coordinate of an ordered pair is twice the x-coordinate. The coordinates are both positive integers. The sum of the x- and y-coordinates is less than 14. How many ordered pairs are there?

Answer _____

5. One natural number is 3 times another natural number. The sum of the numbers is less than 25. How many possible number combinations are there?

Answer _____

6. The product of two integers is ⁻8. How many possible combinations are there?

Answer _____

7. The sum of 5 and a negative integer is greater than ⁻4 and less than 0. How many possible negative integers satisfy the information?

Answer _____

8. The difference between two natural numbers is greater than 6 and less than 11. The greater of the two numbers is 14. How many possible values for the unknown number are there?

Answer _____

Slope

The **slope** of a line tells how steep the line is. The slope is the **ratio** of the vertical change, or **rise,** to the horizontal change, or **run,** from one point to another point on a line.

$$\text{slope} = \frac{\text{change in } y \text{ (rise)}}{\text{change in } x \text{ (run)}}$$

The vertical change, or rise, of this line is 2. The horizontal change, or run, of this line is 5. This line has a slope of $\frac{2}{5}$.

The slope of a line can be positive or negative.

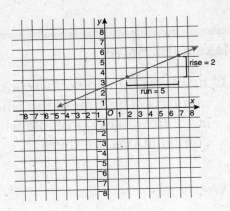

EXAMPLE 1

When a line slants upward from left to right, it has a positive slope.

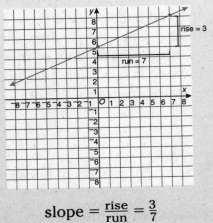

$$\text{slope} = \frac{\text{rise}}{\text{run}} = \frac{3}{7}$$

EXAMPLE 2

When a line slants downward from left to right, it has a negative slope.

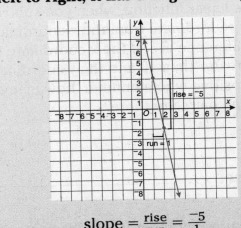

$$\text{slope} = \frac{\text{rise}}{\text{run}} = \frac{-5}{1}$$

PRACTICE

Identify the slope of each line. Write whether the slope is positive or negative.

1.
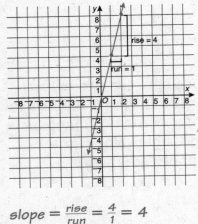

$slope = \frac{rise}{run} = \frac{4}{1} = 4$

The slope is positive.

2.
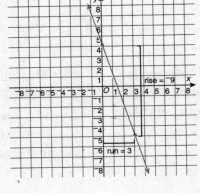

3.
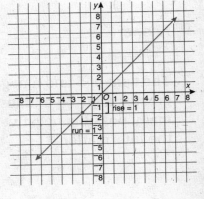

The Slope Formula

Slope is the ratio of rise to run from one point to another point on a line. If you know two points on a line, you can find the slope of the line by using a formula.

Slope Formula

If (x_1, y_1) and (x_2, y_2) are any two points on a line, then the slope of the line is given by:

$$\text{slope} = \frac{\text{rise}}{\text{run}} = \frac{\text{change in } y}{\text{change in } x} = \frac{(y_2 - y_1)}{(x_2 - x_1)}$$

EXAMPLE

Find the slope of the line.

Write the formula.

Substitute the coordinates.

Simplify.

The slope of this line is $\frac{4}{5}$.

$$\text{slope} = \frac{(y_2 - y_1)}{(x_2 - x_1)}$$

$$\text{slope} = \frac{(9 - 5)}{(6 - 1)}$$

$$\text{slope} = \frac{4}{5}$$

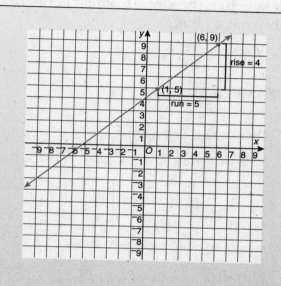

PRACTICE

Find the slope of each line that passes through the given points.

a	b	c
1. $(3, ^-2), (1, 4)$ $\frac{(4 - (^-2))}{(1 - 3)} = \frac{6}{^-2} = {^-3}$	$(^-2, 3), (1, 8)$	$(^-3, ^-2), (5, ^-1)$
2. $(4, 1), (7, 2)$	$(1, ^-5), (6, 0)$	$(^-4, 2), (6, 8)$
3. $(3, ^-1), (6, ^-1)$	$(5, ^-2), (6, 3)$	$(^-2, 1), (5, 1)$
4. $(^-7, 0), (^-1, 5)$	$(^-4, ^-1), (6, 3)$	$(1, ^-2), (4, 4)$

The Slope-Intercept Form

The **slope-intercept form** of the equation of a line is $y = mx + b$, where m is the slope and b is the **y-intercept**. The y-intercept of a graph is the point where the line crosses the y-axis. The ordered pair for the y-intercept is $(0, y)$.

To graph a linear equation using the slope-intercept form, first make sure the equation is in the slope-intercept form. Determine the slope and the y-intercept. Plot the y-intercept as $(0, y)$ and use the slope to plot another point. Then draw a line connecting the two points.

Remember, the slope formula is the ratio of the vertical change to the horizontal change.

$$\text{slope} = \frac{\text{rise}}{\text{run}} = \frac{y_2 - y_1}{x_2 - x_1}$$

EXAMPLE 1

Graph the equation

$y = \frac{1}{2}x + 3.$

$y = mx + b$

y-intercept:
$b = 3$

slope: $m = \frac{1}{2}$

Plot the y-intercept as $(0, 3)$. Since the slope is $\frac{1}{2}$, move right 2 and up 1 and mark the point. Draw the line connecting the two points.

EXAMPLE 2

Graph the equation

$1 = 3x + y.$

First, put the equation in slope-intercept form.

$y = {}^-3x + 1$

y-intercept:
$b = 1$

slope: $m = {}^-3$

Plot the y-intercept as $(0, 1)$. Since the slope is $^-3$ or $\frac{-3}{1}$, move right 1 and down 3 and mark the point. Draw the line connecting the two points.

PRACTICE

Graph each equation using the slope-intercept form.

1. $y = \frac{2}{3}x - 2$

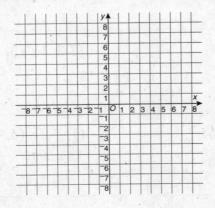

2. $y + \frac{1}{3}x = 4$

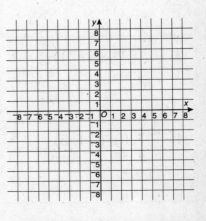

Finding Intercepts

The y-intercept of a line is the point $(0, y)$, where the line crosses the y-axis. To find the y-intercept, substitute 0 for x in the linear equation and solve for y. Likewise, the **x-intercept** is the point $(x, 0)$, where the line crosses the x-axis. To find the x-intercept, substitute 0 for y and solve for x.

EXAMPLE 1

Find the y-intercept of $y = 4x - 7$.

Let $x = 0$.

$y = 4(0) - 7$

$y = {}^-7$

The y-intercept is ${}^-7$.

The ordered pair is $(0, {}^-7)$.

EXAMPLE 2

Find the x-intercept of $y = 3x + 6$.

Let $y = 0$.

$0 = 3x + 6$

${}^-6 = 3x$

${}^-2 = x$

The x-intercept is ${}^-2$.

The ordered pair is $({}^-2, 0)$.

EXAMPLE 3

At what points does the line $y = 2x - 8$ cross the x- and y-axes?

Let $x = 0$.   Let $y = 0$.

$y = 2(0) - 8$ $0 = 2x - 8$

$y = {}^-8$ $8 = 2x$

           $4 = x$

The y-intercept is -8. The x-intercept is 4.

The graph crosses the x-axis at $(4, 0)$ and the y-axis at $(0, {}^-8)$.

PRACTICE

Find the x- and y-intercepts.

a

1. $y = x + 1$

$y = 0 + 1$ $0 = x + 1$
$y = 1$ $x = {}^-1$

The y-intercept is 1. (0, 1)
The x-intercept is ${}^-1$. (${}^-1$, 0)

b

$y = 2x - 4$

c

$y = {}^-2x + 6$

At what points does each line cross the x- and y-axes?

a

2. $y = x - 3$

$y = 0 - 3$ $0 = x - 3$
$y = {}^-3$ $x = 3$

The graph crosses the x-axis at (3, 0) and the y-axis at (0, ${}^-3$).

b

$y = 4x - 3$

c

$y = -x + 5$

Problem-Solving Strategy: Identify Extra Information

The graph of the function $y - 2x = 5$ has no points in the fourth quadrant. Find the slope of the line $y - 2x = 5$.

Understand the problem.

- **What do you want to know?**
  the slope of the line given by $y - 2x = 5$

- **What information is given?**
  $y - 2x = 5$; no points in fourth quadrant

Plan how to solve it.

- **What strategy can you use?**
  You can identify extra information that is not needed to solve the problem.

Solve it.

- **How can you use this strategy to solve the problem?**
  Reread the problem. Cross out any unnecessary facts. Then you can focus on the needed facts to solve the problem.

> ~~The graph of the function $y - 2x = 5$ has no points in the fourth quadrant.~~ Find the slope of the line $y - 2x = 5$.

Write the equation in slope-intercept form. Then determine the slope.

$y - 2x = 5$

$y = 5 + 2x$

$y = 2x + 5$ slope-intercept form

- **What is the answer?**
  The slope is 2, or $\frac{2}{1}$.

Look back and check your answer.

- **Is your answer reasonable?**
  You can check your answer by finding two points and using the formula for slope.

  Let $x = 1$.   Let $x = 2$. $(1, 7)$ and $(2, 9)$

  $y - 2x = 5$ $y - 2x = 5$

  $y - 2(1) = 5$ $y - 2(2) = 5$ slope $= \frac{9 - 7}{2 - 1}$

  $y - 2 = 5$ $y - 4 = 5$

  $y = 7$ $y = 9$ $= \frac{2}{1}$, or 2

  The answer is reasonable.

In each problem, cross out the extra information. Then solve the problem.

1. The x-intercept of the function $2x + 20 = 4y$ is $^-10$. What is the slope of the line given by $2x + 20 = 4y$?

Answer _____

2. Find the slope of the line given by $5y - 15x = 3$. The x-intercept is $\frac{-1}{5}$, and the y-intercept is $\frac{3}{5}$.

Answer _____

3. The following points lie on the line of a function: $(1, 4)$ and $(^-2, 1)$. The y-intercept of the same function is closer to $(1, 4)$ than $(^-2, 1)$. What is the slope of the function?

Answer _____

4. The points where the line of a function crosses the x- and y-axes are $(3, 0)$ and $(0, 3)$. The coordinates of the intercepts are in reverse order. What is the slope of the function?

Answer _____

5. The line given by $3x - 3y = 12$ does not have any points in the second quadrant. What is the slope of the line given by $3x - 3y = 12$?

Answer _____

6. Find the slope of the line given by $10 - 2y = 3x$. The y-intercept of the line is 5, and the point $(2, 2)$ lies on the line of the function.

Answer _____

Unit 5 Functions and Graphs

Identify the domain and the range for each relation. Then tell whether the relation is a function.

a

1. $\{(^-6, 4), (0, 6), (2, 0)\}$

Domain: _____

Range: _____

Function? _____

b

$\{(4, ^-1), (^-1, 3), (^-4, 1), (^-4, 5)\}$

Domain: _____

Range: _____

Function? _____

Solve each equation using the given value of *x* or *y*. Write the ordered pair which makes the equation true.

a

2. $2x + y = 4$ when $x = 3$

Ordered pair _____

b

$5x - 2y = 2$ when $x = 2$

Ordered pair _____

c

$x + y = ^-2$ when $y = 3$

Ordered pair _____

Make a table of 3 solutions. Graph each solution. Draw a straight line through the points.

a

3. $2x + y = 8$

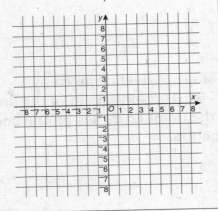

b

$x + 3y = 9$

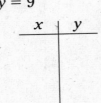

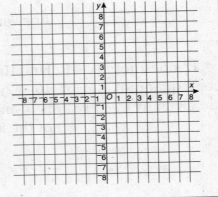

c

$2x - 2y = 16$

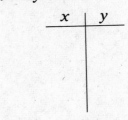

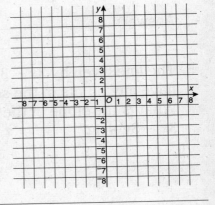

Find the slope of the line that passes through the given points.

a

4. $(^-3, 2), (1, 1)$

b

$(1, ^-2), (4, 1)$

c

$(2, 1), (6, ^-3)$

Evaluate each expression.

a	b	c	d
1. $7 - (2 \times 22)$	$2 \cdot 15 \div 3$	$\dfrac{42 - 2(6)}{5}$	$\dfrac{38 + 18}{4 \times 2}$

Simplify.

a	b	c	d
2. $^-6z + {}^-4y + {}^-9z =$	$(^-7a)(^-7z) =$	$^-3(^-13s - 10) =$	$\dfrac{15q}{-3} \cdot \dfrac{2q}{2} =$
3. $1.8 \times 10^{-2} =$	$(w^3 + 3s)(st - 7) =$	$8.2 \times 10^6 =$	$(mn^4s^3p^2)^4 =$

Solve.

a	b	c
4. $\lvert ^-25 \rvert$	$\dfrac{a}{3} = {}^-18$	$3g - 9 = 3(2g + 5)$
5. $^-9x = 90$	$(4x^2 + 6x + 9)(2 - x) =$	$2k + 3m\overline{)6k^2 + km - 12m^2}$

Graph each equation using the slope-intercept form.

a

6. $x - 2y = 4$

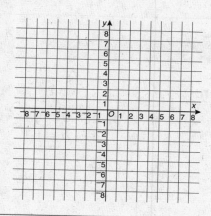

b

$y = {}^-2x + 3$

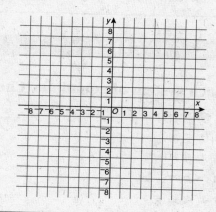

Solve.

7. If three times a number is subtracted from 15, the result will be equal to the number decreased by 21. Find the number.

8. Use the formula $C = (F - 32) \cdot \dfrac{5}{9}$ to find C when F is 104°.

Answer _____

Answer _____

Systems of Equations

Systems of equations are two or more equations that are solved together or at the same time. Sometimes there is a solution that satisfies both equations. Suppose you have two linear equations for lines that intersect. Each equation has 2 variables, x and y. Since both sides of an equation have the same value, you can create a new equation by adding the two equations together or by subtracting one equation from the other. The goal of combining equations in this way is to eliminate one of the variables in order to solve for the other variable. The solution to both equations will be a single ordered pair.

EXAMPLE

Solve: $x + y = 13$
$x - y = 1$

Add.

$$x + y = 13$$
$$\underline{x - y = 1}$$
$$2x + 0 = 14$$
$$x = 7$$

Subtract.

$$x + y = 13$$
$$\underline{x - y = 1}$$
$$0 + 2y = 12$$
$$y = 6$$

Check: Substitute the values of x and y into the original equations.

$x + y = 13$ $x - y = 1$
$7 + 6 = 13$ $7 - 6 = 1$

The solution to the system of equations is (7, 6).

GUIDED PRACTICE

Solve each system of equations. Check by substitution.

1. $a + b = 15$
$a - b = 5$

$$a + b = 15$$
$$\underline{+a - b = 5}$$
$$2a + 0 = 20$$
$$a = 10$$

$$a + b = 15$$
$$\underline{-(a - b = 5)}$$
$$0 + 2b = 10$$
$$b = 5$$

The solution is (10, 5).

Check:
$a + b = 15$ $a - b = 5$
$10 + 5 = 15$ $10 - 5 = 5$

2. $a + b = 13$
$a - b = 5$

3. $a + b = 14$
$a - b = 6$

PRACTICE

Solve each system of equations. Check by substitution.

	a	b	c
1.	$x + y = 17$ $x - y = 7$	$m + n = 27$ $m - n = 17$	$d + e = 51$ $d - e = 9$
2.	$x + y = 37$ $x - y = 7$	$b + c = {}^-55$ $b - c = 17$	$a + b = 23$ $a - b = 9$
3.	$m + n = 35$ $m - n = 15$	$a + b = {}^-44$ $a - b = 10$	$x + y = 25$ $x - y = 15$

MIXED PRACTICE

Find each answer.

	a	b	c	d
1.	$\left| {}^-96 \right| =$	$20 \div (3 + 2) \times 4 =$	${}^-9({}^-2)({}^-2) =$	$g - 7 = 22$
2.	$\frac{x}{3} = {}^-12$	$3m(2m) =$	$(3^2)^3 =$	$\frac{d^5}{d^2} =$

Larger Coefficients

Systems of equations with coefficients greater than 1 are solved
in exactly the same way as before.

EXAMPLE

Solve: $3x + 2y = 26$
$3x - 2y = 10$

Add. $3x + 2y = 26$
$\underline{3x - 2y = 10}$
$6x + 0 = 36$
$x = 6$

Subtract. $3x + 2y = 26$
$\underline{3x - 2y = 10}$
$0 + 4y = 16$
$y = 4$

Check: Substitute the values of x
and y into the original equations.

$3x + 2y = 26$ $3x - 2y = 10$
$3(6) + 2(4) = 26$ $3(6) - 2(4) = 10$
$18 + 8 = 26$ $18 - 8 = 10$

The solution is $(6, 4)$.

PRACTICE

Solve each system of equations. Check by substitution.

a

b

c

1. $2a + 3b = 28$
$2a - 3b = 4$

$3x + 2y = 14$
$3x - 2y = 10$

$5a + 4b = 23$
$5a - 4b = 7$

2. $8y + 6z = 40$
$8y - 6z = {}^-8$

$3r + 7s = 57$
$3r - 7s = {}^-27$

$9x + 5y = 67$
$9x - 5y = {}^-13$

Unit 6 Graphs and Systems of Equations

Changing the Coefficients

Recall that multiplying both sides of an equation by the same number does not change its solution. When you are solving a system of equations, you may need to change the form of one or both equations. By multiplying, you can change the coefficients so that the system can be solved. The following example shows this method. Step 1 shows multiplying the second equation by 2 so that both equations will have the variable x with a coefficient of 2. In Step 2, the new equation is subtracted from the first equation. This eliminates the terms with x so the equation can be solved for y. Then, in Step 3, the value of y is substituted into one of the original equations. When you use this method, remember to check the solution in both original equations.

EXAMPLE

Solve: $2x + 3y = 9$
$ x - 2y = 1$

Step 1.
Multiply by 2.

$2(x - 2y) = 2(1)$
$2x - 4y = 2$

Step 2.
Subtract.

$\begin{aligned} 2x + 3y &= 9 \\ 2x - 4y &= 2 \\ \hline 7y &= 7 \\ y &= 1 \end{aligned}$

Step 3.
Substitute.

$x - 2y = 1$
$x - 2(1) = 1$
$ x = 3$

Check: Substitute the values of x and y into the original equations.

$2x + 3y = 9 \qquad x - 2y = 1$
$2(3) + 3(1) = 9 \qquad 3 - 2(1) = 1$
$ 9 = 9 \qquad 1 = 1$

The solution is (3, 1).

GUIDED PRACTICE

Solve each system of equations.

1. $5a + 2b = {}^-16$
   $a + 3b = 15$

2. $5d - 3e = 5$
   $d - e = {}^-1$

3. $x + 4y = {}^-9$
   $2x - 4y = 6$

PRACTICE

Solve each system of equations. Check.

	a	b	c
1.	$x + y = 4$ $2x + 3y = 10$	$x - y = {}^-4$ $2x - 3y = {}^-14$	$x + y = 4$ $3x - 2y = 7$
2.	$2x - y = 0$ $4x + 2y = 16$	$5x + y = 8$ $2x - 3y = {}^-7$	$3x - y = 1$ $4x - 2y = {}^-2$

MIXED PRACTICE

Find each answer.

	a	b	c	d
1.	$15 - 20 \div 4 + 4 =$	${}^-11 - ({}^-7) =$	$8 + 2y = 30$	$\dfrac{27r}{9} =$
2.	$3m^2(2m + 4) =$	$9(28^0) =$	$2^3 =$	$\dfrac{7}{x} = \dfrac{3}{9}$

Unit 6 Graphs and Systems of Equations

Changing Coefficients in Both Equations

Sometimes it is necessary to change coefficients in both equations in order to solve the equations. Do this by multiplying each equation by a factor that will allow one of its variables to have the same coefficient as the corresponding variable in the other equation. Remember, multiplying both sides of an equation by the same number will not change the solution.

EXAMPLE

Solve: $2x + 3y = 9$
$3x + 2y = 11$

Step 1.

Multiply the first equation by 3.

$3(2x + 3y) = 3(9)$
$6x + 9y = 27$

Step 2.

Multiply the second equation by 2.

$2(3x + 2y) = 2(11)$
$6x + 4y = 22$

Step 3.

Subtract the new equations.

$6x + 9y = 27$
$6x + 4y = 22$
─────────
$5y = 5$
$y = 1$

Step 4.

Substitute $y = 1$ in either equation.

$6x + 9(1) = 27$
$6x = 18$
$x = 3$

Check: Substitute the values of x and y into the original equations.

$2(3) + 3(1) = 9$
$6 + 3 = 9$
$9 = 9$

$3(3) + 2(1) = 11$
$9 + 2 = 11$
$11 = 11$

The solution is (3, 1).

PRACTICE

Solve each system of equations. Check.

1. $5a - 2b = 3$
$2a + 5b = 7$

$2(5a - 2b) = 2(3)$
$^-5(2a + 5b) = ^-5(7)$

$10a - 4b = 6$
$^-10a - 25b = ^-35$
─────────
$^-29b = ^-29$
$b = 1$

$10a - 4(1) = 6$
$10a = 10$
$a = 1$
The solution is (1, 1).
Check:
$5(1) - 2(1) = 3$
$5 - 2 = 3$
$2(1) + 5(1) = 7$
$2 + 5 = 7$

2. $2a + 3b = 14$
$3a - 2b = 8$

3. $3x - 2y = 11$
$4x - 3y = 14$

Problem-Solving Strategy: Use Stem-and-Leaf Plots

The final scores of a local basketball team for the 2000–2001 season were 55, 42, 41, 36, 31, 106, 58, 42, 51, 50, 47, 37, 36, 16, 62, 56, 45, 41, 20, 19, 101, 61, 42, 61, 56, 46, 27, 19, 17. What is the mode, or the number that occurred most often?

Understand the problem.

- **What do you want to know?**
  the mode, or the number that occurred most often

- **What information is given?**
  the final scores of a local basketball team

Plan how to solve it.

- **What strategy can you use?**
  You can use a stem-and-leaf plot to organize the data.

Solve it.

- **How can you use this strategy to solve the problem?**
  Set up a plot for the stems and the leaves. The stems are all the digits in the numbers except the last digits. The leaves are all the last digits. Look at the leaves in the stem-and-leaf plot. Choose the digits that occur most often in the same stem.

Stem	Leaves
10	1 6
6	1 1 2
5	0 1 5 6 6 8
4	1 1 2 2 2 5 6 7
3	1 6 6 7
2	0 7
1	6 7 9 9

- **What is the answer?**
  The mode of the final scores is 42.

Look back and check your answer.

- **Is your answer reasonable?**
  To check your answer, list the scores from lowest to highest and count the repeated scores.
  16, 17, 19, 19, 20, 27, 31, 36, 36, 37, 41, 41, **42, 42, 42,** 45, 46, 47, 50, 51, 55, 56, 56, 58, 61, 61, 62, 101, 106

  42 occurs most often.
  The answer is reasonable.

Make a stem-and-leaf plot to solve.

1. Twenty people who were randomly polled on the street gave their ages as follows: 20, 67, 82, 49, 53, 24, 38, 40, 65, 19, 43, 67, 75, 81, 32, 45, 55, 65, 67, and 32. What is the mode?

2. The scores on a math test were 90, 82, 90, 92, 63, 89, 97, 67, 89, 96, 89, and 100. What is the mode?

Answer _____

Answer _____

3. Chan works out three times a week. He records the length of time of each workout in minutes. Here are the lengths of times for last month's workouts: 75, 90, 60, 30, 120, 90, 60, 30, 75, 90, 90, 60, and 30. What is the mode?

4. The students in Mr. Sutton's class took a physical today. The heights of the students in inches are as follows: 45, 50, 55, 60, 40, 45, 61, 66, 49, 51, 45, 45, 61, 66, 49, 51, 60, 55, and 60. What is the mode?

Answer _____

Answer _____

Solving in Terms of One Variable

Sometimes it is helpful to isolate one of the variables in an equation that has two variables. To isolate a variable, change the form of the equation by adding, subtracting, multiplying, or dividing both sides by the same number or expression. When necessary, multiply both sides of an equation by $^-1$ to change the signs.

EXAMPLE 1

Solve: $2x + 3y = 6$ for y in terms of x

$$2x + 3y = 6$$
$$2x + 3y - 2x = 6 - 2x$$
$$3y = 6 - 2x$$
$$\tfrac{1}{3}(3y) = \tfrac{1}{3}(6 - 2x)$$
$$y = 2 - \tfrac{2}{3}x$$

EXAMPLE 2

Solve: $y - x = 2$ for x in terms of y

$$y - x = 2$$
$$y - x - y = 2 - y$$
$$-x = 2 - y$$
$$^-1(-x) = {}^-1(2 - y)$$
$$x = {}^-2 + y$$
$$x = y - 2$$

PRACTICE

Solve each equation for y in terms of x.

	a	*b*	*c*
1.	$12x - 4y = 48$	$6x + 2y = 10$	$3x + 4y = 60$
2.	$-x + 2y = 8$	$x + 3y = 6$	$4x + 2y = {}^-1$

Solve each equation for x in terms of y.

	a	*b*	*c*
3.	$x - 3y = {}^-1$	$^-2x + 4y = 8$	$3x + y = 9$
4.	$3x - 2y = 3$	$2x - 2y = 20$	$7x + 4y = 28$

The Substitution Method

Another way to solve systems of equations is to use the **substitution method.** This method substitutes for one variable in terms of the other variable.

EXAMPLE

Solve: $x + 2y = 7$
$3x + y = 11$

Step 1.

Solve for x in terms of y in either equation.

$x + 2y = 7$
$x + 2y - 2y = 7 - 2y$
$x = 7 - 2y$

Step 2.

Substitute $7 - 2y$ for x in the second equation.

$3x + y = 11$
$3(7 - 2y) + y = 11$
$21 - 6y + y = 11$
$^-5y = ^-10$
$y = 2$

Step 3.

Substitute 2 for y in either equation.

$x + 2(2) = 7$
$x = 3$

Check: $x + 2y = 7$
$3 + 2(2) = 7$

$3x + y = 11$
$3(3) + 2 = 11$

The solution is (3, 2).

Use the substitution method to solve each system of equations.

a

1. $x + 4y = 12$
$2x - y = 6$
$x = 12 - 4y$
$2(12 - 4y) - y = 6$
$24 - 8y - y = 6$
$^-9y = ^-18$
$y = 2$
$x + 4(2) = 12$
$x + 8 = 12$
$x = 4$ (4, 2)

b

$x - y = 1$
$5x + 3y = 45$

c

$3x + 2y = 13$
$x + y = 5$

2. $x + y = 4$
$x + 3y = 10$

$x - y = 2$
$4x + y = 23$

$2x + 3y = 9$
$x - 2y = 1$

PRACTICE

Use the substitution method to solve each system of equations.

	a	*b*	*c*
1.	$x + 2y = 9$ $x - y = 3$	$x + 3y = 10$ $x + y = 6$	$x + 3y = 11$ $x + y = 7$
2.	$x + 5y = 10$ $x - 2y = 3$	$2x + y = 8$ $x + 2y = 7$	$3x - y = 9$ $2x + y = 11$

MIXED PRACTICE

Multiple or divide.

	a	*b*	*c*
1.	$(1.6)(0.2) =$	$0.03\overline{)1.8} =$	$\frac{3a^3}{7} \cdot \frac{21y^2}{a^3} =$
2.	$\frac{18x^2}{3c} \div \frac{2x^2}{9c^2} =$	$3ax(2a + 2ax + 2x) =$	$2m + k\overline{)6m^2 - mk - 2k^2} =$

You have used several methods to solve systems of equations. Study each system of equations and decide which method is best to use. Then solve.

PRACTICE

Choose a method and solve.

a

b

c

1. $2x + 3y = 16$
$3x - y = 2$

$5x - 2y = 6$
$2x + 5y = 14$

$6x + 5y = 6$
$3x + 5y = {}^-12$

2. $x + y = 5$
$x - 3y = 1$

$4x + 3y = 14$
$2x + 3y = 10$

$3x - y = 3$
$2x - 3y = {}^-19$

3. $10x + 7y = 45$
$3x + 7y = 38$

$2a - b = 5$
$7a + b = 49$

$a + b = {}^-8$
$a - 2b = 1$

Solving Problems with Systems of Equations

Some word problems can be solved by using systems of equations.

EXAMPLE

The sum of two numbers is 13. Their difference is 1. What are the numbers?

Let x = one number.

Let y = the other number.

Then, $x + y = 13$ (the sum)

$x - y = 1$ (the difference)

The two numbers are 7 and 6.

Add.
$$x + y = 13$$
$$\underline{x - y = 1}$$
$$2x = 14$$
$$x = 7$$

Substitute.
$$x + y = 13$$
$$7 + y = 13$$
$$y = 6$$

Check:
$$x + y = 13$$
$$7 + 6 = 13$$

$$x - y = 1$$
$$7 - 6 = 1$$

GUIDED PRACTICE

Use a system of equations to solve each problem.

1. Find the numbers whose sum is 15, if twice the first number minus the second number equals 6.

Answer _____

2. The sum of two numbers is 18. Twice the first number plus three times the second number equals 40. Find the numbers.

Answer _____

3. Four times a number increased by three times a second number is 25. Four times the first number decreased by three times the second number is 7. Find the two numbers.

Answer _____

4. The difference of two numbers is $^-1$. If twice the first number is added to three times the second number, the result is 13. What are the numbers?

Answer _____

PRACTICE

Use a system of equations to solve each problem.

1. Three times the first of two numbers decreased by the second number equals 9. Twice the first number increased by the second number equals 11. Find the two numbers.

Answer _____

2. The first of two numbers decreased by five times the second number equals ⁻10. The first number decreased by two times the second number equals ⁻1. Find the numbers.

Answer _____

3. The first of two numbers added to two times the second number equals 9. The first number decreased by the second number is 3. Find the numbers.

Answer _____

4. Find the numbers whose sum is 9, if three times the first number increased by two times the second number equals 22.

Answer _____

5. The difference of two numbers is ⁻3. Twice the first number increased by three times the second number is 29. Find the numbers.

Answer _____

6. Three times a number increased by two times another number equals 28. Two times the first number increased by three times the second number equals 27. Find the two numbers.

Answer _____

7. Twice Martina's age decreased by Mario's age is 6. Three times Martina's age increased by twice Mario's is 23. What are their ages?

Answer _____

8. Three times the length of a field increased by four times the width equals 24 kilometers. Two times the length decreased by three times the width is ⁻1 kilometer. Find the two dimensions.

Answer _____

Systems of Equations with Fractional Coefficients

The methods for solving systems of equations with fractional coefficients are the same as for solving systems of equations with integer coefficients.

EXAMPLE

Solve: $\frac{1}{2}a + b = 5$

$\frac{1}{2}a - b = 1$

Step 1.
Add.

$\frac{1}{2}a + b = 5$

$\frac{1}{2}a - b = 1$

$\overline{1a + 0 = 6}$

$a = 6$

Step 2.
Subtract.

$\frac{1}{2}a + b = 5$

$\frac{1}{2}a - b = 1$

$\overline{0 + 2b = 4}$

$b = 2$

Check: Substitute the values of a and b into the original equation.

$\frac{1}{2}a + b = 5 \qquad\qquad \frac{1}{2}a - b = 1$

$\frac{1}{2}(6) + 2 = 5 \qquad\qquad \frac{1}{2}(6) - 2 = 1$

$3 + 2 = 5 \qquad\qquad\quad 3 - 2 = 1$

The solution is (6, 2).

PRACTICE

Solve each system of equations.

a

1. $\frac{1}{4}m - n = 1$

$\frac{1}{4}m + n = 3$

$\frac{1}{4}m - n = 1 \qquad \frac{1}{4}m - n = 1$

$\frac{1}{4}m + n = 3 \qquad \frac{1}{4}m + n = 3$

$\overline{\frac{2}{4}m - 0 = 4} \qquad \overline{0 - 2n = {}^-2}$

$m = 8 \qquad\qquad n = 1$

The solution is (8, 1).

b

$\frac{1}{2}x + y = 6$

$\frac{1}{2}x - y = 2$

c

$\frac{3}{4}x + y = 6$

$\frac{1}{2}x - 2y = {}^-4$

2. $\frac{3}{5}x + y = 11$

$\frac{2}{5}x - y = {}^-1$

$\frac{2}{3}x + y = 0$

$\frac{2}{3}x - y = 8$

$\frac{3}{4}x + y = 11$

$\frac{3}{4}x - 3y = 3$

System Problems with Fractional Coefficients

Use a system of equations with fractional coefficients to solve each problem.

1. One half of a number added to a second number equals 4. One half of the first number decreased by the second number equals zero. Find the two numbers.

Answer _____

2. One half of a number increased by a second number equals 8. One half of the first number decreased by the second number equals ⁻2. Find the two numbers.

Answer _____

3. Four tenths of a number increased by the second number equals 19. One tenth of the first number decreased by the second number is equal to 1. What are the two numbers?

Answer _____

4. One third of a number increased by a second number equals 7. One third of the first number decreased by the second number is equal to ⁻3. What are the numbers?

Answer _____

5. Two thirds of the first of two numbers added to the second number equal 6. One third of the first number decreased by the second number is equal to zero. Find the numbers.

Answer _____

6. Three fourths of a number increased by a second number equals 6. Three fourths of the first number decreased by three times the second number equals ⁻6. What are the two numbers?

Answer _____

Problem-Solving Strategy: Use a Graph

Mr. Bristow mixes peanuts that sell for $3.00 a pound with pecans that sell for $4.50 a pound. He wants to make 12 pounds of the mixture to sell for $4.00 a pound. How many pounds of peanuts and pecans should Mr. Bristow use?

Understand the problem.

- **What do you want to know?**
  the number of pounds of peanuts and pecans to use

- **What information is given?**
  peanuts: $3.00 a pound; pecans: $4.50 a pound; 12-pound mixture: $4.00 a pound

Plan how to solve it.

- **What strategy can you use?**
  You can use a graph to find the solution to a system of equations.

Solve it.

- **How can you use this strategy to solve the problem?**
  From the information write two linear equations. Then find and graph 3 solutions for each equation. Draw a line for each equation. The point of intersection of the two lines is the solution to the system of equations.

  Let x = pounds of peanuts and y = pounds of pecans.

  Then, $x + y = 12$ pounds of the mixture.

  $$\$3.00(x) + \$4.50(y) = \$4.00(12)$$

  $$3x + 4.5y = 48$$

$x + y = 12 \qquad 3x + 4.5y = 48$

x	y
0	12
2	10
4	8

x	y
10	4
7	6
4	8

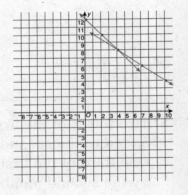

The point of intersection has coordinates (4, 8). So, $x = 4$ and $y = 8$.

- **What is the answer?**
  Mr. Bristow should use 4 pounds of peanuts and 8 pounds of pecans.

Look back and check your answer.

- **Is your answer reasonable?**
  You can check your solution by substituting the x and y values into both equations.

$x + y = 12$	$3x + 4.5y = 48$
$4 + 8 = 12$	$3(4) + 4.5(8) = 48$
$12 = 12$	$12 + 36 = 48$
	$48 = 48$

The answer is reasonable.

Solve by graphing. Write the answer.

1. Twice one number is equal to 1 more than a second number. The sum of the numbers is 5. Find the numbers.

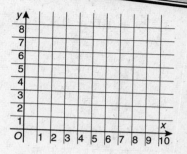

Answer _____

2. The difference between the length and width of a rectangle is 7 cm. The perimeter of the rectangle is 22 cm. Find the length and the width. (Remember, $P = 2l + 2w$.)

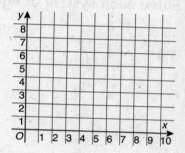

Answer _____

3. The perimeter of a rectangle is 18 inches. The length is twice the width. Find the length and the width.

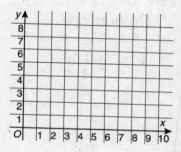

Answer _____

4. The sum of two numbers is 10. Five times the first number plus three times the second number is 36. Find the numbers.

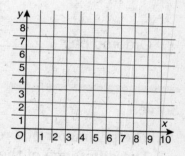

Answer _____

5. Matthew mixes pretzels that sell for $1.50 a pound with cereal that sells for $3.00 a pound. He wants to make 12 pounds of a mixture to sell for $2.00 a pound. How many pounds of each should he use?

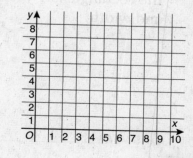

Answer _____

Solve each equation for y in terms of x.

	a	b	c
			$8x = {}^-4y - 32$

1. $2y + 10x = 18$ $\qquad$ $12x - 3y = 24$

Solve each system of equations.

a	b	c

2. $x + y = 12$ $\qquad$ $a + 5b = 14$ $\qquad$ $x + 5y = 13$
   $x - y = 2$ $\qquad\quad$ $a - 5b = 4$ $\qquad\quad$ $2x - 3y = 0$

Ordered pair _____ $\qquad$ Ordered pair _____ $\qquad$ Ordered pair _____

3. $5x + 3y = 45$ $\qquad$ $\dfrac{3a}{8} - b = 2$ $\qquad$ $2x + 3y = 7$

   $x - y = 1$ $\qquad\qquad$ $\dfrac{7a}{8} + b = 18$ $\qquad$ $3x + 2y = 3$

Ordered pair _____ $\qquad$ Ordered pair _____ $\qquad$ Ordered pair _____

Solve.

4. The perimeter of a rectangle is 42 yards. The difference of the length and width of the rectangle is 7 yards. Find the length and width.

5. One half of a number increased by a second number equals 5. One half of the first number decreased by the second number equals 1. Find the two numbers.

Answer _____ $\qquad$ Answer _____

Simplify.

a	*b*	*c*
1. $^-3(12 + 5) =$	$^-12(4) =$	$4(a - 3b) + 9(2a + 4b) =$
2. $\left(\frac{r}{5} - y\right) + \left(\frac{4r}{5} + y\right) =$	$4a^2b - 2a^2b + 10 =$	$\frac{-8x^6}{a^2} \cdot \frac{4a^2}{2x^2} =$
3. $\frac{7}{3} = \frac{x}{9}$	$\frac{-100r^2st^4 + 10rst}{-10rst} =$	$(6x + 3)(2x^2 - 3x - 4) =$

Solve.

a	*b*	*c*
4. $x = 10(3^2)$	$17 - y = 24$	$3x + 2y = 6$ for y in terms of x

Find the slope of the line that passes through the given points.

a	*b*	*c*
5. (1, 4) (3, 3)	(2, 8) (4, 12)	(3, 5) (8, 7)

Solve.

6. Three times a number increased by 9 is equal to twice the number decreased by 4. Find the number.

7. Using the formula $V = \pi r^2 h$, find the volume of a cylinder when the radius is 12 cm and the height is 15 cm. Use 3.14 for π.

Answer _____

Answer _____

UNIT 7 Inequalities, Roots, and Proportions

Inequalities

Sometimes the answer to a problem is a set of numbers. Such a set can be represented by using an **inequality**.

For example, the answer to the inequality $x \geq 3$ is the set of all numbers greater than or equal to 3. Here are the symbols used with inequalities:

> is greater than   < is less than

$\geq$ is greater than or equal to $\leq$ is less than or equal to

On a number line, greater numbers are to the right. If x is greater than y, then $x - y$ is positive. If x is less than y, then $x - y$ is negative.

EXAMPLE 1

Write >, <, or =.

$^-4 \underline{\;<\;} ^-1$

$1.001 \underline{\;>\;} 0.01$

$16 - 7 \underline{\;=\;} 19 - 10$

EXAMPLE 2

Write >, <, or =.

$\left(\frac{1}{2} - \frac{3}{4}\right) \underline{\quad} \left(\frac{3}{4} - \frac{1}{2}\right)$

Find the difference by converting to a common denominator.

$\frac{1}{2} = \frac{2}{4}$

$\left(\frac{2}{4} - \frac{3}{4}\right) \underline{\quad} \left(\frac{3}{4} - \frac{2}{4}\right)$

$-\frac{1}{4} \underline{\;<\;} \frac{1}{4}$

EXAMPLE 3

True or False?

$^-0.14 \leq ^-0.12?$

$^-0.14 - (^-0.12) = ^-0.02$

Since the result is negative, $^-0.14$ is less than $^-0.12$.

True.

PRACTICE

Use >, <, or = to complete each statement.

	a	b	c
1.	$^-10 \underline{\quad} ^-2$	$^-3 \underline{\quad} 4$	$0.56 \underline{\quad} 0.43$
2.	$0.004 \underline{\quad} 0.078$	$\frac{15}{18} \underline{\quad} \frac{61}{72}$	$\frac{10}{48} \underline{\quad} \frac{5}{24}$
3.	$\left(\frac{5}{8} - \frac{1}{6}\right) \underline{\quad} \left(\frac{3}{4} - \frac{1}{8}\right)$	$\left(\frac{2}{3} + \frac{1}{4}\right) \underline{\quad} \left(\frac{5}{12} + \frac{2}{4}\right)$	$\left(\frac{3}{10} - \frac{1}{5}\right) \underline{\quad} \left(\frac{4}{10} - \frac{1}{2}\right)$

Tell whether each statement is true or false.

	a	b	c
4.	$^-14 > ^-10$	$0.08 < ^-0.1$	$^-11 \geq ^-11$
5.	$15 \geq ^-13$	$\frac{3}{4} > \frac{2}{3}$	$\frac{5}{6} \leq \frac{15}{18}$

Solving Inequalities with Addition and Subtraction

Inequalities are solved in much the same way equations are. You can add or subtract the same amount from both sides of an inequality without changing its solution. If you exchange the left and right sides of an inequality, you must reverse the direction. For example, $7 < 9$ and $9 > 7$. Study the following examples.

EXAMPLE 1

Solve: $x - 2 > 12$

$$x - 2 > 12$$
$$x - 2 + 2 > 12 + 2$$
$$x > 14$$

EXAMPLE 2

Solve: $3 \leq x + 15$

$$3 \leq x + 15$$
$$3 - 15 \leq x + 15 - 15$$
$$^-12 \leq x$$
$$\text{or}$$
$$x \geq ^-12$$

EXAMPLE 3

Solve: $-x + 16 \leq ^-2x - 8$

$$-x + 16 < ^-2x - 8$$
$$-x + 16 - 16 \leq ^-2x - 8 - 16$$
$$-x \leq ^-2x - 24$$
$$-x + 2x \leq ^-2x + 2x - 24$$
$$x \leq ^-24$$

PRACTICE

Solve.

	a	b	c
1.	$x - 7 > 15$	$x - 4 \leq 11$	$14 > x - 6$
2.	$x + 9 \leq 10$	$20 < x + 5$	$8 \leq x + 12$
3.	$x - 10 \geq -4$	$^-17 < x + 7$	$x - 3 > -11$
4.	$11 + x < 7$	$^-15 + x < 16$	$^-12 \geq 4 + x$
5.	$2x + 3 < x - 1$	$4x + 2 > 4 + 3x$	$6x - 1 \leq 5x - 5$
6.	$7 + 2x \leq x + 8$	$15 - 4x > 9 - 5x$	$22 + 9x \leq -12 + 8x$

Solving Inequalities with Multiplication and Division

As with equations, you can multiply or divide both sides of an inequality by the same number without changing the solution. However, if you multiply or divide by a negative number, you must change the direction of the inequality sign.

EXAMPLE 1

Solve: $\frac{x}{2} \geq 3$

Multiply both sides by 2.

$$2\left(\frac{x}{2}\right) \geq 2(3)$$

$$x \geq 6$$

EXAMPLE 2

Solve: $^-2x < 6$

Divide both sides by $^-2$ and reverse the sign.

$$\frac{^-2x}{^-2} > \frac{6}{^-2}$$

$$x > {^-3}$$

EXAMPLE 3

Solve: $^-2x + 3 \leq 5x + 17$

$$^-2x + 3 - 3 \leq 5x + 17 - 3$$

$$^-2x \leq 5x + 14$$

$$^-2x - 5x \leq 5x - 5x + 14$$

$$^-7x \leq 14$$

$$\frac{^-7x}{^-7} \geq \frac{14}{^-7}$$

$$x \geq {^-2}$$

PRACTICE

Solve.

	a	b	c
1.	$\frac{x}{5} > 2$	$\frac{x}{2} \leq {^-6}$	$3 \leq \frac{x}{^-4}$
2.	$4x < 8$	$^-10 \geq 2x$	$^-6x \leq {^-18}$
3.	$3x + 2 > 8$	$8x - 13 > 19$	$^-2 - 3x > 7$
4.	$9x - 10 > 7x - 4$	$2 - 5x < 11 + 4x$	$3x - 2 \geq x + 18$
5.	$^-7x + 13 > {^-2x} + 9$	$3x - \frac{2}{5} \leq 5x + \frac{3}{5}$	$4 + 2x < 6 + 6x$

Solving Problems with Inequalities

Some problems can be solved using inequalities.

EXAMPLE

Margaret is 2 years older than Sam, and their combined age is, at most, 20. What is the oldest Sam could be? What is the oldest Margaret could be?

Let x = Sam's age.

$x + 2$ = Margaret's age

Their combined age is, at most, 20.

$$x + (x + 2) \leq 20$$

$$2x + 2 \leq 20$$

$$2x \leq 18$$

$$x \leq 9$$

The oldest Sam could be is 9 years old.

The oldest Margaret could be is $x + 2$ or $9 + 2 = 11$ years old.

PRACTICE

Solve using inequalities.

1. A jockey must weigh in at less than 130 pounds. This includes the jockey's weight plus the weight of the blanket, saddle, and bridle. If the combined weight of the equipment is $\frac{1}{8}$ of the jockey's weight, what is the maximum the jockey can weigh?

Answer _____

2. The Rodriguez family has a fixed income of $4,000 a month. Their fixed expenses are $1,800 a month. They save at least one fourth of the remaining income each month. What is the minimum amount saved by the Rodriguez family in a year?

Answer _____

3. The sum of three consecutive integers is less than 186. What is the maximum value for the first integer?

Answer _____

4. The sum of four consecutive odd integers is greater than 48. What is the minimum value for the first integer?

Answer _____

Problem-Solving Strategy: Make a Table

The sum of the first three consecutive odd integers (1, 3, 5) is 9. What is the sum of the first five consecutive odd integers? the first 50 consecutive odd integers? the first 100?

Understand the problem.

- **What do you want to know?**
  the sums of the first five, 50, and 100 consecutive odd integers

- **What information is given?**
  the sum of the first three consecutive odd integers

Plan how to solve it.

- **What strategy can you use?**
  You can make a table to organize the information and calculations.

Solve it.

- **How can you use this strategy to solve the problem?**
  Find the sum of the first five consecutive odd integers.
  $1 + 3 + 5 + 7 + 9 = 25$

  Record the answer in the table. Notice that $3^2 = 9$ and $5^2 = 25$. Use this observation to complete the table.

Number of consecutive odd integers	3	5	50	100
Sum	9	25	2,500	10,000

- **What is the answer?**
  The sums of the first five, 50, and 100 consecutive odd integers are 25; 2,500; and 10,000.

Look back and check your answer.

- **Is your answer reasonable?**
  You can check your answers by finding the sums of the first six consecutive odd integers and the first ten consecutive odd integers. The sum of the first six consecutive odd integers is: $1 + 3 + 5 + 7 + 9 + 11 = 36$, or 6^2. The sum of the first ten consecutive odd integers is: $1 + 3 + 5 + 7 + 9 + 11 + 13 + 15 + 17 + 19 = 100$, or 10^2. Use a calculator to check the sum of the first 50 odd integers ($50^2 = 2,500$) and the sum of the first 100 odd integers ($100^2 = 10,000$).

  The answer is reasonable.

Make a table. Solve.

1. In January, canned apricots cost 68¢. Canned peaches cost 78¢. During the year, the price of apricots increased 4¢ per month. The price of peaches increased 2¢ per month. Find the month when both items sold for the same price.

Answer _____

2. Domingo had 250 baseball cards, and Jennifer had 82 baseball cards. At the first meeting of the Card Club and at every meeting thereafter, Domingo sold 12 cards to Jennifer. After which meeting did the two have the same number of cards?

Answer _____

3. Stefan took a job at $23,000 the first year with $1,090-a-year raises thereafter. Brenda took a job at $24,020 a year with $950-a-year increases thereafter. During which year will Stefan start earning more than Brenda?

Answer _____

4. In November, the Sport Shop sold 74 pairs of snow skis and 3 pairs of water skis. Each month the shop sold 11 more pairs of water skis and 6 fewer pairs of snow skis than the previous month. When was the first month the shop sold more water skis than snow skis?

Answer _____

5. Briana tore a sheet of paper in half. Then she tore each of the remaining pieces in half. She continued this process 6 more times. How many pieces of paper did she have at the end?

Answer _____

6. Mr. Hassan's house number is composed of 3 consecutive digits. It is a multiple of his age, which is 63. What is Mr. Hassan's house number?

Answer _____

Square Roots

The sign $\sqrt{}$ tells you to find the **square root** of the number under the sign. The expression $\sqrt{9}$ is called a **radical**. The 9 is called a **radicand**, and the $\sqrt{}$ is called a **radical sign.**

The square root of a number is the factor which when multiplied by itself gives the number. The factor can be positive or negative ($\pm$). Here are three examples:

$\sqrt{4} = \pm 2$	$\sqrt{9} = \pm 3$	$\sqrt{81} = \pm 9$

To take the square root of a monomial, first take the square root of the coefficient. Next, take the square root of each variable expression. The following examples use the positive square root of the coefficient.

$\sqrt{4x^2} = 2x$	$\sqrt{9x^4} = 3x^2$	$\sqrt{x^4y^2} = x^2y$
Check:	**Check:**	**Check:**
$2x \cdot 2x = 4x^2$	$3x^2 \cdot 3x^2 = 9x^4$	$x^2y \cdot x^2y = x^4y^2$

Use the chart to help you find larger square roots. To find $\sqrt{400}$, find 400 in the square column. The positive square root of 400 is in the first column. So, $\sqrt{400}$ is 20 since $20 \times 20 = 400$.

Positive Square Root	Square (or Radicand)
1	1
2	4
3	9
4	16
5	25
6	36
7	49
8	64
9	81
10	100
11	121
12	144
13	169
14	196
15	225
16	256
17	289
18	324
19	361
20	400

PRACTICE

Find each positive square root. Use the chart above if needed.

	a	b	c	d	e
1.	$\sqrt{121} = 11$	$\sqrt{49} =$	$\sqrt{144} =$	$\sqrt{25} =$	$\sqrt{169} =$
2.	$\sqrt{225} =$	$\sqrt{81} =$	$\sqrt{16} =$	$\sqrt{324} =$	$\sqrt{196} =$
3.	$\sqrt{a^2} =$	$\sqrt{a^4} =$	$\sqrt{x^6} =$	$\sqrt{y^8} =$	$\sqrt{b^4} =$
4.	$\sqrt{a^2b^2} =$	$\sqrt{x^4y^4} =$	$\sqrt{x^2y^4} =$	$\sqrt{a^2b^2c^2} =$	$\sqrt{x^4b^2c^4} =$
5.	$\sqrt{9a^2} =$	$\sqrt{16b^4} =$	$\sqrt{36a^2b^2} =$	$\sqrt{64x^2y^4} =$	$\sqrt{81a^2b^4c^8} =$
6.	$\sqrt{169x^{10}y^4} =$	$\sqrt{289x^{12}} =$	$\sqrt{324b^4c^6} =$	$\sqrt{400a^2b^6} =$	$\sqrt{100x^4y^2z^6} =$

Unit 7 Inequalities, Roots, and Proportions

Equations with Squares

Some equations have variables that are squared. To solve such an equation, first isolate the squared variable and then find the square root of both sides of the equation. An equation such as $x^2 = 9$ has two solutions. The solutions to $x^2 = 9$ are 3 and $^-3$ because $(^-3)(^-3) = 9$ and $(3)(3) = 9$. These solutions can be written as ± 3. The symbol $\pm$ means positive or negative.

EXAMPLE

Solve: $2a^2 - 7 = 43$

$2a^2 - 7 + 7 = 43 + 7$

$2a^2 = 50$

$\dfrac{2a^2}{2} = \dfrac{50}{2}$

$a^2 = 25$

$\sqrt{a^2} = \sqrt{25}$

$a = \pm 5$

Check both solutions:

$2(5)^2 - 7 = 43$

$2(5)(5) - 7 = 43$

$50 - 7 = 43$

$43 = 43$

and $2(^-5)^2 - 7 = 43$

$2(^-5)(^-5) - 7 = 43$

$50 - 7 = 43$

$43 = 43$

PRACTICE

Solve.

	a	b	c	d
1.	$2x^2 = 200$	$7x^2 = 175$	$3x^2 = 147$	$2x^2 = 32$
2.	$x^2 + 15 = 40$	$x^2 - 12 = 24$	$x^2 + 17 = 81$	$x^2 - 15 = 85$
3.	$3a^2 + 7 = 34$	$5a^2 - 9 = 116$	$2a^2 - 6 = 44$	$4a^2 + 3 = 19$

Combine like terms and solve.

	a	b	c
4.	$3x^2 - 7 = x^2 + 1$	$5x^2 + 3 = 2x^2 + 30$	$7x^2 - 15 = 5x^2 + 17$

Using Equations with Squares

Recall that the area of a rectangle is equal to the length times the width, or $A = lw$. The area is always in square units. If you know the area and something about the length or width, you can use the formula to find both dimensions.

EXAMPLE

The area of a rectangle is 200 square feet. The length is twice the width. Find the dimensions.

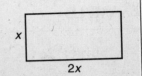

Let x = width.   Since $A = 200$ square ft,   **Check:** $(2x)x = 200$

Let $2x$ = length. $2x^2 = 200$ $(20)10 = 200$

Then $A = (2x)x$ $x^2 = 100$ $200 = 200$

$A = 2x^2$ $x = \pm 10$

The width (x) is 10 ft, and the length ($2x$) is 20 ft. The negative value of $x = -10$ is not a solution because dimensions cannot be negative.

PRACTICE

Solve.

1. Find the dimensions of a rectangle with an area of 288 square cm. The length is twice the width.

Answer _____

2. Find the dimensions of a rectangle with an area of 128 square in. and the length 8 times the width.

Answer _____

3. The area of a rectangle is 100 square m. The length is 4 times the width. What are the dimensions of the rectangle?

Answer _____

4. The length of a rectangle is six times the width, and the area is 2,166 square in. Find the dimensions of the rectangle.

Answer _____

5. Find the dimensions of a rectangle with an area of 125 square cm if the width is one fifth of the length.

Answer _____

6. If the width of a rectangle is one third the length and the area is 48 square ft, find the dimensions of the rectangle.

Answer _____

The sign $\sqrt[3]{}$ tells you to find the **cube root** of the number under the sign. The cube root of a number is used as a factor three times to give the number. Study the following examples.

$\sqrt[3]{8} = 2$

The cube root of 8 is 2, because $2 \cdot 2 \cdot 2 = 8$.

$\sqrt[3]{125} = 5$

The cube root of 125 is 5, because $5 \cdot 5 \cdot 5 = 125$.

$\sqrt[3]{1,000} = 10$

The cube root of 1,000 is 10, because $10 \cdot 10 \cdot 10 = 1,000$.

Cube Root	Cube
1	1
2	8
3	27
4	64
5	125
6	216
7	343
8	512
9	729
10	1,000
11	1,331
12	1,728
13	2,197
14	2,744
15	3,375
16	4,096
17	4,913
18	5,832
19	6,859
20	8,000

To take the cube root of a monomial, first take the cube root of the coefficient. Then take the cube root of each variable expression. Use the chart if needed.

EXAMPLE 1

$\sqrt[3]{216x^3} = 6x$

Check:
$6x \cdot 6x \cdot 6x = 216x^3$

EXAMPLE 2

$\sqrt[3]{1,000x^6y^3} = 10x^2y$

Check:
$10x^2y \cdot 10x^2y \cdot 10x^2y = 1,000x^6y^3$

PRACTICE

Find each cube root. Use the chart above if needed.

	a	b	c	d	e
1.	$\sqrt[3]{27} =$	$\sqrt[3]{64} =$	$\sqrt[3]{1,728} =$	$\sqrt[3]{1} =$	$\sqrt[3]{4,096} =$
2.	$\sqrt[3]{y^3} =$	$\sqrt[3]{y^6} =$	$\sqrt[3]{b^9} =$	$\sqrt[3]{c^{12}} =$	$\sqrt[3]{z^{15}} =$
3.	$\sqrt[3]{8y^3} =$	$\sqrt[3]{2,744x^6} =$	$\sqrt[3]{1,331z^9} =$	$\sqrt[3]{8,000a^3} =$	$\sqrt[3]{4,096b^{12}} =$
4.	$\sqrt[3]{343a^3b^3} =$	$\sqrt[3]{729x^6y^{15}} =$	$\sqrt[3]{8c^{12}d^9} =$	$\sqrt[3]{216x^3y^6} =$	$\sqrt[3]{3,375z^{27}} =$
5.	$\sqrt[3]{512a^3b^3c^6} =$	$\sqrt[3]{1,000x^3y^6z^9} =$	$\sqrt[3]{2,197r^9s^9} =$	$\sqrt[3]{5,832t^{30}} =$	$\sqrt[3]{125x^{15}y^{15}} =$

Equations with Cubes

Some equations have variables that are cubed. To solve such an equation, first isolate the cubed variable and then find the cube root of both sides of the equation. An equation such as $x^3 = 27$ has only one solution. The solution is 3 because $(3)(3)(3) = 27$. The solution cannot be $^-3$ because $(^-3)(^-3)(^-3) = {}^-27$.

EXAMPLE

Solve: $3x^3 + 7 = 88$

$$3x^3 + 7 = 88$$
$$3x^3 + 7 - 7 = 88 - 7$$
$$3x^3 = 81$$
$$\frac{3x^3}{3} = \frac{81}{3}$$
$$x^3 = 27$$
$$x = 3$$

Check: $3(3)^3 + 7 = 88$
$$3(3)(3)(3) + 7 = 88$$
$$3(27) + 7 = 88$$
$$81 + 7 = 88$$
$$88 = 88$$

PRACTICE

Solve.

	a	b	c	d
1.	$3x^3 = 24$	$2x^3 = 250$	$4x^3 = 864$	$2x^3 = 1{,}458$
2.	$x^3 + 7 = 34$	$x^3 + 9 = 17$	$x^3 - 15 = 49$	$x^3 - 81 = 919$
3.	$5x^3 - 15 = 610$	$2x^3 + 25 = 711$	$4x^3 - 8 = 248$	$3x^3 - 100 = 548$

Combine like terms and solve.

	a	b	c
4.	$3x^3 - 5 = x^3 + 11$	$5x^3 - 17 = 3x^3 + 111$	$2x^3 + 5 = x^3 + 221$

Unit 7 Inequalities, Roots, and Proportions

Using Equations with Cubes

Recall that the volume of a rectangular prism is equal to length times width times height, or $V = lwh$. The volume is always in cube units. If you know the volume and information about the length, width, and height, you can use the formula to find the dimensions of the prism.

EXAMPLE

Find the dimensions of a rectangular prism with a volume of 256 cubic meters. The height and the length are each twice the width.

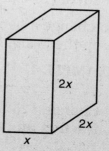

Let x = width.
Let $2x$ = height.
Let $2x$ = length.
Then $V = (2x)(x)(2x)$
$\quad = 4x^3$

Since $V = 256$ cubic m,
$4x^3 = 256$
$x^3 = 64$
$x = 4$
width = 4

Check: $(2x)(x)(2x) = 256$
$(8)(4)(8) = 256$
$256 = 256$

The width (x) is 4 meters, the height ($2x$) is 8 meters, and the length ($2x$) is also 8 meters.

PRACTICE

Solve.

1. Find the dimensions of a rectangular prism with a volume of 512 cubic cm if the width is one-half the length and the height is four times the width.

    Answer _____

2. Find the dimensions of a rectangular prism with a volume of 162 cubic m if the width is one-half the length and the height is three times the width.

    Answer _____

3. Find the dimensions of a rectangular prism with a volume of 384 cubic in. if the length is twice the width and the height is three times the width.

    Answer _____

4. Find the dimensions of a cube with a volume of 125 cubic cm. (Hint: Remember that a cube has equal dimensions because all the sides are squares.)

    Answer _____

5. Find the dimensions of a rectangular prism with a volume of 135 cubic ft if the length equals the width and the height is five times the length.

    Answer _____

6. What are the dimensions of a rectangular prism with a volume of 576 cubic m if the width is three-fourths the length and the height is twice the width?

    Answer _____

The Meaning of Percent

The symbol % is read as **percent**. Percent means *per hundred* or *out of one hundred*. Therefore, 27% means 27 per hundred, 27 out of 100, or 27 hundredths.

We can write a percent as a fraction or as a decimal.

To change a percent to a decimal, move the decimal point 2 places to the left and drop the percent sign (%). Write zeros as needed. For example, 6% = 0.06.

To change a percent to a fraction, place the percent over 100 and drop the % sign. Simplify. For example, $14\% = \frac{14}{100} = \frac{7}{50}$.

EXAMPLE 1

Change 125% to a fraction and a decimal.

$125\% = \frac{125}{100} = 1\frac{25}{100} = 1\frac{1}{4}$

$125\% = 1.25$

EXAMPLE 2

Find 15% of 80.

First change 15% to a decimal. 15% = 0.15

Then solve. Remember, *of* means multiply.

$0.15 \times 80 = 12$

EXAMPLE 3

There are 35 students in Mr. Terrell's math class. 20% of the class got an A on the last test. How many students got an A?

20% = 0.2 $0.2 \times 35 = 7$

7 students got an A.

PRACTICE

Change each percent to a decimal and then to a fraction. Simplify.

a	b
1. $70\% = 0.70 = \frac{70}{100} = \frac{7}{10}$	$100\% =$
2. $98.6\% =$	$4.5\% =$

Find the answer.

a	b
3. 30% of 110 =	15% of 65 =
4. 45% of 200 =	20% of 240 =

Solve.

5. The last class registration showed that 35% of the 500 students preferred an outdoor gym class. How many students preferred an outdoor gym class?

Answer _____

6. Jeffrey purchased a lawnmower at 15% off. The lawnmower was originally $245. How much money did Jeffrey save?

Answer _____

Unit 7 Inequalities, Roots, and Proportions

The Meaning of Ratio

A **ratio** is the comparison of two quantities. It is written as a fraction. For example, there are four quarts in a gallon. The ratio of gallons to quarts is one to four, which is written as $\frac{1}{4}$, or $1:4$. A ratio in fractional form can be reduced just as any fraction can be reduced to lowest terms. Ratios can be used to solve problems.

EXAMPLE 1

Jack is 15 years old. His father is 40 years old. What is the ratio of Jack's age to his father age?

Stated in fractional form, the ratio is $\frac{15}{40}$. Reduced to lowest terms, the ratio is $\frac{3}{8}$. Thus, the ratio of Jack's age to the age of his father is $\frac{15}{40}$, or $\frac{3}{8}$.

EXAMPLE 2

The perimeter of a rectangle is 60 feet. The length and width are in the ratio of 2 to 1. Find the two dimensions.

Let x = width.
$2x$ = length
Then $P = 2(x) + 2(2x) = 6x$
Since $P = 60$ ft,
$6x = 60$
$x = 10$

The width is 10 feet, and the length is 20 feet.

PRACTICE

Find each ratio.

	a	b
1.	1 pound to ounces in a pound 1:16 or $\frac{1}{16}$	a mile to feet in a mile
2.	1 kilogram to grams	a meter to centimeters
3.	millimeters to a centimeter 10:1 or $\frac{10}{1}$	inches to a foot

Solve.

4. Carol is 5 feet 4 inches tall and Adam is 5 feet tall. What is the ratio of Carol's height to that of Adam? (Hint: Change both measurements to inches.)

Answer _____

5. The perimeter of a rectangle is 70 feet. The length and width are in the ratio of 3 to 2. Find the length and width.

Answer _____

The Meaning of Proportion

Consider this situation. On Monday, Stan earned $48 for working 4 hours. On Tuesday, he earned $84 for working 7 hours.

The ratio of Monday's hours to Tuesday's hours is $\frac{4}{7}$. The ratio of Monday's earnings to Tuesday's earnings is $\frac{48}{84}$. Because these ratios are equal, you can write an equation.

Monday's hours $\rightarrow \dfrac{4}{7} = \dfrac{48}{84} \leftarrow$ Monday's dollars
Tuesday's hours $\rightarrow \phantom{\dfrac{4}{7}} \phantom{\dfrac{48}{84}} \leftarrow$ Tuesday's dollars

An equation formed by two fractions is called a **proportion.** The fractions can be ratios or rates. A rate is a kind of ratio that has different units.

Monday's dollars $\rightarrow \dfrac{48}{4} = \dfrac{84}{7} \leftarrow$ Tuesday's dollars
Monday's hours $\rightarrow \phantom{\dfrac{48}{4}} \phantom{\dfrac{84}{7}} \leftarrow$ Tuesday's hours

To solve a proportion that contains an unknown, cross-multiply and solve the resulting equation.

EXAMPLE

Kathryn earns $32 for working 2 hours. How much would she earn for working 6 hours?

Let $x =$ the amount earned in 6 hours.

$\dfrac{32}{x} = \dfrac{2}{6}$

Solve by cross-multiplication.

$32(6) = x(2)$
$192 = 2x$
$96 = x$

Check:

$\dfrac{32}{96} = \dfrac{2}{6} = \dfrac{1}{3}$

Kathryn would earn $96 for working 6 hours.

PRACTICE

Solve each proportion. Use cross-multiplication.

	a	b	c	d
1.	$\dfrac{x}{4} = \dfrac{5}{10}$	$\dfrac{x}{6} = \dfrac{2}{3}$	$\dfrac{2}{x} = \dfrac{6}{9}$	$\dfrac{8}{x} = \dfrac{4}{8}$
2.	$\dfrac{3}{25} = \dfrac{x}{100}$	$\dfrac{4}{5} = \dfrac{x}{20}$	$\dfrac{3}{7} = \dfrac{6}{x}$	$\dfrac{7}{5} = \dfrac{21}{x}$

Solve.

3. If Rolando earned $28.50 in 2 hours, how much would he earn in 8 hours?

4. If it takes 3 hours for a horse to walk 10 miles, how far will the horse walk in 9 hours?

Answer _____

Answer _____

Problems with Percent, Ratio, and Proportion

Solve.

1. Find the dimensions of a rectangle if the area equals 525 square cm and the length and the width are in the ratio of 7 to 3.

Since $l:w = 7:3$,
let $7x =$ length
and $3x =$ width.

$A = lw$
$525 = (7x)(3x)$
$525 = 21x^2$
$25 = x^2$
$\pm 5 = x$
length $= 7x = 7 \cdot 5 = 35$
width $= 3x = 3 \cdot 5 = 15$

Answer _Length = 35 cm   Width = 15 cm_

2. The stereo that Dontay bought was originally priced at $199. Dontay bought the stereo on sale for 20% off. How much money did Dontay save?

Answer _____

3. The area of a rectangle is 96 square ft. The length and the width are in the ratio of two to three. Find the dimensions.

Answer _____

4. When a local office supply store sells 5 packs of paper, it also sells 8 packs of envelopes. How many packs of envelopes would the store sell if it sold 15 packs of paper?

Answer _____

5. The taxes on a piece of property valued at $40,000 were $860. At the same rate, what would be the taxes on property valued at $55,000?

Answer _____

6. During the last survey, 45% of the 700 employees voted in favor of the new company logo. How many employees voted in favor of the new company logo?

Answer _____

7. If Carl drove 65 miles on 5 gallons of gas, how far can he drive on 12 gallons of gas?

Answer _____

8. Good advertising accounts for 35% of a store's revenue. If the store's revenue for last week was $12,400, how much of the revenue was due to good advertising?

Answer _____

Proportion in Angles and Sides

Triangles whose corresponding angles are equal are called **similar triangles**. Similar triangles have the same shape but not necessarily the same size. If two triangles are similar, the measures of the corresponding sides are proportional. For the similar triangles at right you can write these proportions.

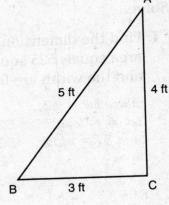

$$\frac{AB}{DE} = \frac{BC}{EF} \qquad \frac{AB}{DE} = \frac{AC}{DF} \qquad \frac{AC}{DF} = \frac{BC}{EF}$$

The lengths of some sides of the triangles are indicated in the drawing. Proportions can be used to find the lengths of the other sides.

EXAMPLE 1

Find the length of EF.

$$\frac{AC}{DF} = \frac{BC}{EF}$$
$$\frac{4}{2} = \frac{3}{EF}$$
$$4 \cdot EF = 6$$
$$EF = 1.5 \text{ ft}$$

EXAMPLE 2

Find the length of DE.

$$\frac{AC}{DF} = \frac{AB}{DE}$$
$$\frac{4}{2} = \frac{5}{DE}$$
$$4 \cdot DE = 10$$
$$DE = 2.5 \text{ ft}$$

GUIDED PRACTICE

Solve.

1. Triangles ABC and DEF are similar. Find the length of EF.

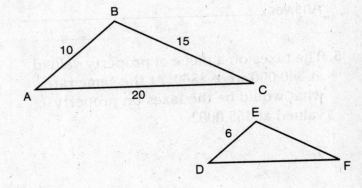

Answer _____

2. When a flagpole 30 feet tall casts a shadow 5 feet long, how tall is a nearby telephone pole that casts a shadow 2 feet long?

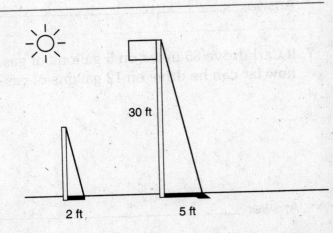

Answer _____

PRACTICE

Solve.

1. The drawing at the right shows a person, 5 feet tall, casting a shadow 3 feet long. The tree is casting a shadow 15 feet long. How tall is the tree?

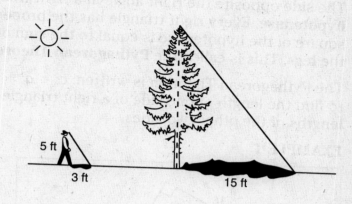

Answer _____

2. Triangles XYZ and MNO are similar. Find the length of MO.

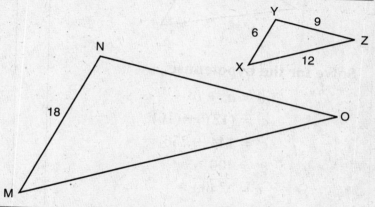

Answer _____

3. When a pole 20 feet tall casts a shadow 15 feet long, how tall is a nearby tree that casts a shadow 24 feet long?

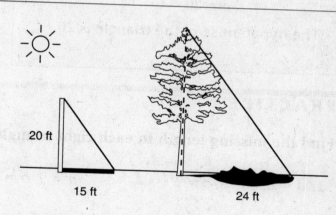

Answer _____

4. Triangles QRS and JKL are similar. Find the length of QR.

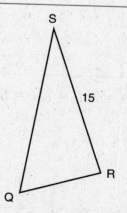

Answer _____

The Pythagorean Theorem

The side opposite the right angle in a right triangle is called the **hypotenuse**. Every right triangle has the property that the square of the hypotenuse is equal to the sum of the squares of the **legs**. This is called the **Pythagorean Theorem**.

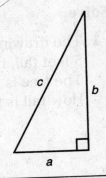

The Pythagorean Theorem is written: $c^2 = a^2 + b^2$. It can be used to find the length of one side of a right triangle if you know the lengths of the other two sides.

EXAMPLE 1

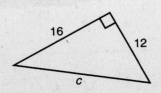

Solve for the hypotenuse.

$$c^2 = a^2 + b^2$$
$$c^2 = (12)^2 + (16)^2$$
$$c^2 = 144 + 256$$
$$c^2 = 400$$
$$c = \sqrt{400}$$
$$c = 20$$

The hypotenuse of the triangle is 20.

EXAMPLE 2

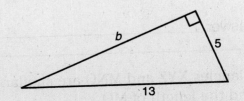

Solve for the missing leg.

$$c^2 = a^2 + b^2$$
$$(13)^2 = (5)^2 + (b)^2$$
$$169 = 25 + b^2$$
$$169 - 25 = b^2$$
$$144 = b^2$$
$$\sqrt{144} = b$$
$$12 = b$$

The missing leg of the triangle is 12.

PRACTICE

Find the missing length in each right triangle, using $c^2 = a^2 + b^2$.

1. $a = 6$, $b = 8$, $c = ?$ | $a = 9$, $b = ?$, $c = 15$ | $a = ?$, $b = 8$, $c = 17$

2. $a = 3$, $b = ?$, $c = 5$ | $a = ?$, $b = 24$, $c = 25$ | $a = 8$, $b = 15$, $c = ?$

Unit 7 Inequalities, Roots, and Proportions

Formula for Distance Between Two Points

The Pythagorean Theorem can be used to find distances on a coordinate plane. Study the graph at right. To find the distance (d) between two points with coordinates (x_1, y_1) and (x_2, y_2) use the formula $d = \sqrt{(x_2 - x_1)^2 + (y_2 - y_1)^2}$.

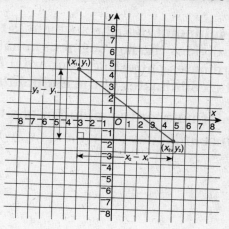

EXAMPLE 1

Find the distance between $(^-3, 4)$ and $(5, ^-2)$.

$d = \sqrt{(x_2 - x_1)^2 + (y_2 - y_1)^2}$

$\quad = \sqrt{[(5 - (^-3)]^2 + [(^-2) - 4)]^2}$

$\quad = \sqrt{(8)^2 + (^-6)^2}$

$\quad = \sqrt{64 + 36}$

$\quad = \sqrt{100}$

$\quad = 10$

EXAMPLE 2

Find the distance between $(^-1, ^-2)$ and $(^-1, ^-9)$.

$d = \sqrt{(x_2 - x_1)^2 + (y_2 - y_1)^2}$

$\quad = \sqrt{[(^-1) - (^-1)]^2 + [(^-9 - (^-2)]^2}$

$\quad = \sqrt{(0)^2 + (^-7)^2}$

$\quad = \sqrt{49}$

$\quad = 7$

PRACTICE

Find the distance between each pair of points.

	a	b	c
1.	(5, 3) and (5, 7)	($^-$4, 9) and (3, 9)	(0, $^-$8) and (0, $^-$1)
2.	(3, 2) and (7, 5)	(1, $^-$3) and (6, 9)	($^-$5, 11) and (4, $^-$1)
3.	(0, 0) and ($^-$6, 8)	(0, $^-$5) and (12, 0)	(5, $^-$4) and (1, $^-$7)

The Midpoint Formula

The **midpoint** of a line segment is the point that divides the line segment in half. The coordinates of the midpoint are the **averages** of the coordinates of the **endpoints**.

The formula for the midpoint of a line segment with coordinates (x_1, y_1) and (x_2, y_2) is:

$$\left(\frac{x_1 + x_2}{2}, \frac{y_1 + y_2}{2}\right).$$

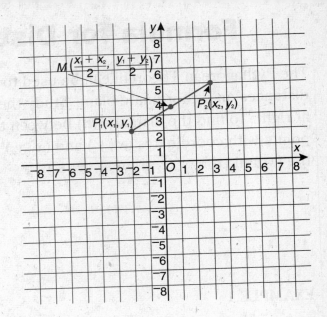

EXAMPLE 1

Find the midpoint between ($^-2$, 2) and (3, 5).

$$\text{midpoint} = \left(\frac{x_1 + x_2}{2}, \frac{y_1 + y_2}{2}\right)$$
$$= \left(\frac{(^-2) + 3}{2}, \frac{2 + 5}{2}\right)$$
$$= \left(\frac{1}{2}, \frac{7}{2}\right)$$
$$= \left(\frac{1}{2}, 3\frac{1}{2}\right)$$

EXAMPLE 2

Find the midpoint between ($^-5$, 2) and ($^-1$, $^-4$).

$$\text{midpoint} = \left(\frac{x_1 + x_2}{2}, \frac{y_1 + y_2}{2}\right)$$
$$= \left(\frac{(^-5) + (^-1)}{2}, \frac{2 + (^-4)}{2}\right)$$
$$= \left(\frac{^-6}{2}, \frac{^-2}{2}\right)$$
$$= (^-3, ^-1)$$

PRACTICE

Find the midpoint between the following points.

a	b	c
1. (2, $^-3$) and (2, 5)	($^-9$, 7) and (3, 7)	($^-5$, 1) and ($^-9$, -1)
2. (13, 11) and (7, 5)	($^-1$, $^-3$) and (7, 1)	(0, $^-8$) and (0, $^-2$)
3. (2, 1) and (4, $^-9$)	(0, $^-5$) and ($^-10$, 3)	($^-4$, $^-6$) and (2, $^-2$)

Unit 7 Inequalities, Roots, and Proportions

The Triangle Midsegment Theorem

The **midsegment** of a triangle is a segment that connects the midpoints of two sides of the triangle. Look at the triangle at right. The midsegment XY connects the midpoints of sides AB and AC. The midsegment lies **parallel** to the third side, BC. It is also $\frac{1}{2}$ the length of BC. This is called the **Triangle Midsegment Theorem.**

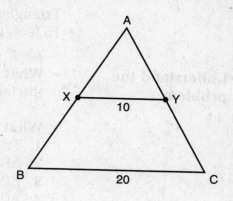

Triangle Midsegment Theorem

The segment joining the midpoints of two sides of a triangle is parallel to the third side, and its length is half the length of the third side.

EXAMPLE 1

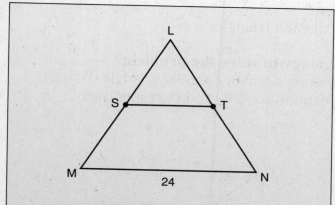

Find the length of ST.

$$ST = \tfrac{1}{2}MN$$
$$ST = \tfrac{1}{2}(24)$$
$$ST = 12$$

EXAMPLE 2

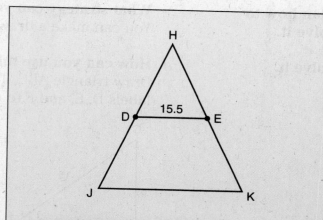

Find the length of JK.

$$\tfrac{1}{2}JK = DE$$
$$\tfrac{1}{2}JK = 15.5$$
$$JK = 31$$

PRACTICE

Find the length of the midsegment of each of the following triangles.

1.

a

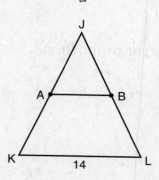

b

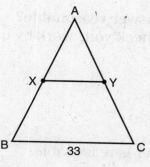

c

Problem-Solving Strategy: Make a Drawing

Triangles ABC and DEF are similar. AB is 12 feet, BC is 9 feet, AC is 15 feet, DE is 8 feet, and DF is 10 feet. Find the length of EF.

Understand the problem.

- **What do you want to know?**
  the length of segment EF

- **What information is given?**
  1. Triangles ABC and DEF are similar.
  2. AB is 12 feet.
  3. BC is 9 feet.
  4. AC is 15 feet.
  5. DE is 8 feet.
  6. DF is 10 feet.

Plan how to solve it.

- **What strategy can you use?**
  You can make a drawing of each triangle.

Solve it.

- **How can you use this strategy to solve the problem?**
  Draw triangle ABC. Then draw a smaller similar triangle. Write labels D, E, and F to correspond to A, B, and C, respectively.

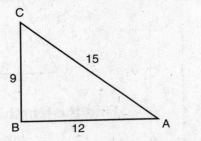 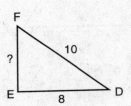

Write a proportion. Substitute.

$$\frac{AB}{DE} = \frac{BC}{EF} \qquad\qquad \frac{12}{8} = \frac{9}{EF}$$

$$12EF = 72$$

$$EF = 6 \text{ feet}$$

- **What is the answer?**
  The length of segment EF is 6 feet.

Look back and check your answer.

- **Is your answer reasonable?**
  You can check your work by using a different proportion.

$$\frac{AC}{DF} = \frac{BC}{EF} \qquad\qquad \frac{15}{10} = \frac{9}{EF}$$

$$15EF = 90$$

$$EF = 6 \text{ feet}$$

The answer is reasonable.

Make a drawing. Solve.

1. Two rectangles are similar. Each of the sides of the small rectangle is half the length of the corresponding side of the large rectangle. How does the perimeter of the small rectangle compare to the perimeter of the large rectangle?

Answer _____

2. When a person 6 feet tall casts a shadow 10 feet long, how tall is a nearby tree which casts a shadow of 45 feet?

Answer _____

3. Triangles XYZ and RST are similar. XY is 24 inches, YZ is 16 inches, XZ is 12 inches, RS is 18 inches, and RT is 9 inches. Find the length of ST.

Answer _____

4. Two rectangles are similar. Each of the sides of the large rectangle is 3 times the length of the corresponding side of the small rectangle. How does the area of the large rectangle compare with the area of the small rectangle?

Answer _____

UNIT 7 Review

Use >, <, or = to complete each statement.

	a		b		c
1. 19 _____ $^-12$		0.003 _____ 0.030		$\left(\frac{1}{2} - \frac{1}{6}\right)$ _____ $\left(\frac{1}{6} + \frac{1}{3}\right)$	

Solve.

	a	b	c
2. $x - 10 < 16$		$3x^2 = 75$	$^-9m + 10 \le ^-7m - 2$
3. $\frac{2}{5} = \frac{x}{15}$		$4a^2 - 20 = 16$	$y^3 - 2 = 6$

Find each square or cube root.

	a	b	c	d
4. $\sqrt{49} =$		$\sqrt[3]{27} =$	$\sqrt{25x^2y^4} =$	$\sqrt[3]{216} =$

Find each answer.

	a	b
5. 60% of 220 =		25% of 85 =

Find the missing length in each right triangle.

	a	b	c
6. $a = ?, b = 7, c = 25$		$a = 8, b = ?, c = 10$	$a = 12, b = 9, c = ?$

Find the distance between each pair of points.

	a	b	c
7. (2, 7) and (5, 3)		($^-6$, 2) and (6, 7)	(0, $^-1$) and (3, $^-1$)

Find the midpoint between the following points.

	a	b	c
8. ($^-2$, 3) and ($^-6$, 1)		(8, $^-2$) and (10, $^-4$)	(5, 8) and (3, 2)

Solve.

9. There are some pencils and erasers in a box. If there are 12 pencils and the ratio of pencils to erasers is 3:2, how many erasers are in the box?

10. When a 40-foot pole casts a shadow of 30 feet, how tall is a nearby tree that casts a shadow of 15 feet?

Answer _____

Answer _____

Simplify.

	a	b	c
1.	$(65 - 11) \div 9 + 100 =$	$46xy + 52xy - 17xy =$	$\dfrac{^{-}36m^2n^2}{18n^3} =$
2.	$\sqrt{a^2b^6} =$	$\left(\dfrac{a}{2} + 3y\right) - \left(\dfrac{a}{2} + 6y\right) =$	$\dfrac{4r^2s^2}{5r} \div \dfrac{16rs}{10r^2} =$

At what points does the line cross the x- and y-axes?

	a	b	c
3.	$y = 3x + 2$	$2x = y - 6$	$^{-}4x + 10 = 2y$

Solve.

	a	b	c
4.	$3(2a - 6) = 24 + 6$	$3k - 3 \geq 15$	$4 - 2x \leq 10$

Solve each system of equations.

	a	b	c
5.	$x + 2y = 7$	$\dfrac{1}{2}x + y = 4$	$3x + 2y = 25$
	$x - 2y = 3$	$\dfrac{1}{2}x - 2y = 7$	$x - 3y = ^{-}21$
	Ordered pair _____	Ordered pair _____	Ordered pair _____

Make a table of 3 solutions. Graph each solution. Draw a straight line through the points.

	a	b	c
6.	$2x - 2y = 10$	$2x + y = 2$	$3x - y = 15$

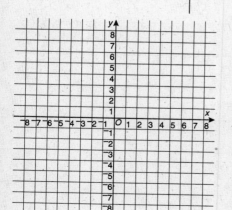
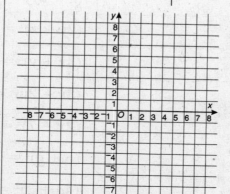
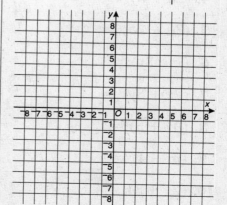

The Square of the Sum of Two Terms

Squaring a binomial is the same as multiplying a binomial by itself. Study Example 1. The first term of the answer is x^2, which is the square of the first term of the binomial. The middle term of the answer is $2xy$, which is twice the product of the two terms of the binomial. The last term of the answer is y^2, which is the square of the second term of the binomial. This leads to the following shortcut for finding the square of the sum of two terms.

RULE: The square of the sum of two terms is equal to the square of the first term, plus twice the product of the first and the second terms, plus the square of the second term.

EXAMPLE 1

Find: $(x + y)^2$

$$(x + y)^2 = (x + y)(x + y)$$
$$= x(x) + x(y) + x(y) + y(y)$$
$$= x^2 + 2xy + y^2$$

EXAMPLE 2

Find: $(a + 2b)^2$

$$(a + 2b)^2 = (a + 2b)(a + 2b)$$
$$= a(a) + 2ab + 2ab + 2b(2b)$$
$$= a^2 + 4ab + 4b^2$$

PRACTICE

Find the square of each binomial.

a

b

1. $(a + b)^2 =$ $(b + a)^2 =$

2. $(m + n)^2 =$ $(r + s)^2 =$

3. $(b + c)^2 =$ $(c + d)^2 =$

4. $(2a + b)^2 =$ $(x + 2y)^2 =$

5. $(2a + 2b)^2 =$ $(2y + z)^2 =$

6. $(x + 3y)^2 =$ $(3x + y)^2 =$

7. $(2x + 3y)^2 =$ $(3x + 2y)^2 =$

8. $(3x + 5)^2 =$ $(2x + 7)^2 =$

9. $(m + 4)^2 =$ $(6 + g)^2 =$

10. $(2x + 3)^2 =$ $(4a + 3)^2 =$

The Square of the Difference of Two Terms

The only difference between squaring the sum of two terms and squaring the difference of two terms is the operation for the middle term of the product. With the sum of two terms, the terms are all added. With the difference of two terms, the middle term is subtracted. Here is a shortcut for squaring the difference of two terms.

> **RULE:** The square of the difference of two terms is equal to the square of the first term, minus twice the product of the first and the second terms, plus the square of the second term.

EXAMPLE 1

Find: $(x - y)^2$

$$(x - y)^2 = (x - y)(x - y)$$
$$= x(x) - x(y) - x(y) + y(y)$$
$$= x^2 - 2xy + y^2$$

EXAMPLE 2

Find: $(2x - 5y)^2$

$$(2x - 5y)^2 = (2x - 5y)(2x - 5y)$$
$$= 2x(2x) - 2x(5y) - 2x(5y) + 5y(5y)$$
$$= 4x^2 - 20xy + 25y^2$$

PRACTICE

Find the square of each binomial.

	a	b
1.	$(x - 4)^2 =$	$(x - 3)^2 =$
2.	$(x - 5)^2 =$	$(x - 8)^2 =$
3.	$(3 - y)^2 =$	$(7 - x)^2 =$
4.	$(a - 12)^2 =$	$(a - 10)^2 =$
5.	$(c - 2d)^2 =$	$(x - 3y)^2 =$
6.	$(x - 6y)^2 =$	$(x - 10y)^2 =$
7.	$(3x - 7y)^2 =$	$(2x - 9y)^2 =$
8.	$(3a - 2b)^2 =$	$(8c - 4d)^2 =$
9.	$(7x - 6y)^2 =$	$(10m - 3n)^2 =$
10.	$(6x - 2y)^2 =$	$(5x - 4y)^2 =$

Factoring the Square of the Sum of Two Terms

The square of a binomial is a perfect square **trinomial,** or polynomial with three terms. For example, $(a + b)^2 = a^2 + 2ab + b^2$. To factor a perfect square trinomial such as $a^2 + 2ab + b^2$, think of the reverse of multiplication. The first term of each binomial will be the square root of the first term of the perfect square trinomial. The second term of each binomial will be the square root of the second term of the polynomial. Since the operation for the middle term of the polynomial is addition, the operation for each binomial also will be addition. Thus, the factors of $a^2 + 2ab + b^2$ are $(a + b)(a + b)$, or $(a + b)^2$.

EXAMPLE 1

Factor: $x^2 + 2xy + y^2$
$= (x + y)(x + y)$
$= (x + y)^2$

EXAMPLE 2

Factor: $25 + 10x + x^2$
$= (5 + x)(5 + x)$
$= (5 + x)^2$

EXAMPLE 3

Factor: $4y^2 + 48y + 144$
$= (2y + 12)(2y + 12)$
$= (2y + 12)^2$

PRACTICE

Factor.

a

1. $a^2 + 2ay + y^2 =$

2. $c^2 + 2cd + d^2 =$

3. $x^2 + 4xy + 4y^2 =$

4. $m^2 + 6mn + 9n^2 =$

5. $x^2 + 8xy + 16y^2 =$

6. $49y^2 + 56y + 16 =$

7. $9 + 6y + y^2 =$

8. $4 + 4x + x^2 =$

9. $64 + 16x + x^2 =$

10. $9x^2 + 12xy + 4y^2 =$

11. $81 + 36x + 4x^2 =$

12. $100 + 20x + x^2 =$

b

$m^2 + 2mn + n^2 =$

$r^2 + 2rs + s^2 =$

$4x^2 + 4xy + y^2 =$

$r^2 + 14rt + 49t^2 =$

$9x^2 + 24x + 16 =$

$x^2 + 10xy + 25y^2 =$

$4z^2 + 12z + 9 =$

$16x^2 + 56xy + 49y^2 =$

$49 + 14x + x^2 =$

$4x^2 + 16xy + 16y^2 =$

$64x^2 + 16x + 1 =$

$36x^2 + 24x + 4 =$

Factoring the Square of the Difference of Two Terms

The polynomial $a^2 + 2ab + b^2$ is a perfect square trinomial and factors into $(a + b)^2$. The polynomial $a^2 - 2ab + b^2$ is also a perfect square trinomial. To factor $a^2 - 2ab + b^2$, follow the same method used for factoring $a^2 + 2ab + b^2$, but use subtraction as the operation in the squared binomial. Since the only difference between $a^2 + 2ab + b^2$ and $a^2 - 2ab + b^2$ is the operation on the middle term, the only difference between their factors should be the operation. Thus, $a^2 - 2ab + b^2 = (a - b)(a - b)$, or $(a - b)^2$.

EXAMPLE 1

Factor: $r^2 - 2rs + s^2$

$= (r - s)(r - s)$

$= (r - s)^2$

EXAMPLE 2

Factor: $9a^2 - 24a + 16$

$= (3a - 4)(3a - 4)$

$= (3a - 4)^2$

EXAMPLE 3

Factor: $4p^2 - 12pq + 9q^2$

$= (2p - 3q)(2p - 3q)$

$= (2p - 3q)^2$

PRACTICE

Factor.

a	b
1. $x^2 - 2xy + y^2 =$	$c^2 - 2cd + d^2 =$
2. $b^2 - 2bd + d^2 =$	$m^2 - 2mn + n^2 =$
3. $r^2 - 2rs + s^2 =$	$y^2 - 2yz + z^2 =$
4. $x^2 - 4x + 4 =$	$4a^2 - 12a + 9 =$
5. $a^2 - 8a + 16 =$	$x^2 - 12x + 36 =$
6. $9x^2 - 36x + 36 =$	$x^2 - 14x + 49 =$
7. $x^2 - 6xy + 9y^2 =$	$16x^2 - 16xy + 4y^2 =$
8. $x^2 - 12xy + 36y^2 =$	$x^2 - 16xy + 64y^2 =$
9. $25a^2 - 30ab + 9b^2 =$	$x^2 - 14xy + 49y^2 =$
10. $4m^2 - 20mn + 25n^2 =$	$x^2 - 22xy + 121y^2 =$
11. $9x^2 - 12x + 4 =$	$16x^2 - 16x + 4 =$
12. $36x^2 - 36x + 9 =$	$49x^2 - 42x + 9 =$

Quadratic Equations and the Zero Product Property

A **quadratic equation** is an equation in which the greatest exponent of any term is 2. An example is $x^2 + 10x + 25 = 0$. This type of quadratic equation has a perfect square trinomial on one side of the equal sign and a zero on the other. The **roots of the equation** are the values of x that make the equation true. To find the roots of the equation, first factor the trinomial. Then use the **zero product property,** which states that any number multiplied by zero equals zero. Therefore, if $ab = 0$, then $a = 0$ or $b = 0$ or both. To use this property, write each factor equal to zero and solve. Check each solution, or root, by substituting it back into the original equation.

EXAMPLE 1

Solve: $x^2 + 10x + 25 = 0$
$(x + 5)(x + 5) = 0$ Factor. Use the zero

$x + 5 = 0$ $x + 5 = 0$ product
$\quad x = {}^-5$ $\quad x = {}^-5$ property.

The root of the equation is $^-5$.

Check: $({}^-5)^2 + 10({}^-5) + 25 = 0$
$\qquad\qquad 25 - 50 + 25 = 0$
$\qquad\qquad\qquad\quad 0 = 0$

EXAMPLE 2

Solve: $8x + 16x^2 = {}^-1$
$16x^2 + 8x + 1 = 0$ Rearrange terms.

$(4x + 1)(4x + 1) \qquad\qquad = 0$
$4x + 1 = 0 \qquad\qquad 4x + 1 = 0$
$\quad 4x = {}^-1 \qquad\qquad\quad 4x = {}^-1$
$\quad\ x = -\frac{1}{4} \qquad\qquad\quad\ x = -\frac{1}{4}$

The root of the equation is $-\frac{1}{4}$.

Check: $8\left(-\frac{1}{4}\right) + 16\left(-\frac{1}{4}\right)^2 = {}^-1$
$\qquad\qquad -\frac{8}{4} + \frac{16}{16} = {}^-1$
$\qquad\qquad\quad {}^-2 + 1 = {}^-1$

PRACTICE

Solve each quadratic equation. Check.

a	b	c
1. $x^2 + 4x + 4 = 0$	$x^2 + 6x + 9 = 0$	$x^2 + 8x + 16 = 0$
2. $x^2 + 14x + 49 = 0$	$9x^2 + 12x = {}^-4$	$16x^2 + 24x = {}^-9$
3. $4x^2 + 12x = {}^-9$	$9 + 18x + 9x^2 = 0$	$16 + 16x + 4x^2 = 0$

More Quadratic Equations and Perfect Square Trinomials

Some quadratic equations involve factoring a perfect square trinomial where the middle term is subtracted. An example is $x^2 - 2x + 1 = 0$.

To solve, or find the roots, factor the trinomial and use the zero product property as before. Check each solution.

EXAMPLE 1

Solve: $x^2 - 2x + 1 = 0$

$(x - 1)(x - 1) = 0$

$x - 1 = 0 \qquad x - 1 = 0$

$\qquad x = 1 \qquad\qquad x = 1$

The root of the equation is 1.

Check: $(1)^2 - 2(1) + 1 = 0$

$1 - 2 + 1 = 0$

$0 = 0$

EXAMPLE 2

Solve: $4x^2 - 12x = {}^-9$

$4x^2 - 12x + 9 = 0$

$(2x - 3)(2x - 3) = 0$

$2x - 3 = 0 \qquad 2x - 3 = 0$

$2x = 3 \qquad\qquad 2x = 3$

$x = \frac{3}{2} \qquad\qquad x = \frac{3}{2}$

The root of the equation is $\frac{3}{2}$.

Check: $4\left(\frac{3}{2}\right)^2 - 12\left(\frac{3}{2}\right) = {}^-9$

$4\left(\frac{9}{4}\right) - \frac{36}{2} = {}^-9$

$9 - 18 = {}^-9$

${}^-9 = {}^-9$

PRACTICE

Solve each quadratic equation.

	a	b	c
1.	$x^2 - 16x + 64 = 0$	$25 - 10x + x^2 = 0$	$16 - 8x + x^2 = 0$
2.	$36 - 12x + x^2 = 0$	$4x^2 - 16x = {}^-16$	${}^-8x + 16x^2 = {}^-1$
3.	${}^-12x + 4 = {}^-9x^2$	$9x^2 - 6x + 1 = 0$	$25x^2 - 20x = {}^-4$

The Product of the Sum and Difference of Two Terms

Example 1 shows the results of multiplying the sum of two terms by the difference of the same two terms. The first term of the product is x^2, which is the square of the first term of each binomial. The second term of the product is y^2, which is the square of the second term of each binomial. The two middle terms added together became zero, so the final product is the difference of the two squares. This leads to the following shortcut for finding the product of the sum and difference of two terms.

> **RULE:** The product of the sum and difference of two terms is equal to the square of the first term of each binomial minus the square of the second term of each binomial.

EXAMPLE 1

Find: $(x + y)(x - y)$

$\quad = x(x) + x(-y) + x(y) + y(-y)$

$\quad = x^2 - xy + xy - y^2$

$\quad = x^2 - y^2$

EXAMPLE 2

Find: $(2x + 1)(2x - 1)$

$\quad = 2x(2x) + 2x(^-1) + 2x(1) + 1(^-1)$

$\quad = 4x^2 - 2x + 2x - 1$

$\quad = 4x^2 - 1$

PRACTICE

Find each product.

	a	b
1.	$(a + b)(a - b) =$	$(y + z)(y - z) =$
2.	$(x + 6)(x - 6) =$	$(x - 7)(x + 7) =$
3.	$(x - 3)(x + 3) =$	$(x + 8)(x - 8) =$
4.	$(5d + g)(5d - g) =$	$(6 - b)(6 + b) =$
5.	$(2x + 3)(2x - 3) =$	$(3m + 5)(3m - 5) =$
6.	$(8x - 2)(8x + 2) =$	$(6x - z)(6x + z) =$
7.	$(5 - 3x)(5 + 3x) =$	$(7 + 6x)(7 - 6x) =$
8.	$(3k + 7m)(3k - 7m) =$	$(9a - 5b)(9a + 5b) =$
9.	$(3x - 4y)(3x + 4y) =$	$(4m + 6n)(4m - 6n) =$

Factoring the Difference of Two Squares

An expression such as $y^2 - 9$ is the difference of two squares. There are only two terms, and one of the terms is subtracted from the other. The factors of $y^2 - 9$ are $(y + 3)(y - 3)$, where the middle terms add to zero.

To factor the difference of two squares, use these steps.

Step 1. Find the square root of each term.
Step 2. Use the sum of these two square roots as the first factor.
Step 3. Use the difference of these two squares roots as the second factor.

EXAMPLE

Factor: $4x^2 - 25$

Step 1. $2x$ = the square root of $4x^2$
 5 = the square root of 25

Step 2. $2x + 5$ = sum of the two square roots

Step 3. $2x - 5$ = difference

The factors are $(2x + 5)(2x - 5)$.

Check: $(2x + 5)(2x - 5)$
 $= 4x^2 + 10x - 10x - 25$
 $= 4x^2 - 25$

PRACTICE

Factor.

	a	b
1.	$x^2 - y^2 =$	$x^2 - 36 =$
2.	$x^2 - 100 =$	$a^2 - 81 =$
3.	$25 - a^2 =$	$m^2 - 9 =$
4.	$225 - x^2 =$	$x^2 - 121 =$
5.	$4x^2 - 49 =$	$64 - a^2 =$
6.	$25a^2 - 16 =$	$900 - z^2 =$
7.	$100x^2 - 9 =$	$36x^2 - 64 =$
8.	$144x^2 - 100 =$	$49a^2 - 49 =$
9.	$9a^2 - 16b^2 =$	$36m^2 - 49n^2 =$
10.	$25x^2 - 25y^2 =$	$16x^2 - 81y^2 =$

The Product of Two Binomials with a Common Term

The factors in $(x + y)(x - y)$ have two common terms, x and y. Sometimes the binomials share only one common term, as in $(x + 5)(x - 3)$. To multiply two binomials with one common term, use either the method of multiplying each term separately or follow these steps.

Step 1. Square the common term.
Step 2. Add the unlike terms and multiply by the common term.
Step 3. Multiply the unlike terms.
Step 4. Combine the results from steps 1–3.

EXAMPLE 1: Multiply each term separately.

Find: $(x + 5)(x - 3)$
$$= x(x) + (^-3)(x) + 5(x) + (5)(^-3)$$
$$= x^2 - 3x + 5x - 15$$
$$= x^2 + 2x - 15$$

EXAMPLE 2: Use the steps shown above.

Find: $(x + 5)(x - 3)$
Step 1. $(x)(x) = x^2$
Step 2. $x(5 + {}^-3) = 2x$
Step 3. $(5)(^-3) = {}^-15$
Step 4. $x^2 + 2x - 15$

PRACTICE

Find each product.

	a	b
1.	$(x + 5)(x + 4) =$	$(x + 2)(x + 6) =$
2.	$(x + 1)(x + 3) =$	$(x + 3)(x + 4) =$
3.	$(x + 7)(x + 2) =$	$(x + 4)(x + 6) =$
4.	$(x + 10)(x + 1) =$	$(x + 6)(x + 7) =$
5.	$(x + 4)(x - 1) =$	$(x + 2)(x - 3) =$
6.	$(x + 8)(x - 2) =$	$(x + 7)(x - 2) =$
7.	$(x - 7)(x + 2) =$	$(x - 10)(x + 1) =$
8.	$(x - 5)(x - 1) =$	$(x - 7)(x - 3) =$
9.	$(x - 4)(x - 5) =$	$(x - 3)(x - 5) =$

Unit 8 Factoring and Quadratic Equations

Factoring for Two Binomials with a Common Term

When two binomials with a common term are multiplied, the product is a trinomial. For example, $x^2 + 8x - 20$ is a trinomial that can be factored into two binomials with a common term, $(x + 10)(x - 2)$. To factor such a trinomial, use these steps.

Step 1. Find the square root of the first term.
Step 2. Find all the factors of the third term.
Step 3. Decide which of these factors can be added to find the coefficient of the middle term.

EXAMPLE

Factor: $x^2 + 2x - 15$

Step 1. x = the square root of first term

Step 2. $(5)(^-3)$ These are factors of the third term.
$(^-5)(3)$ Note that one factor must be
$(^-1)(15)$ negative in this example because
$(1)(^-15)$ the third term (-15) is negative.

Step 3. $5 + (^-3) = 2$ Only the factors 5 and $^-3$ add to 2, the coefficient of the middle term.

Check: $(x + 5)(x - 3)$
$= x(x) + 5x - 3x - 15$
$= x^2 + 2x - 15$

The two binomial factors are $(x + 5)(x - 3)$.

PRACTICE

Factor.

	a	b
1.	$x^2 + 8x + 15 =$	$x^2 + 5x + 6 =$
2.	$x^2 + 3x + 2 =$	$x^2 + 8x + 12 =$
3.	$x^2 + 7x + 10 =$	$x^2 + 9x + 8 =$
4.	$x^2 + 4x - 12 =$	$x^2 - 9x + 18 =$
5.	$x^2 + 2x - 8 =$	$x^2 + 5x - 24 =$
6.	$x^2 - 4x - 12 =$	$x^2 - 8x - 20 =$
7.	$x^2 - 9x - 10 =$	$x^2 - 10x - 24 =$
8.	$x^2 - 7x + 12 =$	$x^2 - 9x + 20 =$

Quadratic Equations and the Difference of Two Squares

To find the roots of a quadratic equation involving the difference of two squares, first factor the difference of the squares. Then use the zero product property.

EXAMPLE 1

Solve: $y^2 - 100 = 0$

$$(y - 10)(y + 10) = 0$$

$$y - 10 = 0 \qquad y + 10 = 0$$

$$y = 10 \qquad\quad y = {}^{-}10$$

The roots of the equation are 10 and $^{-}$10.

Check:

$(10)^2 - 100 = 0$ $\qquad$ $({}^{-}10)^2 - 100 = 0$

$100 - 100 = 0$ $\qquad\quad$ $100 - 100 = 0$

EXAMPLE 2

Solve: $4x^2 - 9 = 0$

$$(2x - 3)(2x + 3) = 0$$

$$2x - 3 = 0 \quad 2x + 3 = 0$$

$$2x = 3 \qquad 2x = {}^{-}3$$

$$x = \tfrac{3}{2} \qquad x = {}^{-}\tfrac{3}{2}$$

The roots of the equation are $\tfrac{3}{2}$ and ${}^{-}\tfrac{3}{2}$.

Check: $4\left(\tfrac{3}{2}\right)^2 - 9 = 0$ $\qquad$ $4\left({}^{-}\tfrac{3}{2}\right)^2 - 9 = 0$

$\qquad\qquad$ $4\left(\tfrac{9}{4}\right) - 9 = 0$ $\qquad$ $4\left(\tfrac{9}{4}\right) - 9 = 0$

$\qquad\qquad\qquad$ $9 - 9 = 0$ $\qquad\qquad$ $9 - 9 = 0$

PRACTICE

Solve each quadratic equation.

a	b	c
1. $a^2 - 49 = 0$	$a^2 - 64 = 0$	$a^2 - 81 = 0$
2. $x^2 - 144 = 0$	$x^2 - 400 = 0$	$x^2 - 16 = 0$
3. $16x^2 - 100 = 0$	$4x^2 - 16 = 0$	$81x^2 - 36 = 0$
4. $4x^2 - 36 = 0$	$25x^2 - 100 = 0$	$9x^2 - 36 = 0$

Quadratic Equations and Factoring Trinomials

Some quadratic equations involve factoring a trinomial that is the product of two binomials with a common term. To find the roots of the equation, factor the trinomial and use the zero product property.

EXAMPLE 1

Solve: $x^2 - 5x - 14 = 0$

$(x - 7)(x + 2) = 0$

$x - 7 = 0 \qquad x + 2 = 0$

$x = 7 \qquad\qquad x = {}^-2$

The roots of the equation are 7 and $^-2$.

Check:

$(7)^2 - 5(7) - 14 = 0 \qquad ({}^-2)^2 - 5({}^-2) - 14 = 0$

$49 - 35 - 14 = 0 \qquad\qquad 4 + 10 - 14 = 0$

$49 - 49 = 0 \qquad\qquad\qquad 14 - 14 = 0$

EXAMPLE 2

Solve: $x^2 + x = 12$

$x^2 + x - 12 = 0$

$(x - 3)(x + 4) = 0$

$x - 3 = 0 \qquad x + 4 = 0$

$x = 3 \qquad\qquad x = {}^-4$

The roots of the equation are 3 and $^-4$.

Check:

$(3)^2 + 3 - 12 = 0 \qquad ({}^-4)^2 + ({}^-4) - 12 = 0$

$9 + 3 - 12 = 0 \qquad\qquad 16 - 4 - 12 = 0$

$12 - 12 = 0 \qquad\qquad\qquad 16 - 16 = 0$

PRACTICE

Solve each quadratic equation.

a	b	c
1. $x^2 + 7x + 12 = 0$	$x^2 + 7x + 6 = 0$	$x^2 + 9x + 20 = 0$
2. $x^2 - 2x - 8 = 0$	$x^2 - 5x = 6$	$x^2 - 9x = 10$
3. $x^2 - 8x = 33$	$x^2 - 7x - 44 = 0$	$x^2 - 10x - 39 = 0$
4. $x^2 - 7x = {}^-6$	$x^2 - 5x + 4 = 0$	$x^2 - 12x = {}^-20$

Multiplying Binomials and the FOIL Method

Knowing the types of binomials multiplied together can allow the use of shortcuts to find the product. It is important to remember, however, that any two binomials can be multiplied together using a simple method.

A general method for multiplying any two binomials is the **FOIL** method. The FOIL method shows how to multiply all terms in a certain order.

F	= First terms
O	= Outer terms
I	= Inner terms
L	= Last terms

EXAMPLE

Find: $(2x + 4)(x - 3)$

$$(2x + 4)(x - 3) = 2x(x) + 2x(^-3) + 4(x) + 4(^-3)$$
$$= 2x^2 - 6x + 4x - 12$$
$$= 2x^2 - 2x - 12$$

PRACTICE

Find each product.

a

1. $(x + 2)(2x + 3) =$

2. $(2x + y)(x + 2y) =$

3. $(x + 5y)(2x + y) =$

4. $(x + 3)(2x - 1) =$

5. $(x + 2y)(2x - y) =$

6. $(3x + 1)(x - 2) =$

7. $(x - 3)(2x - 1) =$

8. $(x - 3y)(2x - y) =$

9. $(2x - y)(x - 2y) =$

b

$(2x + 1)(x + 2) =$

$(2x + 3y)(x + y) =$

$(x + 3y)(2x + y) =$

$(2x + 3)(x - 1) =$

$(2x + y)(x - 2y) =$

$(2x - 4y)(x + 3y) =$

$(x - 4)(2x - 1) =$

$(2x - 3)(x - 1) =$

$(3x - 3y)(2x - y) =$

Unit 8 **Factoring and Quadratic Equations**

Factoring for Two Binomials with Like Terms

The challenge in factoring trinomials such as $2x^2 + 7x - 4$ lies in finding the proper combination of factors that will give the middle term. There are three important facts to keep in mind when factoring all kinds of trinomials. These facts are listed in the box at right.

HINTS FOR FACTORING TRINOMIALS

1. When all the terms of the trinomial are added, the terms in both binomials will be added.

2. When only the middle term is subtracted, the terms in both binomials will be subtracted.

3. When the last term is subtracted, the terms in one binomial are added and the terms in the other binomial are subtracted.

EXAMPLE

Factor: $2x^2 + 7x - 4$

Since the last term is subtracted, the terms in one binomial will be added, and the terms in the other binomial will be subtracted. List the possible factors of the first and third terms (in pairs).

List possible pairs of binomial factors. Find the middle term for each pair of factors. Keep trying until a pair of factors yields $7x$ as the middle term.

So, $2x^2 + 7x - 4 = (2x - 1)(x + 4)$.

Factors for first term
$2x^2 = (2x)(x)$

Factors for third term
$^-4 = (^-2)(2)$
$^-4 = (^-4)(1)$
$^-4 = (4)(^-1)$

Possible factor pairs

Possible factor pairs	Middle term	
$(2x - 2)(x + 2)$	$4x - 2x = 2x$	No
$(2x + 2)(x - 2)$	$^-4x + 2x = ^-2x$	No
$(2x - 4)(x + 1)$	$2x - 4x = ^-2x$	No
$(2x + 1)(x - 4)$	$^-8x + x = ^-7x$	No
$(2x + 4)(x - 1)$	$^-2x + 4x = 2x$	No
$(2x - 1)(x + 4)$	$8x - x = 7x$	Yes

PRACTICE

Factor.

	a	b
1.	$2x^2 + 5x + 2 =$	$3x^2 + 5x + 2 =$
2.	$7x^2 - 15x + 2 =$	$5x^2 + 11x + 2 =$
3.	$2x^2 - 7x + 3 =$	$3x^2 - 8x + 4 =$
4.	$5y^2 - 26y + 5 =$	$7x^2 - 16x + 4 =$
5.	$2x^2 + 3x - 2 =$	$3x^2 + x - 2 =$
6.	$5y^2 - 7y - 6 =$	$7x^2 - 10x - 8 =$

Problem-Solving Strategy: Use Guess and Check

Rhonda has 7 coins, none of which are pennies or half dollars. She has more dimes than nickels. The total value of the coins is $0.80. How many quarters, dimes, and nickels does Rhonda have?

Understand the problem.

- **What do you want to know?**
  how many quarters, dimes, and nickels Rhonda has

- **What information is given?**
  Clue 1: Rhonda has 7 coins with no pennies or half dollars.
  Clue 2: Rhonda has more dimes than nickels.
  Clue 3: The total value of the coins is $0.80

Plan how to solve it.

- **What strategy can you use?**
  You can guess an answer that satisfies the first two clues. Then check to see if your answer satisfies the third clue.

Solve it.

- **How can you use this strategy to solve the problem?**
  Choose seven coins and find the value. Make sure you choose more dimes than nickels. If your guess is incorrect, guess again. Try to guess in an organized way so that each of your guesses gets closer to the exact answer.

  (Let Q = quarter, D = dime, and N = nickel.)

Guess Seven Coins	Check Value in Cents	Evaluate
Q, Q, D, D, D, D, N	$2(25) + 4(10) + 5 = 95$	too high
Q, Q, D, D, D, N, N	$2(25) + 3(10) + 2(5) = 90$	too high
Q, D, D, D, D, N, N	$25 + 4(10) + 2(5) = 75$	too low
Q, D, D, D, D, D, N	$25 + 5(10) + 5 = 80$	satisfies all clues

- **What is the answer?**
  Rhonda has 1 quarter, 5 dimes, and 1 nickel.

Look back and check your answer.

- **Is your answer reasonable?**
  Check your answer to make sure it satisfies each clue. The value is $0.80 with no pennies or half dollars, and there are more dimes than nickels.

  The answer is reasonable.

Solve. Use the guess-and-check strategy.

1. The square of a number is 729. What is the number?

Answer _____

2. The square of a number is 2,916. What is the number?

Answer _____

3. The cube of a number is 13,824. What is the number?

Answer _____

4. The cube of a number is 68,921. What is the number?

Answer _____

5. Using each of the digits 2 through 5 only once, write 2 two-digit whole numbers whose product is as large as possible.

Answer _____

6. Using each of the digits 3 through 8 only once, write 2 three-digit whole numbers whose product is as large as possible.

Answer _____

7. The product of three whole numbers is 135. The sum of the same three whole numbers is 17. What are the numbers?

Answer _____

8. The cube of a whole number is 48 more than the square of the same number. What is the number?

Answer _____

Quadratic Equations and Coefficients Other Than 1

Sometimes a quadratic equation might have a squared term with a coefficient other than 1. To find the roots of the equation, follow the same factoring method used for finding two binomials with a like term.

EXAMPLE

Solve: $2x^2 - 10x + 12 = 0$

$(2x - 4)(x - 3) = 0$

$2x - 4 = 0 \qquad x - 3 = 0$

$2x = 4 \qquad\qquad x = 3$

$x = 2$

The roots of the equation are 2 and 3.

Check: $2(2)^2 - 10(2) + 12 = 0$

$8 - 20 + 12 = 0$

$^-12 + 12 = 0$

and

$2(3)^2 - 10(3) + 12 = 0$

$18 - 30 + 12 = 0$

$^-12 + 12 = 0$

PRACTICE

Solve each quadratic equation.

a	b	c
1. $2x^2 + 5x + 2 = 0$	$2x^2 + 11x + 5 = 0$	$5x^2 - 14x - 3 = 0$
2. $7x^2 + 13x - 2 = 0$	$3x^2 - 14x - 5 = 0$	$2x^2 - 5x + 3 = 0$
3. $5x^2 + 9x - 2 = 0$	$2x^2 - 3x - 2 = 0$	$2x^2 + x - 3 = 0$
4. $3x^2 - 2x - 5 = 0$	$5x^2 - 3x - 2 = 0$	$3x^2 + 14x - 5 = 0$

Mixed Practice Solving Quadratic Equations

You have seen five general types of products of two binomials.

- The square of the sum of two terms:
- The square of the difference of two terms:
- The product of the sum and difference of two terms:
- The product of two binomials with a common term:
- The product of two binomials with like terms:

$$(x + y)^2 = x^2 + 2xy + y^2$$
$$(x - y)^2 = x^2 - 2xy + y^2$$
$$(x + y)(x - y) = x^2 - y^2$$
$$(x + 5)(x + 1) = x^2 + 6x + 5$$
$$(x + 2)(2x + 1) = 2x^2 + 5x + 2$$

PRACTICE

Solve each quadratic equation.

a	b	c
1. $x^2 - 49 = 0$	$x^2 - 4x + 4 = 0$	$x^2 + 4x - 5 = 0$
2. $x^2 + 10x + 25 = 0$	$x^2 - 64 = 0$	$x^2 - 15x + 50 = 0$
3. $x^2 - 2x = {}^-1$	$x^2 - 7x = 30$	$2x^2 + 5x + 3 = 0$
4. $2x^2 + 5x = {}^-2$	$3x^2 + 2x = 5$	$x^2 - 16x = {}^-64$
5. $x^2 - 20x = {}^-75$	$x^2 + 6x + 9 = 0$	$3x^2 - 6x - 9 = 0$

Writing and Solving Quadratic Equations

Write an equation and find the solutions.

1. Find the number which when added to the square of the number equals 30.

Let x = the number
and x^2 = the square of the number.

$x^2 + x = 30$
$x^2 + x - 30 = 0$
$(x + 6)(x - 5) = 0$

$x + 6 = 0$ or $x - 5 = 0$
    $x = {}^-6$ or $x = 5$

Check: $({}^-6)^2 + ({}^-6) = 30$ $5^2 + 5 = 30$
                $36 - 6 = 30$ $25 + 5 = 30$

Answer _____${}^-6$ or 5_____

2. The product of two consecutive integers is 90. Find the integers.

Let x = the first integer
and x + 1 = the second integer.

$(x)(x + 1) = 90$
$x^2 + x - 90 = 0$
$(x + 10)(x - 9) = 0$

  $x + 10 = 0$ or $x - 9 = 0$
            $x = {}^-10$ or $x = 9$
so $x + 1 = {}^-9$ so $x + 1 = 10$

Check: $({}^-10)({}^-9) = 90$ $9(10) = 90$

Answer _____${}^-9$ and ${}^-10$, or 9 and 10_____

---

3. Find the number which when added to its square equals 20.

Answer _____

4. Find the number which when subtracted from its square equals 56.

Answer _____

---

5. The product of two consecutive even integers is 80. Find the integers. (Hint: Let x and $x + 2$ be the integers.)

Answer _____

6. The product of two consecutive odd integers is 99. What are the integers?

Answer _____

---

7. The square of a number added to twice the number equals 24. What is the number?

Answer _____

8. The length of a rectangle is 5 m greater than the width. The area is 300 sq m. Find the dimensions. Remember, dimensions cannot be negative.

Answer _____

---

9. The length of a rectangle is 20 cm greater than the width. The area is 125 sq cm. Find the dimensions of the rectangle.

Answer _____

10. The width of a rectangle is 10 m less than the length. The area of the rectangle is 200 sq m. Find the length and width.

Answer _____

Completing the Square

One method for solving certain quadratic equations is called **completing the square.** The method works even when the trinomial cannot be factored. It involves changing the equation to make a perfect square trinomial on one side. Consider the equation $x^2 - 2x - 3 = 0$. First, rewrite the equation so that both terms containing variables are on one side of the equal sign and the constant (a number) is on the other. Then add the square of one-half the coefficient of x to both sides of the equation. This would be $\left(\frac{1}{2} \cdot 2\right)^2$, or 1. Finally, factor and find the roots, or solutions, of the equation. Sometimes the solutions might contain square roots.

EXAMPLE

Solve: $x^2 - 2x - 3 = 0$

$x^2 - 2x = 3$	Rearrange terms.	**Check:** $(3)^2 - 2(3) - 3 = 0$
$x^2 - 2x + 1 = 3 + 1$	Add $\left(\frac{1}{2} \cdot 2\right)^2$, which equals 1, to both sides.	$9 - 6 - 3 = 0$
		$9 - 9 = 0$
$(x - 1)^2 = 4$	Factor.	and
$\sqrt{(x - 1)^2} = \sqrt{4}$	Find the square root of both sides.	$(^-1)^2 - 2(^-1) - 3 = 0$
$x - 1 = \pm 2$		$1 + 2 - 3 = 0$
		$3 - 3 = 0$
$x - 1 = {}^+2 \quad x - 1 = {}^-2$	Solve each equation.	
$x = 3 \qquad\quad x = {}^-1$		

PRACTICE

Solve. Use the method of completing the square.

a	b	c
1. $x^2 - 4x = 3$ $x^2 - 4x + 4 = 3 + 4$ $(x - 2)^2 = 7$ $x - 2 = \pm\sqrt{7}$ $x = 2 + \sqrt{7}$ or $x = 2 - \sqrt{7}$	$m^2 = {}^-6m - 7$	$x^2 - 2x - 3 = 0$
2. $y^2 + 2y - 8 = 0$	$m^2 - 4m - 32 = 0$	$p^2 - 4p - 5 = 0$

The Quadratic Formula

The **quadratic formula** can be used to find the roots of a quadratic equation. It is particularly useful when a quadratic equation cannot be solved by factoring.

Every quadratic equation can be written in the general form $ax^2 + bx + c = 0$. Hence, in the equation $x^2 - 7x + 6 = 0$, $a = 1$, $b = {}^-7$, and $c = 6$. Using the general form and the method of completing the square, solving for x gives this formula:

$$x = \frac{-b \pm \sqrt{b^2 - 4ac}}{2a}$$

Use the quadratic formula by first writing each equation in the form $ax^2 + bx + c = 0$. Then substitute for a, b, c in the formula.

EXAMPLE

Solve: $x^2 - 7x + 6 = 0$

$ax^2 + bx + c = 0$

Substitute $a = 1$, $b = {}^-7$ and $c = 6$ in the quadratic formula.

$$x = \frac{-b \pm \sqrt{b^2 - 4ac}}{2a}$$

$$x = \frac{{}^-({}^-7) \pm \sqrt{({}^-7)^2 - 4(1)(6)}}{2(1)}$$

$$x = \frac{7 \pm \sqrt{49 - 24}}{2}$$

$$x = \frac{7 \pm \sqrt{25}}{2} = \frac{7 \pm 5}{2}$$

$$x = \frac{7 + 5}{2} \qquad x = \frac{7 - 5}{2}$$

$$x = 6 \qquad x = 1$$

The roots of the equation are 6 and 1.

Check: $(6)^2 - 7(6) + 6 = 0$

$36 - 42 + 6 = 0$

$^-6 + 6 = 0$

$(1)^2 - 7(1) + 6 = 0$

$1 - 7 + 6 = 0$

$^-6 + 6 = 0$

PRACTICE

Use the quadratic formula to solve each quadratic equation.

a	b	c
1. $x^2 + 5x + 6 = 0$	$2x^2 + 5x + 2 = 0$	$4x^2 - 9x + 2 = 0$
2. $2x^2 - 7x + 3 = 0$	$2x^2 - 13x + 6 = 0$	$5x^2 = x + 4$
3. $2x^2 + x = 1$	$3x^2 = 20 - 7x$	$x^2 + 2x - 15 = 0$

More Practice with the Quadratic Formula

On the previous page, the exercises could also have been solved by factoring methods. Some quadratic equations, however, cannot be solved by factoring. The roots of these equations may be fractions and may contain square roots.

EXAMPLE

Solve: $2x^2 + x - 2 = 0$

Substitute $a = 2$, $b = 1$, and $c = {}^-2$.

$$x = \frac{-b \pm \sqrt{b^2 - 4ac}}{2a}$$

$$x = \frac{{}^-(1) \pm \sqrt{(1)^2 - 4(2)({}^-2)}}{2(2)}$$

$$x = \frac{{}^-1 \pm \sqrt{1 + 16}}{4}$$

$$x = \frac{{}^-1 + \sqrt{17}}{4} \quad x = \frac{{}^-1 - \sqrt{17}}{4}$$

The roots of the equation are $\frac{{}^-1 + \sqrt{17}}{4}$ and $\frac{{}^-1 - \sqrt{17}}{4}$.

PRACTICE

Use the quadratic formula to solve each quadratic equation.

a	b	c
1. $x^2 - 2x - 2 = 0$	$2x^2 - 8x + 3 = 0$	$2x^2 + 3x - 1 = 0$
2. $3x^2 - 4x - 2 = 0$	$6x^2 = 5x + 3$	$3x^2 = 2x + 3$
3. $3x^2 = 5x - 1$	$5x^2 - 3 = 3x$	$2x^2 + 5x = 1$

Problem-Solving Strategy: Select a Strategy

A wall measures 26 feet by 9 feet. It took exactly three cans of paint to cover the wall with one coat of paint. How many square feet were covered with each can of paint?

Problem-Solving Strategies	
Make a Table	Use a Formula
Make a List	Choose an Operation
Work Backwards	Identify Substeps
Find a Pattern	Identify Extra Information
Make a Drawing	Write a Number Sentence
Use Estimation	Use Guess and Check
Use Logic	

Understand the problem.

- **What do you want to know?**
  how many square feet of wall each can of paint covered

- **What information is given?**
  The wall is 26 feet by 9 feet. It took 3 cans of paint to cover the wall with one coat.

Plan how to solve it.

- **What strategy can you use?**
  You can identify substeps to find how many square feet of wall were covered with each can of paint.

Solve it.

- **How can you use this strategy to solve the problem?**
  There are 2 steps needed:
  1. Find the area of the wall.
  2. Divide the area of the wall by the number of cans used.

  > 1. $A = 26 \times 9 = 234$ square feet
  > 2. 234 square feet $\div$ 3 cans = 78 square feet per can

- **What is the answer?**
  Each can covers 78 square feet.

Look back and check your answer.

- **Is your answer reasonable?**
  You can check your work by multiplying and dividing.

  3 cans $\times$ 78 square feet = 234 square feet

  234 square feet $\div$ 9 feet = 26 feet

  The answer is reasonable.

Read each problem. Select a strategy. Solve.

1. Deshawn has a nickel, a dime, a quarter, and a half dollar. How many different values can he make using combinations of one or more of the coins?

Answer _____

2. On her new job, Melissa earned $10.50 per hour, which was $3.80 per hour less than twice what she earned at her previous job. What was the hourly wage at her previous job?

Answer _____

3. It takes 3 workers 1 hour to pack 6 boxes. At that rate, how long will it take 9 workers to pack 36 boxes?

Answer _____

4. The cube of a whole number is 100 more than the square of the same number. What is the number?

Answer _____

5. The occupations of Diane, Ella, and Felicia are lawyer, doctor, and teacher, although not necessarily in that order. Ella does not work in medicine. Neither Ella nor Diane is a lawyer. Which person is in which profession?

Answer _____

6. A rectangular field with a width of 48 feet has an area of 3,456 square feet. Inside the field is a rectangular fenced-in area with length and width that are each one-fourth as long as the corresponding side of the field. What is the area of the fenced-in area?

Answer _____

Using the Quadratic Formula in Solving Problems

Some problems can be solved using the quadratic formula. Use guess and check or a calculator to find the square root of large numbers.

EXAMPLE

> **The square of a number added to three times the number is equal to 28. What number or numbers satisfy these conditions?**
>
> Let x = the number.
>
> Write an equation:
>
> $x^2 + 3x = 28$.
>
> Rearrange into $ax^2 + bx + c = 0$
>
> $\qquad x^2 + 3x - 28 = 0$
>
> Find a, b, c: $a = 1$, $b = 3$, and $c = {}^-28$.
>
> Substitute into the quadratic formula.
>
> $x = \dfrac{-b \pm \sqrt{b^2 - 4ac}}{2a}$
>
> $x = \dfrac{{}^-(3) \pm \sqrt{(3)^2 - 4(1)({}^-28)}}{2(1)}$
>
> $x = \dfrac{{}^-3 \pm \sqrt{9 + 112}}{2} = \dfrac{{}^-3 \pm \sqrt{121}}{2} = \dfrac{{}^-3 \pm 11}{2}$
>
> $x = \dfrac{{}^-3 + 11}{2} = 4 \qquad x = \dfrac{{}^-3 - 11}{2} = {}^-7$
>
> Both $^-7$ and 4 satisfy the conditions of the problem.

PRACTICE

First write an equation. Then solve using the quadratic formula.

1. One-half the square of a number is equal to 16 more than twice the number. What is the number?

   Answer _____

2. Find the two consecutive odd integers whose product is 143.

   Answer _____

3. The product of two consecutive odd integers is 323. What are the integers?

   Answer _____

4. Find the number which when subtracted from its square equals 72.

   Answer _____

5. The length of a rectangle is 10 more than twice the width. The area of the rectangle is 672 square inches. Find the length and width. (Remember, dimensions cannot be negative.)

   Answer _____

6. The width of a rectangle is one-half the length minus 11 cm. The area of the rectangle is 700 square centimeters. Find the length and width.

   Answer _____

Find each product.

1.
   a. $(x - y)(x + y) =$
   b. $(4 - 6t)^2 =$
   c. $(2x - y)(x + 4y) =$

Factor.

2.
   a. $x^2 + 2xy + y^2 =$
   b. $25x^2 - 40x + 16 =$
   c. $64 - 16x^2 =$

3.
   a. $x^2 - 2x - 8 =$
   b. $x^2 - 3x - 4 =$
   c. $3x^2 + x - 2 =$

Solve by factoring.

4.
   a. $x^2 + 10x + 25 = 0$
   b. $x^2 + 16x = {}^-64$
   c. $4x^2 + 32x + 64 = 0$

5.
   a. $4x^2 - 4x + 1 = 0$
   b. $4x^2 - 64 = 0$
   c. $x^2 + 5x + 4 = 0$

Solve by completing the square.

6.
   a. $m^2 - 4m + 1 = 0$
   b. $y^2 - 2y - 1 = 0$
   c. $x^2 - 4x = 5$

Solve using the quadratic formula.

7.
   a. $2x^2 + 7x + 6 = 0$
   b. $x^2 - 6x = 2$
   c. $x^2 - 8x = {}^-3$

First write an equation. Then solve.

8. The length of a rectangle is 10 inches greater than the width. The area of the rectangle is 75 square inches. Find the dimensions.

9. Find the number which when added to its square equals 12.

Answer _____

Answer _____

Simplify.

a	*b*	*c*
1. $9x^2 + 6x + 4y + x =$	$2a(^-12ab - 3ab) =$	$\sqrt{16x^2}$
2. $\dfrac{^-90x^2y^3}{10x^3y^2} =$	$\dfrac{6x - 9y}{-3} =$	$\left(\dfrac{m}{2} - n\right) + \left(\dfrac{3m}{2} + n\right) =$

Find the distance between each pair of points.

a	*b*	*c*
3. $(^-3, 5)$ and $(5, 11)$	$(^-4, 9)$ and $(4, 9)$	$(1, 10)$ and $(1, 14)$

Solve.

a	*b*	*c*
4. $2x^2 = 32$	$\dfrac{3r}{100} = \dfrac{9}{10}$	$5x - 1 = 3x + 15$

Find the slope of the line that passes through the given points.

a	*b*	*c*
5. $(2, ^-2), (5, ^-11)$	$(4, 8), (5, 15)$	$(3, ^-10), (^-3, 10)$

Solve by factoring.

a	*b*	*c*
6. $x^2 + 8x + 12 = 0$	$x^2 - 10x = ^-21$	$4x^2 + 2x - 6 = 0$

Make a table of solutions. Graph each equation. Draw a straight line through the points.

a

7. $2x - y = 0$

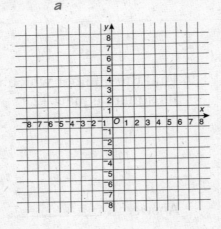

b

$2x + y = 3$

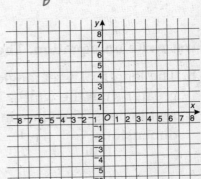

Name all the sets to which each of the following numbers belong. Choose from *natural numbers*, *whole numbers*, *integers*, **and** *rational numbers*.

a	*b*	*c*	*d*
1. 7	$^-16$	$3\frac{5}{11}$	5.3

Find the absolute value of each number.

a	*b*	*c*	*d*
2. $\left|\,^-39\right| =$	$\left|7\right| =$	$\left|\frac{^-1}{2}\right| =$	$\left|\,^-1.05\right| =$

Simplify.

a	*b*	*c*
3. $(18 - 6) - 4 + 10 =$	$(7 - 4) \div 9 \times \frac{1}{4} =$	$54 \div 8 - \frac{3}{4} \times 2 + 4 =$

Write an algebraic expression for each verbal expression.

a	*b*
4. the product of *a* and 9 _____	5 decreased by *n* _____

Evaluate each expression if *r* = 8, *s* = 3, **and** *t* = 6.

a	*b*	*c*	*d*
5. $r + st =$	$\frac{rs + t}{s} =$	$t - 2s =$	$r + 5s =$

Solve.

a	*b*	*c*	*d*
6. $n = 2(3 + 6)$	$10k = 200$	$7(5) - 4(3) = b$	$12 + w = 55$

Simplify.

a	*b*	*c*	*d*
7. $7 + (^-1) =$	$6(^-3) =$	$\frac{^-65}{5} =$	$^-5 + (^-25) =$
8. $\frac{12b + 40}{4} =$	$m + 9 - (3m + 6) =$	$\frac{3}{8}(16c - 32) =$	$3r - 2(r + 5) =$

Solve.

9. In the formula $A = lw$, find A when l is 10 meters and w is 12 meters.

Answer _____

10. In the formula $A = \pi r^2$, find A when r is 8 inches. Let $\pi = 3.14$.

Answer _____

11. In the formula $I = prt$, find I when p is $250, r is $6\frac{1}{2}\%$, and t is 1 year.

Answer _____

12. In the formula $C = (F - 32)\frac{5}{9}$, find C when F is 77°.

Answer _____

Final Review

Solve.

	a	b	c	d
13.	$2x + 11 = {}^-7$	$3y - 5y = {}^-6$	$16z = 96$	$\frac{m}{4} = 12$
14.	$4x - 4 = 2x + 8$	$\frac{x}{2} + 4 = \frac{x}{3} + 5$	$6b - 4 = 2(2b + 1)$	$\frac{8}{x} = \frac{4}{3}$

Simplify.

	a	b	c
15.	$4 \cdot ({}^-1)^3 =$	$6a^2b(4c) =$	$(7xy^2)({}^-7x^2y) =$
16.	$(r^3s^5)^2 =$	$\frac{5a^6}{a^4} =$	$\frac{{}^-30mn^3}{15m^2n} =$
17.	$(3x - 2y)(x - 3y) =$	$(3a - b)(2c + b) =$	$(2x^2 - y^2 - 3)(xy - y) =$

Change each number from scientific notation to standard form.

	a	b	c
18.	$5.32 \times 10^4 =$	$0.00071 \times 10^{-6} =$	$45.01 \times 10^{-3} =$

Divide.

	a	b	c
19.	$x - 2\overline{)x^2 - 5x + 6}$	$2x + y\overline{)2x^2 - xy - y^2}$	$2a - 2b\overline{)2a^2 - 8ab + 6b^2}$

Make a table of solutions. Graph each equation.

a

20. $4x - 2y = 6$

x	y
$^-2$	
0	
1	

b

$3x + y = 1$

x	y

Circle which of the given points lie on the graph of the given function.

21. $3x + 3y = 3$ (3, 0)   (2, ⁻1)   (0, 1)

Find the slope of the line that passes through the given points.

a   *b*   *c*

22. (0, 7), (2, 13) | (3, 9), (⁻2, ⁻6) | (1, 8), (⁻3, ⁻8)

At what points does each line cross the x- and y-axes?

a   *b*   *c*

23. $4x - y = 3$ | $2y + 3x = 2$ | $2x = 3y + 4$

Solve each system of equations.

a   *b*   *c*

24. $x + 2y = 9$ | $2x + 3y = 14$ | $\frac{3x}{4} + \frac{y}{2} = 5$

      $x - y = 3$ | $x + 2y = 18$ | $\frac{x}{4} + \frac{y}{2} = 1$

Ordered pair _____ | Ordered pair _____ | Ordered pair _____

Simplify.

a   *b*   *c*

25. $(2x - y)^2 =$ | $(3x - 1)(3x + 5) =$ | $\sqrt[3]{27a^6} =$

Solve.

a   *b*   *c*

26. $\frac{b^2}{2} = \frac{27}{6}$ | $7 - 2a \geq {}^-3$ | $3x^3 + 28 = 220$

Write the equations. Solve.

27. Carlos is three times as old as Maria. The sum of their ages is 56 years. How old is each?

28. The sum of three numbers is 180. The second number is twice the first, and the third number is three times the first. Find each number.

Answer _____ | Answer _____

Final Review

Find the percent.

	a	b	c	d
29.	20% of 86 =	10% of 200 =	35% of 170 =	16% of 49 =

Find the length of the missing side of each right triangle. Use $a^2 + b^2 = c^2$.

	a	b	c
30.	$a = 5$, $b = 12$, $c = ?$	$a = ?$, $b = 12$, $c = 15$	$a = 6$, $b = ?$, $c = 10$

Find the distance between each pair of points.

	a	b	c
31.	(4, 16) and (4, 25)	(0, ⁻2) and (6, 6)	(⁻2, 0) and (6, ⁻3)

Find the midpoint between the two points.

	a	b	c
32.	(2, 20) and (0, 4)	(2, 7) and (6, 1)	(3, 10) and (1, ⁻8)

Factor.

	a	b	c
33.	$x^2 + 5x + 4 =$	$4x^2 - 49 =$	$25 - 70x + 49x^2 =$

Solve.

	a	b	c
34.	$x^2 + 49 = {}^-14x$	$16x^2 - 24x + 9 = 0$	$2x^2 + x - 3 = 0$

Solve.

35. The length and the width of a rectangle are in the ratio of 5 to 2, and the area is 1,000 sq. ft. Find the dimensions.

36. The length of a rectangle is 10 m greater than the width, and the area is 600 sq. m. Find the two dimensions.

Answer _____

Answer _____

absolute value the distance a number is from 0 on a number line (pp. 12, 39)

addend a number being added (p. 19)

algebra the study of variables and operations with variables (p. 10)

algebraic expression a combination including one or more variables and possibly one or more numbers and operations (p. 16)

area number of square units in a figure (p. 22)

average the sum of a set of numbers divided by the number of addends (p. 168)

base a number that is the repeated factor of a number written in exponential form (p. 86)

binomial the addition or subtraction of two monomials (p. 97)

Celsius a commonly used temperature scale (p. 29)

circumference the perimeter of a circle (p. 26)

clearing fractions the process of eliminating fractions by multiplying both sides of an equation by a common denominator (p. 77)

coefficient a number multiplied by a variable in an expression (p. 48)

common denominator an integer that is divisible by each of the denominators of two or more fractions (p. 77)

common monomial factor a factor of all the terms in a polynomial (p. 106)

completing the square a method for solving a quadratic equation by changing the equation to make a perfect square trinomial on one side (p. 193)

constant the term in an expression that does not contain variables (p. 48)

coordinate plane a reference system used to locate points (p. 113)

coordinates the numbers in an ordered pair that determine the position of a point on a graph (p. 113)

cross-multiply to clear fractions by multiplying each numerator in a proportion by the denominator on the opposite side of the equation (p. 78)

cube a rectangular prism that has equal dimensions (p. 87)

cube root a number that when multiplied by itself three times results in a given number (p. 157)

cubic made up of three dimensions (p. 24)

cylinder a three-dimensional figure with two parallel and congruent circular bases (p. 28)

diameter a straight line segment that crosses through the midpoint of a circle and has its endpoints on the circle (p. 26)

distribute to give something to each member of a group (p. 56)

distributive property the rule for multiplying a number or a variable by each term in an expression that is within parentheses; $a(b + c) = ab + ac$ (p. 56)

dividend an amount being divided (p. 44)

divisor a number that divides a dividend (p. 44)

domain the set of all x-values in a function (p. 112)

endpoints the points at the ends of a line segment (p. 168)

equation a mathematical sentence that shows that two expressions are equal (p. 18)

evaluate to find the simplest value for an expression (p. 15)

exponent a number that indicates the number of times a given base is used as a factor (p. 86)

expression one or more terms, usually with one or more operations (p. 48)

factor a number that when multiplied by another number forms a product (p. 19)

Fahrenheit a commonly used temperature scale (p. 29)

fixed rate a rate that does not change over the course of a loan (p. 30)

FOIL a general method for multiplying any two binomials; first terms, outer terms, inner terms, last terms (p. 186)

function a set of ordered pairs in which each *x*-value has only one *y*-value (p. 112)

greater than (>) a comparison of two numbers, where the greater number is left of the > symbol (p. 13)

horizontal axis the left-right axis on a coordinate plane (p. 113)

hypotenuse the side opposite the right angle in a right triangle (p. 166)

inequality a mathematical sentence that compares amounts that are not equal (p. 148)

integers the set of whole numbers and their opposites (pp. 11, 38)

interest an amount of money that is paid for borrowed money (p. 30)

intersect to cross at one point (p. 113)

inverse operation an operation that undoes another operation; the inverse operation of addition is subtraction and the inverse operation of multiplication is division (p. 19)

legs the two sides that form the right angle of a right triangle (p. 166)

less than (<) a comparison of two numbers, where the lesser number is left of the < symbol (p. 13)

like terms two or more terms with the same variable or variables (p. 49)

linear equation a two-variable equation whose solutions may be graphed on a straight line (p. 117)

linear function a function whose graph is a straight line (p. 114)

midpoint the point on a line segment that divides the line segment into two equal halves (p. 168)

midsegment the segment that connects the midpoints of two sides of a triangle (p. 169)

monomial a number, variable, or product of numbers and variables that make a single term (p. 48)

natural numbers the set of numbers 1 and above used for counting (p. 11)

negative less than zero (p. 38)

opposites two numbers that, when added together, have a sum of zero (p. 38)

order of operations the order in which operations in an expression should be performed (p. 14)

ordered pair a pair of numbers in the form (x, y) (p. 112)

origin the point (0, 0) on a coordinate plane where the axes cross (p. 113)

parallel lines lines that never intersect and are always the same distance apart (p. 169)

percent (%) out of one hundred, per hundred (p. 160)

pi (π) the ratio of the circumference of a circle to the diameter, about $\frac{22}{7}$, or 3.14 (p. 26)

polynomial an expression that can be written as a sum or difference of monomials (p. 99)

positive greater than zero (p. 38)

power an expression in the form a^n that is read "a to the nth power" (p. 88)

principal an amount of money loaned or borrowed (p. 30)

proportion an equation stating that two ratios are equal (p. 162)

Pythagorean Theorem the rule that the square of a right triangle's hypotenuse equals the sum of the squares of the legs ($c^2 = a^2 + b^2$) (p. 166)

quadrants the four sections formed by the x- and y-axes on a coordinate plane (p. 113)

quadratic equation an equation in which the greatest exponent of any term is 2 (p. 178)

quadratic formula a formula that can be used to solve any quadratic equation; $x = \frac{-b \pm \sqrt{b^2 - 4ac}}{2a}$ (p. 194)

radical an expression containing one or more numbers under a radical sign (p. 154)

radical sign ($\sqrt{\ }$) the symbol used to indicate the calculation of a positive square root of the term under the sign (p. 154)

radicand the number under the radical sign (p. 154)

radius a straight line from the center point of a circle to a point on the circle (p. 26)

range the set of all y-values in a given function (p. 112)

ratio a fraction used to compare two quantities (pp. 120, 161)

rational numbers the set of numbers that can be written as fractions of the form $\frac{a}{b}$, where a and b are integers and $b \neq 0$ (p. 11)

reciprocal the number that when multiplied by another number results in 1 (p. 58)

relation a set of ordered pairs (p. 112)

rise the vertical change between two points (p. 120)

roots solutions to a quadratic equation (p. 178)

run the horizontal change between two points (p. 120)

scientific notation a method of writing numbers using powers of 10 (p. 89)

set a group (p. 11)

similar triangles triangles with corresponding angles of equal measures and corresponding sides of proportional lengths (p. 164)

simple interest the amount obtained by multiplying the principal, or money borrowed, by the rate and by the time (p. 30)

simplest form the form of an expression with no like terms and no parentheses, usually arranged in alphabetical order and with constants last (p. 52)

simplify to write an expression in simplest form (p. 52)

slope the ratio of vertical change (rise) to horizontal change (run) that indicates the incline of a line (p. 120)

slope-intercept form the equation of a line written in the form $y = mx + b$, where m is the slope and b is the y-intercept (p. 122)

solution a number that, when substituted for a variable, makes an equation true (p. 18)

standard form the customary method of writing whole numbers (p. 89)

substitution method a method for solving systems of equations by solving for one variable, substituting its value into the equation, and then solving for the other variable (p. 137)

square made up of two dimensions (p. 22)

square root a number that when multiplied by itself results in a given number (p. 154)

systems of equations two or more equations that are solved together (p. 128)

term a number, variable, or combination of a number and variable(s) between the operation signs of an expression (p. 48)

Triangle Midsegment Theorem a rule stating that a segment joining the midpoints of two sides of a triangle is parallel to the third side and has a length that is half the length of the third side (p. 169)

trinomial a polynomial with three terms (p. 176)

variables letters or symbols that are used to represent numbers (p. 10)

vertical axis the up-down axis on a coordinate plane (p. 113)

volume number of cubic units that will fit inside a three-dimensional area (p. 24)

whole numbers the set of natural numbers (counting numbers) and 0 (p. 11)

x-axis the horizontal axis on a coordinate plane (p. 115)

x-intercept the point on a coordinate plane where a line crosses the x-axis (p. 123)

y-axis the vertical axis on a coordinate plane (p. 115)

y-intercept the point on a coordinate plane where a line crosses the y-axis (p. 122)

zero product property the rule that if $ab = 0$, then $a = 0$ or $b = 0$ (p. 178)